D1458902

After the Evil

White Crucifixion, 1938, by Marc Chagall, 1887–1985, Gift of Alfred S. Alschuler. 1946.925. © ADAGP, Paris and DACS, London 2003. Photograph © 2003 The Art Institute of Chicago.

After the Evil

*Christianity and Judaism
in the Shadow of the Holocaust*

Richard Harries
Bishop of Oxford

OXFORD
UNIVERSITY PRESS

OXFORD
UNIVERSITY PRESS

Great Clarendon Street, Oxford OX2 6DP

Oxford University Press is a department of the University of Oxford.
It furthers the University's objective of excellence in research, scholarship,
and education by publishing worldwide in

Oxford New York

Auckland Bangkok Buenos Aires Cape Town Chennai
Dar es Salaam Delhi Hong Kong Istanbul Karachi Kolkata
Kuala Lumpur Madrid Melbourne Mexico City Mumbai Nairobi
São Paulo Shanghai Taipei Tokyo Toronto

Oxford is a registered trade mark of Oxford University Press
in the UK and in certain other countries

Published in the United States
by Oxford University Press Inc., New York

British Library Cataloguing in Publication Data

Data available

Library of Congress Cataloging in Publication Data

Data available

ISBN 0–19–926313–2

1 3 5 7 9 10 8 6 4 2

Typeset by Hope Services (Abingdon) Ltd
Printed in Great Britain
on acid-free paper by
Biddles Ltd, Guildford & King's Lynn

For friends who were members of the Manor House
Group and also for office holders and members of staff of
the Council of Christians and Jews

Contents

Contents

Note on the Jacket
Illustration/Frontispiece

Marc Chagall painted *White Crucifixion* in 1938 after he had travelled widely in Europe and experienced the rise of Nazi brutality. In that year, 1500 Jews were taken to concentration camps; in the same month and in August that year synagogues in Munich and Nuremberg were destroyed, and pogroms carried out. *White Crucifixion* was originally even more specific than it is now. Before over-painting, the old man at the lower left-hand side had 'Ich bin Jude' (I am a Jew) written on the plaque which he wears around his neck. The painting shows in vivid detail, in an iconic way, the destruction of the closed but joyous Jewish world Chagall had known in Russia as a child.

At the foot of the Cross is the *Menorah*, the seven-branch candlestick of Judaism—although here, it seems, with only six candles and only five of these alight. Then (in an anti-clockwise direction) a mother hugs her child to her chest as she flees the destruction. Above her is a Torah scroll with white light streaming from it and a figure stepping over the light. This must be Elijah.

Above Elijah a synagogue is being burned by a Nazi brownshirt, while behind this Nazi flags can be seen. The sacred furniture and books are thrown out into the street. Above the door of the synagogue are two lions, a familiar image in Eastern European synagogues. Here, though, there may also be a personal reference, for Chagall's first name Marc has in Christian symbolism the lion as its image.

At the top, Jewish figures lament and flee while on the left of the picture, a Jewish Shtetl (village) is put to the torch by Communist troops with red flags. Flames flare from the roof-tops and the homeless sit on the ground outside. Below this scene there are some trying to escape in a boat—to Palestine. At the bottom left, Jewish figures clutching the sacred scrolls flee from the destruction. Dominating the picture in the centre is the figure of Christ crucified—but this is very much a Jewish Christ. Over his head written in Hebrew are the words 'King of the Jews', while around his body is wrapped a Jewish prayer shawl.

It is truly remarkable that it is the figure of Jesus on the Cross which is at the centre of this picture. The suffering of the Jewish people is being summed up in a Christian icon. The agony of Jesus is seen as the agony of all Jewish people. This is startling, even shocking, when we remember that for many Jews the Cross has been a symbol of Christian oppression of Jewish people. Many Jews have, quite under-standably, felt very uneasy about Chagall's painting. But from a Christian point of view, it points to a terrible paradox: in the suffering of the Jewish people, so much of it inflicted by Christians, it is the Christian God who suffers.

Richard Harries
Bishop of Oxford
February 2003

Introduction

When people express definite views on controversial issues we sometimes think 'I wonder where he's coming from?' Such a question
assumes that we all have a personal history which has affected our feelings and shaped our outlook. This assumption is hardly an invention
of the modern world but it is certainly one which has been heightened
by so-called postmodernism. Nothing in this life is value-free, nothing
is neutral. There is no eagle's eye view from which we can survey the
world in a detached and totally objective manner. I therefore begin
with some personal memories which indicate why the issues discussed
in this book are of concern to me and which indicate some of the experiences which have shaped my outlook. I list them very briefly because
their implications form the substance of my book.

Towards the end of World War II my family returned from the
United States and we were billeted on a Yorkshire family in
Huddersfield. One Saturday afternoon I was taken to the pictures by
Mrs Broadbent, in whose house we were living. Before the main film
was shown, as was the custom in those days, there was the Pathé
News. I was told to keep my eyes shut. Nevertheless, I did have one
quick peek through my fingers and glimpsed the emaciated figures of
prisoners in Belsen being released. The sombre events of the 1930s and
1940s that led up to Belsen and the other extermination camps have,
quite properly, hung like a black cloud over my generation. For
Christians their significance has become of increasing significance.

My next memory comes from my time at school as a boy of about
14. Another boy in my dormitory was being taunted with shouts of

'Jew boy'. I found the scene distasteful and unpleasant. He was perhaps the only Jewish boy in the school. No doubt some of this was the result of the usual schoolboy tendency to pick on anyone who was different. But there was nothing very obviously different about this boy and he had a very English name. There was one black boy in the school but as he was a prince of ancient lineage with a remarkably sunny disposition, he was not picked on. Many years later a Jewish friend told me that at about the same period her father had applied to a well-known school on her behalf. The headmistress told her father that they already had their quota of Jews and they never took the daughters of local tradesmen. An attitude breathtaking in its combination of snobbery and antisemitism. There was something in the adult air that children breathed in without knowing it.

My third memory dates from time at Cuddesdon Theological College from 1961 to 1963. It was the custom for the after-dinner session at least once a week to be occupied by a visiting speaker. One week we had James Parkes to talk to us, the man whose pioneering work revealed the extent of antisemitism in Christian history and who strove for a new relationship between Church and Synagogue. It was only many years later that I became aware of the true importance of Parkes. But it was symptomatic that what he had to say to us should have been, as it were, fitted in as an optional extra. It is still the case that the radical reappraisal that is required of Christianity's approach to Judaism is not reflected in the main curriculum of biblical studies, in Church history and systematic theology. Most ordinands, in most denominations, still go through their training with the old stereotypes about the Pharisees, Jewish legalism and with Judaism simply presented as a foil to Christianity.

When I was at theological college I was fortunate enough to be able to spend one term in East Jerusalem, at a time when it was governed by Jordan. The city was divided by barbed wire and still bore the marks of shells and bullets. I heard the stories of Palestinians who nostalgically remembered their homes in the orange groves of Jaffa. Then we spent some days in Israel and saw something of that dynamic society. Israel—the great sign of hope for European Jewry shattered by the Holocaust, and 'the Catastrophe' for Palestinians—still torments all those working for a new relationship between Judaism and Christianity.

During the 1980s I became a member of the Manor House Group. This small group of Jewish and Christian theologians used to meet regularly in London and go away for one weekend a year together at Charney Bassett. The group came to know each other very well, like one another enormously, and in that freedom could get beyond politeness to real exchanges. It was membership of this group, more than anything, which began to shape my whole understanding of Judaism. I think all members of the group would testify to the effect it has had on us. As Rabbi Tony Bayfield has written, 'I have been changed immeasurably by the process'.[1] Not least were the moments of humour, when we realized that the differences were cultural rather than theological. I can remember for example going out for a walk on the Ridgeway near the White Horse on a winter's day with snow covering the ground. The Christians were out in their walking boots or gumboots, our Jewish members had shiny black shoes on.

We used to take it in turns to read papers to one another, which would then be followed by a discussion. But when one of our Jewish members read a paper, he had usually only got a few sentences into it before he was interrupted and questioned by another Jewish member. Having since then been to a good number of seders, in which constant dialogue, questioning, and interruption is all part of the scene, I can now understand how it is that Jewish people always like to question both one another and God. Out of the Manor House Group experience came a book *Dialogue with a Difference*. This has four main theological concerns: making theological space for each other; text, tradition, and historical criticism; Shoah, suffering, and theodicy, and religion and the transformation of society.[2]

More controversial issues erupted into my life about that time. In 1988 the Lambeth Conference met in Canterbury. Many hundreds of Anglican Bishops from all over the world gathered for a month's reflection, talking, and making resolutions. There is a sharp contrast in

---

[1] Marcus Braybrooke, *Christian-Jewish Dialogue: The Next Steps* (SCM, 2000), 121.

[2] Tony Bayfield and Marcus Braybrooke (eds.), *Dialogue with a Difference: The Manor House Group Experience* (SCM, 1992).

the way that the Lambeth Conference and a Vatican Council operate. At the last Vatican Council papers carefully prepared over years beforehand were the basis for discussion, alteration as necessary, and then promulgation at the end. Although a Lambeth Conference has preparatory papers these are genuinely preparatory. They are not meant to provide the basis of authoritative documents at the end. This has always seemed to me a weakness resulting in a lot of free-wheeling discussion, last-minute writing of papers at the conference itself, and endless resolutions hurried through. Aware of that weakness I was asked to chair a small group of Christians, with a Jewish adviser, who would prepare in advance some guidelines on Jewish/Christian relations for Anglicans. This carefully prepared document would then, we thought, be discussed and hopefully endorsed by the Lambeth Bishops. However, the document encountered immediate opposition from two quarters. Evangelicals opposed the guidelines because it ruled out the idea of mission to the Jews. The Middle Eastern Bishops and their friends were very unhappy about a document going out that dealt only with Judaism and not with Islam. As a result of this the document had to be totally recast in order to relate to Muslims as well as Jews. Fortunately, there were some Islamic specialists amongst the advisers at Lambeth and together with them the whole document was rewritten. Even so, there was still much criticism and it was by no means certain that it would receive any kind of welcome. I was extremely worried, as worried as I have been in my life, for one simple reason. The Jewish community had built up a great sense of expectation about this document. Knowing the incredible influence that the second Vatican Council and the documents that had come from the Vatican since then had had on the Roman Catholic Church, they looked to the Lambeth Conference to do something similar for the Anglican Communion. This expectation might have been totally unrealistic, because there is no central authority in the Anglican Communion and the resolutions of the Lambeth Conference are only persuasive at best, not mandatory. Nevertheless, unreal or not, that expectation was there and I could imagine the damage that could be done to Jewish/Christian relations when the *Jewish Chronicle* reported that Lambeth had refused to accept any guidelines on Jewish/

Christian relations. In the end, thanks to the good offices of David Penman, the then Archbishop of Melbourne, who had both the trust of the Evangelicals and the support of the Palestinians, the document was commended for study by churches in the Anglican Communion who were also asked to produce guidelines for their own context.

My subsequent experience has only confirmed what I encountered at Lambeth, the real difficulty of achieving any kind of agreement on contentious issues such as mission to the Jews and Israel.

The last experience which has shaped my outlook was the nine years I had as Chairman of the Council of Christians and Jews.[3] This enabled me to enter into and appreciate the Jewish community in many parts of the country. It also brought home to me how the work of Jewish/Christian relations, especially what the Vatican calls the right presentation of Christianity in relation to Judaism, needs to be done afresh in every generation.

These are just some of the experiences which have helped to form my approach to Jewish/Christian relations. They underpin the themes of this book and have set in motion the thoughts it contains. It only remains to be said in this introduction that this book sets out to be a work of Christian theology. In interfaith dialogue it is fundamental that we allow the other partner to speak for themselves and to define themselves in their terms. Nevertheless, I believe that both Judaism and Christianity have a consistent and coherent view of the universe and this will inevitably mean that they will see the other and interpret the other also in their own categories, with their own perspective, and in terms of their own theology. I would expect Judaism to do this to Christianity and there is one chapter in this book which explores Jewish attempts to see Christianity in a positive light. But this work is of course written by a Christian on Christian premisses and therefore whilst I hope it does justice to Judaism, in Jewish terms, it is also an attempt to see Judaism, positively, in Christian terms. The main issues in the book are I hope conveyed by the chapter titles listed on the contents page.

---

[3] Marcus Braybrooke, *Children of One God: A History of the Council of Christians and Jews* (Vallentine Mitchell, 1991).

Introduction

In recent decades there have been highly significant changes in the relationship between Judaism and Christianity. For example in the Good Friday rite it has been said, 'We see not a gradual evolution but a dramatic change'.[4] The Church of England Prayer Books of 1549, 1552, and 1662 prayed 'Have mercy upon all Jews, Turks, infidels, and heretics'. The services for Lent, Holy Week, and Easter now contain a prayer for Good Friday which reads:

> Let us pray for God's ancient people, the Jews,
> the first to hear his word—
> for greater understanding between Christian and Jew
> for the removal of our blindness and bitterness of heart
> that God will grant us grace to be faithful to his covenant
> and to grow in the love of his name.

No doubt this prayer will be interpreted by different people in different ways but there is a profound sense within it of Jews and Christians belonging together.

The equivalent Roman Catholic prayer for Good Friday reads:

> Let us pray for the Jewish people,
> the first to hear the word of God,
> that they may continue to grow in the love of his name
> and in faithfulness to his covenant.

Those prayers express the spirit in which this book is written. Nevertheless, although there have been highly significant changes, a number of controversial issues remain unresolved within the Christian community. Some of these will be discussed in this book. Furthermore, as will be made clear, a huge task still remains to be done if the bitter legacy of centuries is to be healed.

---

[4] Martin Dudley, Pastoral Commentary 1, 'The Jews and the Good Friday Liturgy', *Anglican Theological Review* (Mar. 1994).

The Unspeakable Evil   1

In the introduction I mentioned how as a boy I was taken to the cinema and peeped between my fingers during the Pathé News to get a glimpse of emaciated figures being liberated at Belsen. The reality is described by Rabbi Isaac Levy, who as senior Jewish chaplain to the British Liberation Army was one of the first people into Belsen.

Heaps of corpses were lying in the main pathways. Those who still had a little life in them were crawling on all fours in search of scraps of food. Haggard, starved bodies, bulging eyes, pitifully appealing for help.

I entered some of the huts which accommodated hundreds of emaciated bodies lying in the tiered bunks. The nauseating smell was unbearable. These wretched victims were lying in indescribable filth. At first sight it was impossible to distinguish between the barely living and dead, for those who still had the barest trace of life looked lifeless. . . . Hundreds died everyday and little or no effort had been made to remove the corpses. To enter these huts was like a descent into Dante's *inferno*. . . . Within the first two or three weeks after liberation, no less than 20,000 corpses were removed from the huts and from the heaps lying in the main paths.

. . . Owing to the vast numbers involved, the most expedient method of burial was to commit them to mass graves which were prepared by bulldozers provided by the Royal Engineers. The indignity of these burials was deeply disturbing . . . To recite the Kaddish over such a heap of emaciated bodies cast helter-skelter into pits, each containing 5000 such corpses, seemed to negate the concept of man created in the divine image.[1]

---

[1] Isaac Levy, *Witness to Evil: Bergen-Belsen 1945* (Peter Halban Publishers, 1995), 10–12.

No words can convey the suffering and evil of the Shoah.[2] Here is, literally, unspeakable horror. The only possible response is grief and anger and silence. Yet as Elie Wiesel has written,

For us today—
'How is one to speak of it?
How is one not to speak of it?'

The Shoah, has quite properly, shocked the Christian churches into asking searching questions about its responsibility for what happened and about its historic relationship to Judaism. Some Jewish scholars, such as Norman Solomon, object to Christianity's new relationship to Judaism being built upon a sense of guilt for the Holocaust. They argue that Judaism is a vital, living religion and they want a new relationship to Christianity built upon respect for this fact. That Judaism is a living religion to be respected is fundamental to this whole book. Nevertheless, we cannot consider the relationship between Christianity and Judaism without looking at the Shoah and taking cognizance of the long history of 'the teaching of contempt'. The situation might be compared to a man whose life began to fall apart. He overworked, drank too much, neglected his family. Then one day driving the car he was responsible for a crash which killed his wife and two children. In prison he reflected long and hard not only on the terrible destruction of the people dearest to him, for which he was responsible, but what had gone wrong in the years before which led up to the catastrophic event. A profound reappraisal of his life took place. The Christian Church is in the process of a similar reappraisal.

---

[2] The word 'Holocaust' primarily means 'something wholly burnt up' and because it translates the Hebrew term for whole-burnt offering, is strictly speaking, an objectional word to describe what happened because it gives the attempts to exterminate the Jewish people a religious connotation. The word Shoah is now used by most scholars and writers because this simply refers to the devastation and catastrophe that happened without any religious connotation. Most Yiddish speakers refer to the Nazi period as the *Churban*, a Rabbinic term describing the destruction of the first and second temples. However, despite unsatisfactory connotations, the word Holocaust has entered into popular usage and so both it and the word Shoah are used fairly indiscriminately here. Franklin Littell was using the word Holocaust freely while an officer in the American military government in Germany in 1949; see his *Inventing the Holocaust: A Christian's Retrospect* (Jerusalem, 1993).

Recently there has been a major controversy in the Jewish community caused by Norman Finkelstein's book *The Holocaust Industry: Reflection on the Exploitation of Jewish Suffering.* Without going into the details of his accusation there is the apparently strange fact that in the immediate post-World War II years the Holocaust was little talked about but in the last two decades it has received a great deal of attention. There are I think perfectly understandable reasons for this time lag. It has been noted that those who survived the terrible carnage of the Gallipoli campaign and who went to the trenches in France were very reluctant to talk about their devastating experience. It was only later that the full story of Gallipoli emerged. At the time those who had been through it were reluctant to talk about it and the people they were with were not ready to hear about their experience. Marcus Braybrooke has written:

It is easy now—with the rapid growth of Holocaust studies—to forget that for 20 years or more there was great reluctance to discuss the subject. For example, in 1961, CCJ refused to support an exhibition about the concentration camps because it was felt likely that the exhibition would only perpetuate hatred and bitterness.[3]

In addition to this initial reluctance there was the fact that people who had survived the Holocaust were getting old and some of them were dying. As Rabbi Julia Neuberger has written 'In 1995, on the 50th anniversary of the liberation of Auschwitz, my mother, and many of her generation, really began to talk and tell us what happened. . . . Suddenly, they wanted us to know, before they died, more of "their story". . . . This was a sense of wanting their lives to mean something, wanting those who had perished not to be forgotten.'[4]

Then, in addition to these two factors, the initial reluctance of people to speak about their experiences or others to hear about them, and a realization by survivors that they wanted to tell their story before they died, there is the general experience that sometimes, even terrible

[3] Marcus Braybrooke, 'The Impact of the Holocaust on the Church of England', in John K. Roth and Elizabeth Maxwell (eds.), *Remembering for the Future: The Holocaust in an Age of Genocide* (Palgrave, 2001), ii. 545–60.

[4] Julia Neuberger, *Evening Standard* (12 July 2000), 13.

things do take a long time to sink in and for people to realize all the consequences. So it was that Dr Elizabeth Maxwell, who has been indefatigable in trying to help people remember what happened at the Holocaust in order to avoid anything like it happening again, organized the first major conference on the subject in Britain in 1988, *Remembering the Future*,[5] with the follow-up in Berlin in 1994 and, *Remembering the Future 2000* in the millennium year, again in Britain.

Despite what the Pope has called 'the unspeakable iniquity' of the Holocaust, or perhaps just because that evil was so horrendous, I intend to begin in a rather different place from other writers on this subject. The Holocaust exhibition at the National War Museum is superbly organized. Those who visit are quite properly reduced to silence, horror, anger, and tears. But I venture to make one criticism. There is no section there dealing with what Judaism calls 'Righteous Gentiles'. It is to the credit of the state of Israel that in recent years they have been collecting the stories of Gentiles who tried to help Jews and honour them in a special way. The reason why it is important to do this and why it is sad that there is no section in the Holocaust exhibition dealing with such people, is that humanity desperately needs good role models. It would be a pity if people came away from such exhibitions feeling that everyone was complicit, that there is no alternative to capitulating to evil. In fact there is a whole section on righteous Gentiles in the Holocaust Museum at Beth Shalom near Newark. There is an alternative and there were people even at the height of the Shoah who chose at the risk of their own life to help Jewish people. Sir Martin Gilbert, the distinguished historian of the Holocaust, has written:

Despite the terrifying dangers of helping Jews during the war, there were many, many Christians who risked their lives and many suffered death for trying to help. There was an effort in every town, in every countryside that I have been able to study or read about. Even in Berlin there are dozens of examples,

[5] Yehuda Bauer, Alice Eckardt, Franklin H. Littell, Elizabeth Maxwell, Robert Maxwell, and David Patterson (eds.), *Remembering for the Future* in three volumes (Pergamon Press, 1989). Vol. i in particular deals with the response of the churches and the implications of the Holocaust for Christian theology, though some late papers appear in vol. iii.

actually hundreds of examples, of Christians who hid Jews at the risk of their own lives, or smuggled them through Germany to safe houses or even out of Germany.[6]

What interests me about so many of these examples, is that the acts of courage were done by ordinary people, sometimes quite simple people, certainly people without any great philosophical or theological framework. For example, during the war a French farmer, Victor Guichard, and his wife Josephine, hid Jewish children on their farm, saving them from certain death by the Nazis who were rounding up Jews in their area. Recently one of the children who survived returned and met her protectors. The farmers were asked why they did what they did. 'Why do you ask?' they responded. It was obvious to them that something needed to be done, that children needed to be protected. For all the books that have been written by philosophers and theologians there is in the end a simple capacity in every human being to distinguish good from evil.

The distinguished artist Roman Halter was a slave worker in a factory in Dresden. After the factory was hit they were marched south. Three Jews managed to escape and were employed as Poles by Mr and Mrs Fuchs. When they left Roman Halter told them that he wasn't a Roman Catholic Pole but was a Jew with another name. 'They both laughed and Mr Fuchs replied that he had news for me too. He said, "And I am not a Nazi although I am a German." The Nazis found out that the Fuchs had been sheltering Jews and Mr Fuchs was shot. Mr and Mrs Fuchs knew what they were doing and deliberately took the risk.'[7]

Nicole David-Schneider has now organized three international conferences for Jewish children who were hidden to keep them safe. The first attracted 1,600 participants. She herself was hidden by a family called Champagne. Every morning the family went to mass and young Nicole wanted to be confirmed so that she too could receive communion but the family tactfully tried to distract her. Every

[6] Martin Gilbert, Address to the AGM of the Council of Christians and Jews, 3 Dec. 1997, reprinted in *Common Ground*. The full story is contained in Martin Gilbert, *The Righteous: the Unsung Heroes of the Holocaust*, Doubleday, 2002.
[7] Roman Halter, 'The Kindness of Strangers', *Guardian Weekend* (9 Oct. 1993).

evening when they came to wish her goodnight one of the family would say, 'Don't forget to say the *Shema*, your Jewish prayer.' Why did the Champagnes and other righteous Gentiles do what they did? Nicole believes the crucial factor was the deep sense of good and evil a rescuer shared with others who sheltered Jews. Their attitude was, 'That was the thing to do. How could we do anything else?'[8]

The point of recounting these stories is not in any way to diminish the enormity of what happened. They do indeed give us a good role model, they show that the most ordinary person is capable of distinguishing good and evil. But these examples also serve to highlight the fact that what failed was a whole so-called Christian civilization. For those who saved or tried to help Jews in any way were a minority. The fact is that the majority, in one way or another, were complicit. Despite the heroic, courageous efforts of the few, an enormity was perpetuated which involved the majority of a country that was at least Christian in name.

By February of 1933 Reinhold Niebuhr had already concluded that the Nazis intended to destroy the Jewish people. 'They are bent upon the extermination of the Jews.'[9] Niebuhr wrote more articles and editorials on the subject of the Nazi assault on the Jews than any other American Christian. He campaigned ceaselessly to counteract American isolationism, calling for American intervention in the struggle against Nazism.[10] Niebuhr knew what was happening in 1933. What did the Germans know, how much, and when? It has even been argued, not altogether convincingly, that Albert Speer was not fully cognizant of what was happening when it came to the Final Solution. Gitta Sereny quotes W. A. Visser 't Hooft's judgement that probably applies not only to Speer but many other people as well.

People cannot find a place in their consciousness . . . their imagination . . . or finally have the courage to face (or allow themselves to remember) unimagin-

---

[8] Emma Klein, 'A Survivor's Story', the *Tablet* (4 Mar. 1995).

[9] Reinhold Niebuhr in the *Nation*, 154 (21 Feb. 1933), 214.

[10] Franklin Littell, 'Reinhold Niebuhr and the Jewish People', the 1990 Niebuhr Lecture at Elmhurst College. This contains a full bibliography of Reinhold Niebuhr's writings on Jews and Judaism.

able horror. It is possible to live in a twilight between knowing and not knowing.[11]

Historians have attributed Hitler's rise and popularity to a combination of factors, the possibility of a new national pride after the humiliation of Versailles, the need for economic stability, in law and order, or a bulwark against communism and so on. Hitler had huge support particularly among younger voters and 95 per cent of Germans at the time were registered as members of a church. Willie Schelke, who rejoined Hitler's team in 1935, said that he was aware of course of the Nazis' antisemitism: 'How could one not be? Of course, one had no idea—I mean just no idea at all—that they might actually kill, murder people . . . but antisemitism as a central issue of the campaign—yes, that one *couldn't* not see.'[12]

Despite this, as General Sir Hugh Beach has written:

Between 1933 and 1945 the majority of German Christians approved of national socialism, found it moral in its values and impressive in its achievements. Communists were defeated, order and honour restored, brothels shut down, youth taught the virtues of community and self-sacrifice. The sense of unity and pride exhilarated them. The Protestant middle class was the very core of Hitler's popular support. When war came in September 1939 all the German churches supported their government: this was a war for the Fatherland, a patriotic duty. Only a handful of Christians resisted national socialism; they were ruthlessly persecuted, many executed and the one serious heroic attempt to act against Hitler failed in confusion.[13]

It's a disturbing picture. As much as anything else it was a failure of theology. One way in which the theologians failed the people of Germany was by the excessive emphasis upon the duty of Christians to submit obediently to the ruling powers. It was only after World War II that German theologians reminded people that in addition to Romans 13, with its inculcation of obedience, there is Revelation 13,

---

[11] Gitta Sereny, *Albert Speer: His Battle with Truth* (Macmillan, 1995), 335. Other references that substantiate this point in relation to Speer can be found on pp. 407, 463, 465, 546, and 706.

[12] Ibid. 97.

[13] General Sir Hugh Beach, *The Door* (Diocesan Church House, Oxford, OX2 0NB, May 1995).

in which the state is depicted as demonic, for when it has become demonic it has no claim to be a true state to which obedience is due.[14] But there was no hint of that teaching in the German Church. So when Georg Neuber, a typical apolitical youngster, was called up for military service his mother, a decent Catholic lady, told him to keep his nose clean and his mouth shut. 'I warned my boy at Christmas in 39 never to protest, always to obey his superiors no matter what and to pray to God that he would never be forced to do anything wrong.' Georg duly kept quiet when he witnessed the mass murder of 80 Jews. He was an unprotesting observer at the execution of 100 Polish prisoners. His unit found the bodies of at least 50 Polish children shot in the back of their head in their school house and nobody rebelled.[15]

It was not of course only Jews who were the object of Hitler's extermination plans. Six million Jews were killed but in addition to this there were ten million others, including gypsies, people who were mentally subnormal, homosexuals, and Soviet prisoners of war (it is believed that more than three million of them were murdered while in captivity by the SS).[16] In fact the majority of people who were killed were non-Jewish civilians and the great majority of these were Christian. So some people have wondered why Christian teaching should be specially singled out as responsible for what happened.

Hitler's own ideology was not only not Christian, it was anti-Christian. He sought to create a master, Aryan race, freed of all defectives, weaklings, dissidents, and deviants as well as Jews. This outlook was not only rooted in nineteenth-century philosophies of the strong man arrogating to himself a responsibility for the future against all moral and religious codes, it was fed quite specifically by a pagan philosophy as it came to him through the music of Wagner. Hitler himself was anti-Christian. 'Christianity is an invention of a sick brain', he said. Again, 'I am myself a heathen to the core.'[17]

[14] See Helmut Thielicke, *Theological Ethics* (A. and C. Black, 1969), vol. ii.

[15] Bernt Engelmann, *In Hitler's Germany* (Methuen, 1988).

[16] These figures have been confirmed by Sir Martin Gilbert in a personal letter to the author.

[17] Quoted by Margaret Brearley, 'Hitler and Wagner: The Leader, the Master and the Jews', *Patterns of Prejudice*, 22/2 (Institute of Jewish Affairs, Summer 1988).

Nevertheless he frequently used Christian vocabulary to describe his aims and actions and argued that his antisemitism had not only the posthumous approval of Martin Luther but also the blessing of God. 'I believe I would be no Christian, but a very devil if I felt no pity for (my people), if I did not, as did our Lord 2000 years ago turn against those by whom today this poor people is plundered and exploited.'[18] When some German churchmen in 1936 went in person to Hitler to protest 'g..inst the mistreatment of the Jews he replied, 'Why do you complain? I am only following through on what you have taught for centuries.' Indeed not only did Hitler's attacks on Jews and Judaism consciously echo the language of traditional antisemitism, but the infamous laws of Nuremberg are consciously modelled on the legislation of the medieval Church.[19]

In addition to this, Margaret Brearley has argued there was a deeper religious/anti-religious impulse behind his hatred. Hitler was enthralled by Wagner from the age of 12, seeing *Tristan* and *Die Meistersinger* over 100 times each as well as many performances of the other operas. Wagner was a systemic anti-Semite and his operas became in subtle and unsubtle ways vehicles of those feelings. He looked for the rebirth of humanity and that involved the overthrowing of the Jewish God and Jews. In March 1936 Hitler asked for the prelude of *Parsifal* to be played and later declared, 'I have built up my religion out of *Parsifal*. Divine worship in solemn form, without pretences of humility . . . one can serve God only in the garb of the hero.' So as Margaret Brearley concludes:

In obliterating the Jews, Hitler, like Wagner, hoped to eradicate all traces of their humane values and their God, the God of Israel, creating in their stead a terrifying world based on ruthless instinct and man himself as his only God. Once the physical, racial and spiritual presence of the Jews had been removed, Christianity completely divorced from its Jewish roots would itself be the more easily obliterated or simply subverted into a disguised paganism, as happened with the German church.[20]

---

[18] Ibid.

[19] Norman Solomon, *Jewish Responses to the Holocaust* (Centre for the Study of Judaism and Jewish–Christian Relations, Birmingham, 1988), 17.

[20] 'Hitler and Wagner'.

It is this religious/anti-religious drive in Hitler, nourished by Wagner's music, that goes someway I think to explain the fanaticism with which he spoke and the mesmeric hold he had on crowds of people. But, as Margaret Brearley again observes:

By and large the church did not stand forth as a defender of the Jews. Centuries of false Christian teaching that Jews were children not of God but of the devil had left Jews physically defenceless and Christians theologically defenceless in the face of attack by genuine forces of evil, all the more so since in the case of both Wagner and Hitler evil was cloaked in religious garb.[21]

It is therefore important at this stage to make a distinction between anti-Judaism and antisemitism. Antisemitism is primarily a hatred that is directed against the Jews as a race and its modern form arose in the nineteenth century as part of various racial theories. Anti-Judaism is hostility to a religion. Gavin Langmuir, quoted by Geoffrey Alderman, has argued that the difference is between hostility to the Jewish religion (anti-Judaism) and hostility to Jews (antisemitism), and that one slipped into the other in the twelfth century when Western Christianity started to become undermined by self-doubt.[22] Whether that more sophisticated historical analysis is true or not, the important point is to make a distinction between anti-Judaism and what emerged under Hitler. And the question is how far the Church's traditional anti-Judaism, its centuries-long teaching of contempt, prepared the ground and dulled people's hearts and minds, so that antisemitism could take hold with so little resistance in the population as a whole.[23]

In 1928 James Parkes went to work with the International Students Service in Geneva, where he quickly became aware of the rising tide of antisemitism and began a serious study of this phenomenon. He was, he wrote later, 'Completely unprepared for the discovery that it was the Christian church and the Christian church alone, which turned a normal xenophobia and normal good and bad community relations

[21] Ibid.
[22] Geoffrey Alderman, 'Anti-Judaism and Antisemitism', *Jewish Journal of Sociology*, 33/2 (Dec. 1991).
[23] It is a pity that *The Oxford Companion to Christian Thought* (OUP, 2000), such an admirable volume in so many ways, confuses the issue by subsuming anti-Judaism under the heading of antisemitism as though they were the same thing.

between two human societies into the unique evil of antisemitism, the most evil, and as I gradually came to realise, the most crippling sin of historic Christianity.'[24] He published the results of his conclusions in his pioneering study *The Conflict of Church and Synagogue* in 1934.[25] The major responsibility for antisemitism rested, in Parkes's view, 'upon the theological picture created in Christian literature of the Jews perpetually betraying God and ultimately abandoned by him'.[26] Parkes summarized his study in the words:

The Christian public as a whole, the great and overwhelming majority of the hundreds of millions of nominal Christians in the world, still believe that 'The Jews' killed Jesus. That they are a people rejected by their God, that all the beauty of the bible belongs to the Christian church and not to those by whom it was written; and if on this ground, so carefully prepared, modern anti-Semites have reared a structure of racial and economic propaganda, the final responsibility still rests with those who prepared the soil, created the deformation of the people, and so made these ineptitudes credible.[27]

St John Chrysostom, who lived during the fourth century in Antioch, now in south Turkey, and in Constantinople was a great man. A superb orator, a fearless champion of the poor and opponent of those in political power, he was loved by the ordinary people. He also said and wrote devastating things about Jews and Judaism. Antioch, whilst predominantly Christian, had a substantial, well-organized, and confident Jewish population. Furthermore, in 363 the pagan emperor Julian had started on a programme to rebuild the temple at Jerusalem with government help and restore the Jewish sacrificial system. Julian died before this could happen but Judaism in Antioch was popular. What stirred Chrysostom into his outbursts against the Jews in 386 was the approach of the great Jewish autumn feasts. The Antioch Jews celebrated these publicly and welcomed outsiders. Many Christians flocked to watch them, even to participate in them. Many, as he ruefully admitted, 'hold Jews in deep respect and regard their way of life as deserving reverence'. John preached eight sermons

---

[24] John Hadham (Parkes's nom de plume) *Voyages of Discovery* (Victor Gollancz, 1969), 123.

[25] James Parkes, *The Conflict of Church and Synagogue* (Soncino Press, 1934).

[26] Ibid. 375.   [27] Ibid. 376.

which are now entitled *Against the Jews*. In addition, his other writings are riddled with anti-Jewish references. For example, in his commentary on John's Gospel there are two long columns in the index devoted to references to the Jews, all hostile.

J. N. D. Kelly has written that 'These tirades reveal John as master of unscrupulous, often coarse invective.'[28] These sermons are distressing to a modern reader but Kelly has observed, 'In his own day, however, there was nothing exceptional about them—except, of course, their oratorical bravura. So far from being original, the arguments they deploy reflect a tradition of Christian polemic which can be traced back, in East and West alike, to the first century, when the church separated itself from the synagogue.'[29] There is no point in going through Chrysostom's sermons in detail; however, the main theological structure of the Church's anti-Judaism down the ages, from the second century through to the twentieth, can be summarized as follows:

1. The Jews as Christ killers. 'It is because you shed the precious blood that there is now no restoration, no mercy anymore and no defence . . . through your madness against Christ you have committed ultimate transgression' (St Chrysostom, *The Sixth Oration Against the Jews*).

'Why was the temple made desolate? . . . It was because they killed the son of their benefactor, for he is coeternal with the Father' (St Hippolytus, *Contra Judaas 7*).

2. Israel has been replaced by Christianity. 'On the rejection of Israel and the election of the gentiles, the Lord said to Moses, "Let me alone that I may destroy these people and make of you a great nation" . . . it thus follows clearly that everything concerning these people is an adumbration, image, prefiguration and symbol of that which had been written for *us*—"Upon whom the end of the ages have come" ' (St Jerome, *On the Promised Land*).

3. The wandering Jew. 'You can hear the wailing and lamentations of each of the prophets . . . over the calamities which will overtake the Jewish people because of their impiety to him who had been foretold

[28] J. N. D. Kelly, *Golden Mouth: The Story of John Chrysostom Ascetic, Preacher, Bishop* (Duckworth, 1995), 63.
[29] Ibid. 66.

. . . how their kingdom would be utterly destroyed after their sin against Christ . . . and they would be dispersed among the gentiles throughout the whole world, with never a hope of any cessation of evil or breathing space from troubles' (Eusebius of Caesarea, *Demonstrations of the Gospel* 1.7).

4. The Jews eternally reprobate. 'Groaning and trembling shall you be upon the earth'; here no one can fail to see that in every land where the Jews are scattered, they are in terrified subjection to the immensely superior number of Christians . . . to the end of the seven days of time the continued preservation of the Jews will be a proof to believing Christians of the subjection merited by those who, in the pride of their kingdom, put the Lord to death (St Augustine, *Reply to Faustus the Manichaean*).

5. Jewish depravity. 'The demons inhabit the very souls of the Jews as well as the places where they gather. If you call the synagogue a brothel, a den of vice, the devil's refuge, Satan's fortress, a place to deprave the soul, an abyss of every conceivable disaster, or whatever you will, you are still saying less than it deserves' (St John Chrysostom, *Sixth Oration Against the Jews*).

This theological outlook was reflected in legislation. Although some church laws at some times were enacted to protect Jews and allow them to practise their own religion, the majority were hostile; forbidding marriage or adultery with Jews, eating with them, using fields blessed by them, receiving gifts from them, entering synagogues or converting to Judaism, the penalty for which was death. At the Reformation Martin Luther's extreme hostility to Jews is notorious but he was not the only one then or later to indulge in such polemic. Not surprisingly all this hateful teaching and legislation resulted in very direct suffering for Jewish communities. There were massacres of Jews along the Rhine in 1096 by the crusader army. There was a massacre of Jews at York in 1190. In 1290 all Jews were expelled from England. In the fifteenth century Jews were first massacred and then expelled from Spain and there were pogroms and massacres in Russia and Eastern Europe throughout the nineteenth century. As part of the background to all this Jews were depicted in art and literature as the personification of evil. Allegedly Jewish features were caricatured in order to depict the negation of everything that was Christian and good. Judas Iscariot became a symbol for Jews.[30]

My concern, however, is with the Church's teaching, its view that the Jews collectively continued to be guilty of killing Christ; that because of this worst of all crimes they were to receive the worst of all punishments; as a sign that God was indeed punishing them, the temple had been destroyed in CE 70 and Jewish people scattered throughout the world, where they lived in subjection to the majority population; there they were to be subject to every kind of ignominy and harassment, again as a sign of the divine displeasure.

There is probably no way in which a direct link can be shown to exist between the Church's traditional anti-Judaism and what happened in Nazi Germany. Nevertheless, it is inconceivable that this centuries-long poisoning of minds did not have its effect. Christian teaching has had positive effects. I think, for example, of how stories of Jesus healing, which make up so much of the Gospels and which have been read Sunday by Sunday in the churches of Europe, have influenced the founding of Christian hospitals and hospices. The Gospels together with the associated teaching have inculcated an attitude that we should look after the sick and this shaped a whole culture. Conversely, and terribly, the negative statements in the New Testament about the Jews as interpreted by the Church's teaching of contempt, cannot but have poisoned minds and shaped a whole culture. It was a culture so shaped and minds so poisoned, that were receptive to Nazi antisemitism. It was not just the German habit of obedience, what Franklin Littell has termed 'schooled docility', but the fact that those minds all too readily saw the Jews as cursed Christ killers deserving of punishment. Whether we like it or not we are shaped for both good and ill by our culture. I find myself, for example, always disturbed when I hear German spoken, particularly if it is spoken loudly. Even in Mozart's *Die Zauberflöte*, the spoken parts offend my unconscious. For I have been shaped by a good number of war films when young, in which brutal Germans soldiers would be heard shouting in German. Then there is the ranting of Hitler at the

---

[30] Hyam Maccoby, *Judas Iscariot and the Myth of Jewish Evil* (Peter Halban, 1992).

Nuremberg rallies and at the 1936 Olympics which has gone into my unconscious and which again makes German a difficult language to listen to sympathetically. So although it is difficult to prove that the Church's anti-Judaism must bear significant responsibility for the way Nazi antisemitism took hold, our own experience in other matters makes it difficult to resist the conclusion that it does. As Archbishop Robert Runcie said at a Kristallnacht meeting,

Without centuries of Christian antisemitism, Hitler's passionate hatred would never have been so fervently echoed . . . and why this blindness? Because for centuries Christians have held Jews collectively responsible for the death of Jesus. On Good Fridays Jews have, in times past, cowered behind locked doors with fear of a Christian mob seeking 'revenge' for deicide. Without the poisoning of Christian minds through the centuries, the Holocaust is unthinkable.[31]

So although it is true that there may have been as many as ten million non-Jews who were exterminated by Hitler, the result of his programme of cleansing the German people of what he conceived to be alien elements and the expression of an utter brutality arising out of the concept of a super race that knows no moral limits, Hitler's hatred of the Jews was quite specific. It was part of his programme from the beginning and, if it did not always meet with a ready reception, nor did it always meet with the kind of moral and spiritual rejection that should have been mounted.

Few Christians today would take the same attitude to Judaism that was summed up in the five propositions stated above. Nevertheless, the idea that Christianity has simply superseded Judaism and that Judaism is at best a cul-de-sac or a fossil that has somehow survived, is still very much there in the Christian psyche. The challenge presented by the long history of the teaching of contempt, which paved the way for twentieth-century antisemitism, is whether Christianity can be taught without even a hint of supersessionism. One way of doing this would be to adopt a total relativism, to say that it is simply impossible to choose between one religion and another. But truth matters both to

---

[31] Marcus Braybrooke, *Children of One God: A History of the Council of Christians and Jews* (Vallentine Mitchell, 1991).

the Jewish partners in the dialogue and the Christian ones. Nor is it possible to overcome supersessionism by maintaining that all religions are really saying the same thing and therefore it doesn't matter which one we belong to. In fact, the religions of the world are sometimes saying very different things, incompatible things. Another way of avoiding the problem altogether would be to eliminate or at least downplay to the point of insignificance, all distinguishing features of Christianity so that in essentials it becomes like Judaism. But again this would make a mockery of true dialogue, which involves bringing our differences into the relationship as well as our desire to find any common ground there might be. So the challenge remains: How to preach and teach a Christian faith that is recognizably at one with historic Christianity, but which is not, even implicitly, anti-Judaic?

Some might argue that this challenge does not really have to be met today, because power relationships between Christianity and Judaism are totally different and we have democratic structures which safeguard human rights, including the right for people to practise their own religion. It is certainly true that power relationships are the crucial factor. In Western Europe it is Christianity that has been in a position to enforce its view and Jews have been a powerless minority in a society which had no way of enforcing basic human rights, even if such rights were acknowledged, which in the case of the Jews they were not. It is of course now very different when, as much due to Enlightenment values as to values drawn from religion, religions are forced to rub along together more or less peacefully in democratic societies. Nevertheless the issue of Christian supersessionism still remains. Antisemitism is still rampant in Russia and many Eastern European countries and there is no doubt that this is being fed by the anti-Judaism implicit in so much that is taught from the pulpits. In this country antisemitism is 'A very light sleeper' to use the fine phrase of Conor Cruise O'Brien.[32] It does not take much to arouse it.

---

[32] See the Runnymede Commission on antisemitism, *A Very Light Sleeper* (The Runnymede Trust).

The poet Swinburne put these words to Jesus:

> Say, was not this thy passion, to foreknow
> In death's worst hour the works of Christian men?

The least we can do, in the light of those works of Christian men, is to look again at Christianity's relationship with Judaism and see whether, whilst retaining Christian identity, it is possible to say something theologically affirming and positive: much more affirmative.

After the Evil—What?   2

In planning the first Holocaust Memorial Day in Britain in 2001 there was much discussion about whether this should only focus on the Holocaust or whether it should also call to mind other twentieth-century genocides. Many in the Jewish community were unhappy about focusing exclusively on the Holocaust and wanted it to be seen as part of a wider problem. Nevertheless, it is important to remind oneself first of the scale of the disaster which hit European Jewry. It was not just the loss of individual lives, on however massive a scale, but of a whole culture and way of life. A third of world Jewry had gone up in flames: the busy townships of Eastern Europe, the Talmudic academies, the courts of the Jewish mystics, the Yiddish-speaking masses, the highly cultured Jews of Germany, the Jews of Poland who had lived among their Gentile neighbours for 800 years, the legendary synagogues and houses of study—all these perished.

Secondly, in addition to this utter destruction of a people and its culture the Nazi plan was quite literally for extermination, not a single Jewish person was meant to survive. Jews were singled out simply because they were Jews. The mass killing of Poles and Russians was on a different basis. With the possible exception of gypsies, defectives, and homosexuals, it was only Jews that had committed the 'crime of existing at all'. The Final Solution was not a pragmatic project to serve economic or political ends. It was an end in itself and at the final stage of Nazi domination when Eichmann diverted trains to Auschwitz from the Russian front it was the only end that remained. Only a minority of the perpetrators were sadists or perverts. For the most part they were ordinary people who thought of themselves as good citizens. In addition to this there was the studied and perverse way in which the Nazis sought to humiliate, dehumanize, and induce self-disgust in the Jews even before killing them.

These factors combine to suggest that from a historical point of view there was indeed something uniquely evil about the Shoah.

For twenty years or so after the Holocaust there was a stunned, appalled theological silence. The enormity of what had happened could not be registered in ordinary theological terms and indeed the very attempt to do this seemed an act of gross insensitivity. Nevertheless, in the course of time there were those who began to put forward again some of the traditional 'answers' to the problem of evil and human suffering. Some amongst the ultra orthodox took the view, a view often taken in the Hebrew scriptures, that the people of Israel had suffered because of their sin. Only there were very divergent accounts as to the nature of this sin. For some it was the fact that Jews in Europe had assimilated so well to the prevailing culture. They had not asserted their Jewish identity and in particular they had not made the return to Israel. For others, the sin was precisely the opposite. There have always been ultra orthodox who regarded the setting up of a Jewish state in Palestine as an attempt to force the hand of God, therefore an act of hubris. Only God himself, in his own good time, would bring the ingathering of the people of Israel to Israel. For such people it was Zionism itself which was the sin for which people were being punished. For most people, however, Jews and non-Jews alike, the attempt to account for a million children being thrown into the gas ovens as God's punishment for the sin of Israel, seemed utterly grotesque.

Other traditional Jewish thinkers took the other approach put forward by Job's comforters, namely seeing suffering as a form of purgation and preparation. The people of Israel did not suffer for their own sin but this suffering had a place within the divine purpose drawing the people closer to him and helping to prepare the world for its Messianic redemption. But again, such a view seemed appalling to most dispassionate thinkers. The idea of a God who exterminates six million of his chosen people in order to bring about a higher good suggested such a sadistic God that no one with any conscience could put their trust in him. When we come to the next chapter, which looks at traditional responses to suffering in Judaism and Christianity, it will be seen that these traditional responses have certainly not gone unchallenged in Jewish history. Those who reject them now can find support from a number of ancient Rabbinic discussions.

It is understandable, in the light of the Holocaust and the total inadequacy of the two main traditional accounts of suffering, that some should have abandoned their belief in God altogether. The best known figure was Richard Rubenstein, who later came to a kind of mystical Pantheism but who continued to reject any traditional concept of God as being the lord of history. Rubenstein became loosely associated with the Christian so-called 'Death of God' movement which, paradoxically, tried to assert the death of God and the full assumption of human responsibility as a Christian option. In 1966 *Time* magazine had the 'Death of God' on its cover. Yet three years later, in 1969, *Time* produced another edition with a cover indicating that God was still around. The intervening years had seen the emergence both of the theology of hope associated with Jurgen Moltmann and liberation theology associated with a range of mainly Latin American Christian thinkers. In Judaism too, there was a series of attempts to face the Holocaust theologically and still hold on to faith. Elie Wiesel, in his autobiography, *All Rivers Run to the Sea*[1] wrote:

I have risen against his justice, protested his silence and sometimes his absence, but my anger rises up within the faith and not outside it.

When asked whether he had ever doubted God's existence he replied

You question his existence if you have the background to such questions. If you come from my background—I lived only for Cheder and later, Yeshivah, for nothing else—you don't. When I went to Auschwitz, I had more books in my bag than clothes or food. So the very possibility that God didn't exist didn't exist, so to speak. Therefore all I did was from within.

In the interview from which that quotation came Wiesel said that in the late 1960s he began to study philosophy and he was aware of the

---
[1] Elie Wiesel, *All Rivers Run to the Sea* (HarperCollins, 1996).

'God is Dead' movement. He resented the way those thinkers used his work for their theories because he himself never came to that conclusion. When asked why not, he said, 'Not because of God but because of my father and my grandfather.' He then listed a long line of pious forebears. 'I didn't want to be the last. They believed and I said: "I will be the last, the last who believed in what they believed? That he existed?" That is why I never went that far.'[2]

Wiesel's motivation to continue to ask questions about God from within the tradition of religious belief rather than from outside it is based upon a sense of loyalty to his believing forebears. He also remembers that when he went to Auschwitz he had more religious books than clothes or food. He sought to practise his religion even in the death camps, and so did millions of others.

The subject of faith in the death camps has had an element of controversy about it. Tales have been told of the most heroic affirmations of faith even in the face of death. But these have been dismissed by some Jewish thinkers as fairy tales. Zev Garber in a detailed examination of the practice of Judaism during the Holocaust argues that such tales need to be taken into account. 'In evaluating the practice of Judaism during the Holocaust, that is, we must examine not only what happened but what people perceived to have happened or believed to have been possible and appropriate.'[3] That may be so but it is no less important to acknowledge realistically that, understandably, a fair number of Jews despaired of God during the Holocaust and ceased in any meaningful sense to be believers. The reason why it is necessary to recognize this is that there is always the danger of posthumously legitimizing suffering because of the moral and spiritual qualities it brought about. Some people did indeed show a heroic perseverance in the practice of their faith but it is important not to give even a hint of a suggestion that suffering can somehow be willed by God in order to bring this about. The fact is that suffering crushes as much as it might, in some people, ennoble. Nevertheless, as the Holocaust took hold, many Jews sought to maintain a religious life as best they could under

---

[2] *Jewish Chronicle* (7 June 1996), 23.

[3] Zev Garber, 'The Practice of Judaism During the Holocaust', *The Encyclopedia of Judaism* (Brill, 2000), i. 420–34.

the circumstances with an education system, services of worship, and study of the Torah. Even in the camps people did what they could to maintain observance. As Zev Garber has written,

Hundreds of testimonies bear witness to children's observing of the religious commandment of honouring parents: said prayers in secret, either from memory or by imitating another's recitation, repeating words or simply listening and responding 'Amen'; they followed the Jewish calendars as best as possible, fasting on Yom Kippur . . .

At great personal peril, Phylacteries was smuggled into the camp and people prayed in community. Verses from the psalms became personal credos.[4]

What is perhaps the most remarkable of all is the way that people continued to come to Rabbis, even in the camps, for them to settle difficult religious questions. Rabbi Ephraim Oshry survived the Holocaust in the ghetto of Kovno in Lithuania. He committed the questions and answers that he gave to people on paper torn from cement sacks and hid the writing in cans which somehow survived the war. They reveal that people asked questions about what to do if forced to shed a Torah scroll, whether they should save themselves with a baptismal certificate, whether they should use contraceptives, and so on. Was it proper, for example, as slave labourers, to recite the customary blessing in the morning prayers thanking God 'Who has not made me a slave'? The Rabbi ruled that people might not skip or alter this blessing under any circumstances. 'On the contrary, despite our physical captivity, we were more obligated than ever to recite the blessing to show our enemies that as people we were spiritually free.'[5]

It is loyalty to this inheritance of faith, which perhaps above everything else, should motivate Christians, as well as Jews, not to abandon faith in God even in the face of the terrible evil of the Holocaust. Great numbers of those who perished and great numbers of those who survived still, somehow, against all the odds, retained faith that behind

[4] Zev Garber, 'The Practice of Judaism During the Holocaust', *The Encyclopedia of Judaism* (Brill, 2000), i.420–34.

[5] Quoted by Norman Solomon, *Jewish Responses to the Holocaust* (Centre for the Study of Judaism and Jewish–Christian Relations, Birmingham, 1988), 6.

this strange, agonized universe, there is a wise and loving power. Who are we Christians to assert that God is dead?

Since the 1960s there have been a number of attempts by Jewish thinkers, of all traditions, to interpret the Holocaust in theological terms.[6] I will just briefly mention some of the leading ideas that have emerged from this discussion. One of the most influential views has been that of Emil Fackenheim who has suggested that through the Holocaust God issued the 614th commandment (traditionally there were thought to be 613): Jews are forbidden to grant posthumous victories to Hitler. Jews are instructed to survive as Jews, they are forbidden to deny or despair of God however much they may have to contend with him. They are forbidden finally to despair of the world as a place which is to become the Kingdom of God. Fackenheim points out that some camp inmates were unwilling to become 'muselmann', a term used to describe those who allowed themselves to become totally passive, emotionally and spiritually dead whilst still remaining physically alive. For example, resistance was exhibited by pregnant mothers who refused to abort their pregnancies, hoping their offspring would survive and frustrate the plans of the Nazis to eliminate every Jew. Jewish partisans took to the woods to fight and Hasidic Jews prayed even though they were forbidden to do so. These acts of resistance are of primary importance, for if the Holocaust is to be resisted in thought it must first be resisted in deed. The first act of resistance is the determination to survive or die as a human being. Fackenheim upholds those who said that if they had to die at Auschwitz it would be as a human being, with dignity, and this meant not simply dying passively as a martyr but always inwardly resisting and outwardly resisting where possible. The establishment of the State of Israel was to be seen as part of this act of resistance, this determination to survive, this attempt to make the world a place where Jews could still honour God.[7] This same attitude

---

[6] The most accessible survey is by Dan Cohn-Sherbok, *Holocaust Theology* (Marshall Morgan and Scott, 1989). An assessment of this is in J. Pawlikowski, *What are they Saying about Christian–Jewish Relations?* (Paulist Press, New York, 1980), ch. 6.

[7] Emil Fackenheim, *God's Presence in History: Jewish Affirmations and Philosophical Reflections* (Harper and Row, New York, 1972), and *To Mend the World: Foundations of Future Jewish Thought* (Schocken Books, New York, 1982).

After the Evil—What?

is very much present in the novels of Primo Levi. For example in *If not now, when?* one of the partisans says:

In this sense you could call us Socialists, but we didn't become partisans because of our political beliefs. We are fighting to save ourselves from the Germans, to get revenge, to clear the way for ourselves; but most of all—and excuse the solemn word—for dignity.[8]

The attitude of Emil Fackenheim, though much admired, has also been criticized on the grounds that the survival of the Jewish people has been seen as an end in itself. Whereas, traditionally, the survival of the Jewish people has been important as part of a larger divine purpose, to honour the divine name and bring the light of religious and moral truth to the world. But I think the Chief Rabbi is right when he writes:

And the stubborn people has shown its obstinacy again. Faced with destruction, it has chosen survival. *Lo amut ki echyeh*, says the psalm: 'I will not die, but I will live.' And in this response there is a kind of courage which rises beyond theology's reach.[9]

If one wanted to gloss Dr Sacks's statement it would be that this kind of courage, the determination to survive with dignity, and for many Jews with faith also, is grounded in a religious conviction that is itself supported by a view of the world which is theological. It is a witness to the fact that life, despite everything, is a gift and a blessing. This too is a form of witness, a way of sanctifying the divine name. It may take a secular form as it has with so many secular Jews both in the Diaspora and in Israel, but the implication in it and the assumption underlying it, is the conviction that life is worth living.

Another influential writer has been Eliezer Berkovits.[10] His theme is the silence of God, the hiddenness of God. In biblical terminology this concept of divine silence is expressed by the Hebrew phrase *hester panim*, hiding of the face. Sometimes this hiddenness of God is linked to an ancient Jewish story of God creating the world. Because God is

[8] Primo Levi, *If not now, when?* (Abacus, 1987), 195.

[9] Jonathan Sacks, 'On God and Auschwitz', *Faith in the Future* (Darton, Longman and Todd, 1995), 242.

[10] Eliezer Berkovits, *Faith After the Holocaust* (KTAV, New York, 1973).

God, he is everywhere present and fills all things. Therefore in order to give human beings genuine freedom and the opportunity to take responsibility for their own lives, God has, as it were, to lift up a corner of his cloak in order that there might be a tiny space which he does not envelop. In that space he appears to be absent. But his absence is the condition for human freedom and growth. As the remarkable French woman Simone Weil once put it, 'God can only be present in creation under the form of absence.' Obviously this theme of God's silence, of his absence which makes human life as a created life possible, but an absence in which paradoxically there is also the divine presence, needs a great deal of thinking through. It also needs relating to Christian thought on the subject. Berkovits has been criticized as offering no real comfort for people. How can the thought of God's silence, his absence, be of any consolation to those who are suffering? But this rather misses the point. Fundamental to any modern approach to suffering in general, let alone the Holocaust, must be the genuine autonomy which God has given to the created order, an autonomy which comes to consciousness in human freedom. Human freedom can still be exercised before God and with God. However that freedom is our birthright as well as our birth anguish. Sometimes it is the apparent silence of God which forces us to shoulder our proper responsibilities.

If, in our time, human responsibility is to the fore, then what matters is the kind of creative response which we make to calamity. Jonathan Wittenberg has shown how every Jewish disaster has been met by a response that has enabled Jewish life to survive in a new form. The prophet Jeremiah's contemporaries in the sixth century BCE expected God to protect the sacred temple. But it was sacked and burned and Jeremiah challenged that false assumption. God is not tied down to buildings, even to lands. When the second temple fell some 650 years later in the year 70 of the Christian era, it engendered soul-searching, repentance, and a commitment to responsibility. Then in 135 when Jerusalem itself was razed to the ground Rabbinic Judaism as we know it today was established. God was thought to be present wherever the sacred community establishes a framework of Jewish life and observance. The expulsion of the Jews from Spain in 1492 also

31

brought forth a creative response. Amongst the exiles from Spain in the small community of Safed in the sixteenth century, was Isaac Luria. According to his influential interpretation of Kabbalah, God, as well as the Jewish community, could be somehow seen as scattered. There had been a disaster in the very process of creation as a result of which sparks of divinity were flung far and wide and they were scattered and concealed in every husk of creation. The spiritual task of every human being was to remove the material garb in which they were hidden and to uncover their light. Only then could they be reconnected to the source of all light.

Jonathan Wittenberg suggests that we stand too near in time to the Holocaust to affirm a new response to God but the Jewish community will do so for 'Why should our enemies take this from us? After all, we never allowed them to do so in the past.' He suggests that a new response will be found in the testaments that have come to light from ordinary people, for example the diary of Etty Hilsum. When she faced the prospect of deportation from Amsterdam she wrote:

I shall try to help you, God, to stop my strength ebbing away, though I cannot vouch for it in advance. But one thing is becoming increasingly clear to me— that you cannot help us, that we must help you to help ourselves. And that is all we can manage these days, and also all that really matters: that we safeguard that little piece of you God, in ourselves—and in others as well. Alas there does not seem to be much you yourself can do about our circumstances, about our lives. Neither do I hold you responsible. You cannot help us, but we must help you and defend your dwelling place inside us to the last.

So as Jonathan Wittenberg concludes, we are to regard every single life as God's sacred temple, and God's power in this world lies substantially in what each of us chooses to do with that part of the divine which is delegated to us.[11]

Another influential Rabbi, Irving Greenberg, takes a similar point of view, arguing that the classic Jewish response to every catastrophe in the past has been to renew life. Essential to this renewal has been according a proper place to grief and mourning. The Rabbis created a string of mourning rituals. They ordained that a glass be broken at

---

[11] Jonathan Wittenberg, *Jewish Chronicle* (16 July 1999).

every wedding, in empathetic grief with the catastrophe of the destruction of the temple. But the weddings were not to be stopped: life, family, children must go on. So the Jewish community mourned after the destruction of the temple and after the expulsion of Jews from Spain. The secret of survival for Jews has been this capacity to use the memory of tragedy to spur themselves to come back again and again after defeat. He sees this not just simply in the capacity of Jews to survive but in their willingness to become more sensitive to those who still suffer and those who need help.[12]

Theodore Adorno wrote in 1949: 'After Auschwitz, it is no longer possible to write poetry'. If it is no longer possible to write poetry, it might well be thought that it is no longer possible to do theology. Any response, aesthetic or religious, that comes between us and the unspeakable horror of what happened, has to be eschewed. The full quotation from Adorno was:

After Auschwitz, it is no longer possible to write poetry . . . The aesthetic principle of stylisation . . . makes an unthinkable faith appear to have had some meaning; it is transfigured, something of its horror is removed. This alone does an injustice to the victims.

Thirteen years later Adorno revised his earlier statement and said:

I have no wish to soften the saying that to write lyric poetry after Auschwitz is barbaric . . . but . . . it is now virtually in art alone that suffering can still find its own voice, consolation, without immediately being betrayed by it.[13]

There are important points here which apply not just to poetry but to theology. What Adorno rejected was lyric poetry, poetry that is soft and sweet and takes us into another world away from the barbarities of this one. Any theology that seemed lyrical in that sense must also be totally rejected. But Adorno rightly identified a problem in his earlier statement that goes beyond simply the rejection of lyrical poetry. He rightly points out that any work of art 'makes an unthinkable faith appear to have had some meaning; it is transfigured, something of its

---

[12] Irving Greenberg, *Jewish Chronicle* (4 Aug. 1995).
[13] Quoted by Zev Ben-Shlomo, *Jewish Chronicle* (1 Sept. 1995) as is the previous quotation.

horror is removed. This alone does injustice to the victims.' That is true, and is one of the difficulties for example associated with paintings of the crucifixion. The crucifixion was a brutal form of torture. But down the ages painters have depicted this, and even if they have retained a sense of its horror, as did Grünewald, the very act of producing a work of art transfigures what is depicted. So any work of art on the Holocaust, in any medium, is fraught with danger. All works of art depend on form of one kind or another and form means assembling materials, words, paint or music, stone or movement, into a whole which is characterized by some element of symmetry, balance, and wholeness. So if what is depicted is suffering, that suffering is inevitably transposed to a new key.[14] There is I believe hope, spiritual hope, in the capacity of genuine art to transfigure its object. But there is always danger. Nevertheless, as Adorno says, in a world like our own which is 'suffocated in the cultivation of kitsch', works of art can still enable suffering to be heard without betrayal. That should be the goal of theology as well. Theology, like art, transfigures. It sets the world, even the world of suffering, in a larger context. Therefore it gives meaning. But the challenge in relation to all forms of suffering, but especially the Holocaust, is to give that meaning without in any way stopping us hearing the cries of anguish. For, as has also been said, all theology after Auschwitz has to be done in the face of children being thrown, sometimes alive, into the flames. It is for this reason that for many people silence, especially a theological silence, is the only appropriate response. Rabbi Berel Berkovits has written:

Just as God was silent, so we, too, should be silent. For is not speech trite in the face of the silent scream of six million? Is it not a blasphemy to talk in the face of the unutterable?[15]

Nevertheless Rabbi Berkovits goes on to argue that there are questions that cry out for an answer. We do our best to think our way through all the possible answers and explanations and none carries conviction.

---

[14] I have explored this dilemma in Richard Harries, *Art and the Beauty of God* (Mowbray, repr. 2000 in the Contemporary Christian Insights series).

[15] Rabbi Berel Berkovits, *Jewish Chronicle* (15 Dec. 1989); also the next quotation.

But we come through in the end to a more profound silence which can also be an expression of belief.

Eventually we may come to a true understanding—*the understanding that in fact we do not understand*. That is a deep and profound level of understanding. When we reach that point, when we attain that level, we begin to understand and we begin to believe. But at that point only—and only after we have struggled, after we have tried, after we have agonised—will we really be able to believe and to understand. . . . This time however, it is a silence not of defeat, but of response: a true silence, an evocative silence, a meaningful silence. Not the silence of suffering man, of overwhelmed man, but the silence of accepting man, of believing man . . . where, then, was God in the Holocaust? He was there. Why did we not hear him? Because he was silent. But in his silence he was present. He spoke in his silence. And if we seek, as we ought to, to emulate God—if we, too, are silent—we may be able to hear him.

Together with this silence there is action, constructive action. Some have seen such actions, however small, as part of the mystical process of repairing the world, *tikkun olam*. Among the many who were killed in Auschwitz was a woman of 26 called Charlotte Salomon. Before she died, however, as a refugee in France from 1940 to 1942, she painted nearly a thousand pictures of her life. Many of us like to leave a diary or a photo album of our life. Charlotte Salomon had a deeper motive. A number of the women in her family, including her mother and grandmother, had committed suicide, she herself was prone to severe depression. It's as though she felt she could somehow preserve her balance through recording and recreating her life in painting. When she left for almost certain death she said to the local doctor, 'Keep them well. It's my whole life.' It's now thought that Charlotte Salomon had a deeper meaning than simply recording her life. For she solemnly dated her works '1940–42 or between heaven and earth outside our time in year 1 of the new salvation'. It's now thought that she saw this way of overcoming the past not only as a means of keeping her sane but of making a contribution to the remaking of the world, restoring the unity which was lost in primeval times, *tikkun olam*.

I agree with Rabbi Norman Solomon's judgement that the Shoah is historically unique, for the reasons indicated at the beginning of this chapter. But, nevertheless, the problem it poses for belief in a wise and

35

loving power behind this universe is not fundamentally new. Norman Solomon argues that the traditional answers were never satisfactory and that, furthermore, traditional beliefs have been under attack in modern times for reasons that have nothing to do with the Shoah, not least the new strains placed on the concept of a life after death. 'Thus it is not a question of a new challenge posed to theology by the Shoah, but rather that the Shoah came at a time when theology was already in a greater ferment than ever before in its history, but a ferment occasioned by the intellectual movement of the modern world.'[16]

The two most obvious traditional answers to the problem of suffering, as divine punishment or divine disciplining for his chosen ones for some larger purpose, may never have been satisfactory. But there has been a very strong element in the Jewish tradition on this subject which has recognized that and has sought for other ways of looking at the matter. In the next chapter I shall look in more detail at Jewish responses to suffering down the ages, reflecting also on what congruence there might be with Christian approaches. It will also be necessary to look in more detail at the point mentioned by Norman Solomon, the fading of any strong belief in a life after death. Rabbi Dan Cohn-Sherbok has been highly critical of all the major Jewish responses to the Holocaust because they left out any consideration of an afterlife. It remains to be seen though whether this can be taken into account and if so whether this can be done in such a way that does not take away from the stark reality and horror of those who suffered and died.

From this Jewish wrestling with the Shoah, however, I would want to make the following points. First, human responsibility. As the late Rabbi Hugo Gryn used to say, the question in relation to Auschwitz is not where was God but where is man? To exist at all is to exist with a life of one's own: that is what it means to be created. God has handed over our destiny to us. Out of love for us he has quite consciously limited what he will do for us.

Secondly, because of this we experience the silence of God, his absence. This absence may also be a presence but we need to explore further what kind of presence that might be.

---

[16] Norman Solomon, *Jewish Responses to the Holocaust*, 23.

Thirdly, the imperative to remain human, to live or, if all else fails, to die, with dignity is of surpassing importance. For Jews it has meant surviving as a Jewish people. But there is a wider lesson here for all of us. Fourthly, there is always the possibility of a responsible, creative response to tragedy, however terrible. This has been exhibited down the ages by the Jewish people in response to the destruction of the first temple, the destruction of Jerusalem and the expulsion from Spain. It is also being exhibited today even if the final shape of that response has not yet emerged. More mystically, and related to Jewish views of the redemption of the world, those creative responses, by individuals and the community as a whole, are part of the process of redeeming the world, and preparing for its ultimate Messianic redemption.

Jewish and Christian   3
Responses to Suffering

The Protest against Suffering

According to the author of an article in a two-volume Jewish encyclopaedia published in 1921, it is in their attitude towards suffering that we see one of the major differences between Judaism and Christianity. Even today the popular perception would be that the two religions have a very different approach. In the Jewish mind Jews have just suffered too much, too often at the hands of Christians. The last thing they want is any kind of justification of suffering. They believe that Christianity, with its central icon of the crucifixion, has been unhealthily obsessed with finding meaning in suffering. I do not believe that this contrast holds true in either of the traditions of the two religions today. There are, as we shall see, some differences of emphasis, but the central ground is shared.

The starting point for any consideration of suffering and its relationship to God today will be very different from that of any other period in the past. Our instinctive reaction is that all suffering has describable causes and our prime concern is to locate them in order to eliminate or mitigate that suffering. If we have a pain we go to the doctor. If there is poverty we look for political and economic remedies. Our basic presupposition is that suffering is attributable to specific causes, human or natural. Our attempts to square this with belief in God is not what first comes to mind.

It was different in the past. Then people assumed that the world was under the direct, immediate control of God. For although of course everything, or almost everything, had a secondary cause (people also went to doctors then), those secondary causes were less crucial than the prime cause in the will of God. This meant that suffering was directly attributable to God and the question was, why had God brought this particular form of suffering about.

Our starting point, on the contrary, is the independence of the world, the autonomy of its natural processes and the genuine freedom of human beings to shape their destiny. None of this of itself implies any lack of faith in God. To be created is to have a life of one's own; that is what it means, whether for an electron, a cell, or a multi-cellular structure such as ourselves. That said, there still remains the question: How do we relate the suffering of this autonomous order, not least in the Shoah, to the God who holds it in being and who, we believe, loves each human being? It is a question that still has to be answered, for how else can we hold on to faith: not with knock-me-down answers but with enough to go on to continue on our way in faith and hope and love. This chapter is a response to that question drawing on Rabbinical discussions referred to in *Responses to Suffering in Classical Rabbinic Literature*, by David Kraemer and *Evil and Suffering in Jewish Philosophy* by Oliver Leaman.[1] Both claim to be the first systematic study of its subject. For ease of reference the Rabbinic quotations are drawn from Kraemer's book. Following another distinguished Jewish scholar, Jacob Neusner, Kraemer is concerned to see each text as a whole, rather than isolating individual sayings of particular Rabbis. He seeks to discover the overall thrust of the discussion in question, in its context. He shows both the variety of views and their development from the Mishnah through to and including the Babylonian Talmud. This chapter is a personal response in dialogue with those Rabbinic writings, giving a Christian evaluation of points of view, rather than that of the text in question, and relating them to the responses to the Shoah discussed in the previous chapter.

---

[1] David Kraemer, *Responses to Suffering in Classical Rabbinic Literature* (Oxford University Press, 1995), and Oliver Leaman, *Evil and Suffering in Jewish Philosophy* (Cambridge University Press, 1995).

The predominant theme in the Bible and Rabbinic writings as indicated in the previous chapter is that suffering is a result of sin. If a person suffers then they must have sinned. If that suffering seems disproportionate, this is to be seen as an expression of God's mercy, for the suffering now will be much less than the suffering of the wicked in the hereafter.[2]

At an individual level, as an explanation of all suffering, this answer has always been unacceptable. Time and again it is the relatively innocent who suffer. Civilians suffer most in wars. All round the world it is the poor who are malnourished, starving, experiencing manifold diseases and dying young. The rich, some of whom are hard and exploitative, live lives of comfort, relatively unscathed. Nor does it help to say that in the age to come the wicked will suffer severely whilst the relatively innocent, who have suffered in this life, will be rewarded. For it is the disproportionate nature of the suffering which is the affront. 'All right, I am not perfect,' a person might say. 'But to be punished by losing both my children in a car accident is grotesque—and what about them?' The idea that there is a strict correlation between sin and suffering, the latter being an exact penalty for the former, must be firmly rejected. In the case of the Shoah such a connection between sin and suffering at an individual level is grotesque and cruel.

It is, however, vital to hold on to the Scriptural and Rabbinic conviction that at a *general* level, there is a connection between sin and suffering. Actions have consequences: and wrong actions have destructive consequences. They cause harm, bring about suffering. At a general level the suffering of people in the former Yugoslavia as a result of the fighting, as in all wars, is the result of human sin. The suffering of so many children as a result of family disharmony and break-up is the consequence of sin. The fact that it is the poor who suffer throughout the world again is a result of sin, as expressed and maintained through unjust economic systems and political regimes. It is the poor who always suffer most as a result of natural disasters. The rich live away from earthquake zones or reinforce their houses, the poor

---

[2] Kraemer, *Responses*, 87.

can't. The only land available to the poor, as in Bangladesh, is too often that which is swept by floods. We live in a world darkened by sin, with the resultant terrible suffering falling so often on the most vulnerable and powerless.

Some biblical and Rabbinic writers of course recognized that it is very difficult to believe that in the case of a particular individual there is an exact equation between sin and suffering. They therefore asserted that God had a rather different purpose in mind. The suffering was to test and strengthen the character, as gold is tested in the furnace, to use an image they often repeated, to make it better fitted for the world to come. This is not punishment but 'the sufferings of love', as the Rabbis termed them. Again, there is an important truth in this at a general level. We recognize that many of the qualities we most admire in human beings, their courage, patience, sympathy, and love are given an opportunity to arise just because life is not always easy. In Eden there was no need for courage, because there was no fear; no need for patience because there was no hardship to endure; no need for sympathy because there was no suffering; no need for a love that bears all things, because there was nothing to bear. We can therefore agree, however reluctantly, that if we want these qualities which we so much admire, earthly life cannot be a paradise. If it is a 'vale of soul-making', then that vale must have its rocks as well as its green pastures.

All this may be true at the general level but it simply does not work in relation to individuals. Suffering can break people as much as it improves them. We work on the assumption, quite rightly, that a good home, with enough to live on, will be more likely to produce decent people than one wracked by poverty. Good breeds more good than evil ever can. Furthermore, whilst it might be very good for me to be tested and strengthened, often the price is much too high. I may develop all kinds of good qualities as a result of the loss of my children—but I would rather have them back. And what about them? They had no say in whether they were willing to lose their lives that I might grow in courage and sympathy. And in the end can we believe in a God who is always about to pull the carpet from under us? Someone who claimed to be a friend but who deliberately tripped us up on the stairs in order to break our leg and see whether we would

41

develop qualities of patience in adversity, would not long remain our friend. So with God.

We therefore come to one of the most important insights of the biblical and Rabbinic writings: the protest against this whole way of thinking. Protest against the idea that a particular individual is suffering because of his or her sins; protest against the idea that God has sent the suffering that they might develop in character. Classically it is expressed by Job in reaction to the false comfort offered him. In the Rabbinic writings, although the general tendency is that people should be encouraged to accept suffering as a test, protest is allowed to break through. In a Midrash from the later Palestinian period on the Song of Songs Rabbi Yohanan became ill. When he was told that his great suffering would bring great rewards he replied: 'I want neither them nor their reward.'[3] In the Babylonian Talmud the question 'Is suffering dear to you?' is answered with even more emphasis, 'Neither its nor its reward.'[4] Then in the discussion on death, the connection between sin and suffering is even more decisively refuted. The discussion focuses on Adam, whose death was regarded as a punishment for sin and Moses who lived a righteous life but who still died. A conclusion of the dialogue is 'There is death without sin and there is suffering without transgression' and the refutation of the contrary opinion is a 'Definitive refutation'.[5]

A dramatic example of the willingness of faithful people to carry the argument to God himself occurs in the Rabbinic reading of the Book of Lamentations. This concerns God contemplating destroying the temple and sending the Israelites into exile in Babylon. Abraham pleads with God not to do this, so do Isaac, Jacob, and Moses, all to no avail. Then 'Rachel, our mother, leapt to the fray' and pointed out to God that she had waited for Jacob for seven years and that after those seven years when the time came for her wedding, her sister took her place in bed. But having compassion for her sister, Rachel crawled under the bed on which Jacob was lying with her sister. As she said to God:

I made all the replies so that he would not discern the voice of my sister. I have paid my sister only kindness, and I was not jealous of her, and I did not allow

---

[3] Kraemer, *Responses*, 132.   [4] Ibid. 196.   [5] Ibid. 185.

her to be ashamed, and I am a mere mortal, dust and ashes . . . but you are the king, living and enduring and merciful. How come that you are jealous of idolatry which is nothing, and so have sent my children into exile. . . . Forthwith the mercy of the Holy One, blessed be he, welled up, and he said: 'For Rachel I am going to bring the Israelites back to their land.'[6]

This moral protest against what are alleged to be the decrees of God has found expression many times in response to the Holocaust, notably in the work of Elie Wiesel already quoted. Another example is his autobiographical memoir *Night*. Elie Wiesel describes himself as a young boy fascinated with God's mystery, studying Talmud. When he was in Auschwitz and the Jews gathered together to celebrate Rosh Hashanah, he thought angrily to himself, 'Where are you, my God?'

Why, but why should I bless him? In every fibre I rebelled. Because he had had thousands of children burnt in his pits? Because he kept six cemeteries working night and day, on Sundays and feast days?

Suddenly Wiesel feels strong, stronger than God:

This day I have ceased to plead. I was no longer capable of lamentation. On the contrary, I felt very strong. I was the accuser, God the accused.[7]

Although it is Elie Wiesel who has made this kind of protest so well known, it is a theme that is present elsewhere, for example in some of the Polish and Yiddish poetry that came out of the camps.[8] Until recently this kind of argument with God, springing from a profound sense of moral protest, has not been so strongly part of the Christian tradition. It emerged through Ivan Karamazov in Dostoevsky's great novel, *The Brothers Karamazov* and in the final poems of Gerard Manley Hopkins. It is there in a secular form with Christian sympathies in *The Plague* by Albert Camus but this attitude has not been a prominent part of the Christian tradition. The tendency of all monotheistic religions is to emphasize submission to the divine. One of the great strengths of Judaism, as these quotations show, is its

[6] Lamentations Rabbati Petihta 24. Discussed by J. Neusner in *Telling Tales* (Westminster/John Knox, 1993) 109 f.   [7] Elie Wiesel, *Night* (Penguin, 1981), 78–81.

[8] Frieda Roan, 'Yet the Song Continued: Polish and Yiddish Poetry in the Ghettos and Concentration Camps', *Remembering for the Future* (Pergamon, 1989), ii. 1407.

anguished protest, its shift away from sheer submission to argument and dialogue, to having it out with God. The honesty of this response is particularly important for the possibility of faith in our times.

Suffering is not 'sent' directly from God, either for punishment or testing. We need to look at the matter very differently. Suffering is rooted in pain and this capacity to be hurt is simply part of our survival mechanism, as much as our eyes or ears. Without this sensitivity to pain we would walk into fires, jump off cliffs, and fail to seek medical attention when we needed it. Pain is nature's early warning system: an essential feature of our existence as physical creatures, if we are to survive at all.

Our Relationship to God: A More Important Question?

Oliver Leaman, in the book already referred to, roots his discussion of the subject in the book of Job and analyses the response to the dilemmas there presented by Jewish thinkers, who, whilst they may not be professional philosophers, have sought to give a systematic, philosophical answer. He discusses Philo (25 BCE–50 CE), Saadya Gaon (887–942), Maimonides (1135–1204), Gersonides (1288–1344), Spinoza (1632–77), Mendelssohn (1729–86), Hermann Cohen (1842–1918), Martin Buber (1878–1965), and a range of modern writers who reflected on the evil of the Holocaust. Though these responses have been very varied, Leaman suggests that the most profound and distinctive Jewish approach is not in fact a philosophical one at all, but a further question about what constitutes a right relationship to God. Job questioned God and received, not an intellectual answer to his questions, but an assurance of his presence. Rabbi Akiba was burnt at the stake and while reciting *Shema* before death, as Jews are supposed to do, he is said to have reflected with joy that for the first time he understood the part of the familiar prayer which refers to loving God with all one's might. So Leaman writes:

Akiba and Job have different views on the nature of evil and suffering, and yet they are both rewarded. How can we explain this? It may well be because they both understand that what the issue of evil and suffering is really about is our relationship with God. This issue is in fact a misplaced metaphor. It seems to concern evil and suffering, but this can be very misleading. The development of this issue in Jewish philosophy throws light not so much on the nature of evil but more of the nature of God and on our relationship with him. What both Job and Akiba end up emphasising is the way in which we relate to God as to someone who is the source of grace.[9]

In this understanding Leaman seems to have been particularly influenced by Rosenzweig and Buber. Both criticize a remote God and emphasize that the disclosure of God to Moses is 'His being-present for you and with you, now and in the future'. For Buber God is like a father who holds the hand of his child in the dark, where the purpose is not only to guide but to communicate his presence. God is the one who is continually with us. The child has to take his own decisions and go his own direction but he will be supported by the continuing presence of his father.

Two questions arise in relation to this approach. First, whether this is in fact a distinctively Jewish understanding or whether it is also shared by Christians and, secondly, how adequate it is to the dilemmas originally posed? In answer to the first question I suspect that the response which Leaman delineates in the Jewish philosophical tradition as scholars reflected on the experience of Job is in fact characteristic of a particular kind of devout mind as likely to be found within Christianity as in Judaism. Christian sermons down the ages have reiterated the response of Job after he had experienced the wondrous splendour of God (Job 42: 1–6):

I know that you can do all things
and that no purpose is beyond you.
You ask: who this is obscuring counsel yet lacking knowledge?
But I have spoken of things which I have not understood,
things too wonderful for me to know.
Listen, and let me speak.
You said:
I shall put questions to you, and you must answer.
I knew of you then only by report,
but now I see you with my own eyes.

[9] Leaman, *Evil and Suffering in Jewish Philosophy*, 248.

Therefore I yield,
repenting in dust and ashes.

There are many Christians who would want to affirm with Pascal

'God of Abraham, God of Isaac, God of Jacob', not of the philosophers and
    savants,
Certitude. Certitude. Feeling. Joy. Peace.
God of Jesus Christ.
My God and thy God
'Thy God shall be my God.'

I do not myself, however, believe that this approach, by itself, is an
adequate response to the agonizing issue of evil and suffering. First,
very few people have had the kind of overwhelming encounter with
God that Job and Pascal reported, an experience that stills all intellectual questioning. Secondly, for any thinking person, unless there is
some intellectual understanding that at least enables one to live with
the questions rather than be overwhelmed by them, they will not be
open to the experience of God as God. Or, if they do believe that they
have a real relationship, that relationship can be eroded by a persistent
failure to achieve a coherent and consistent view of human existence
which can understand the place of evil and suffering.

In fact, mind and heart cannot be separated in quite the way that
what Leaman distinguishes as a Jewish approach suggests. Faith, as
Anselm said, is always faith seeking understanding. No arguments or
bad arguments about the role of suffering can close the heart to
God. Some real and honest attempt to account for suffering as an
inescapable part of the created order will at least keep open the possibility of a wise and loving power behind it. Leaman suggests that the
kind of experience that Job had establishes a certain relationship with
God and that the next stage is to work out how what one can know
about God explains the way things are in the world. But the reality and
depth of our relationship with God and our attempt to understand the
world are much more interconnected than this suggests. Many people
believe they have a relationship of some kind with God but their faith
can be terribly knocked by personal tragedy or the daily catalogue of
human evil and suffering.

Responding Creatively

When we suffer, we have to respond. First, in practical ways to try to eliminate or reduce the suffering. Then, if that is totally impossible, as for example when someone we love has died, other responses become necessary. One instinctive, early response may be protest and anger and this, as I have suggested, is all part of enabling our relationship vith God to be real. But a person might work through this to other, creative responses. The point about this is that as human beings we are free to make a response. It is up to us. There is a possibility of something genuinely, creatively new. It's not all laid down in advance. When we look at a shoreline we see the waves breaking endlessly on the beach. As a result of millions and millions of interactions throughout time those particular waves beat there on that beach and will go on doing so for as long as we can imagine. There is an impersonality about those waves. But we can make a personal response to them in a variety of ways. Some will go surfing, others will simply gambol in the shallows. Others will draw or paint. Some will pray, thanking God for their beauty and others will reflect on the mystery of nature and life. None of these responses excludes the others. There is a creative interaction between the mind and spirit of the person, on the one hand, and the impersonal forces of nature, on the other. The pain we experience through a broken leg or cancer is a result of forces no less impersonal than those which brought the waves to the shore. And we have the same opportunity for a personal, creative response. For a believer this response will be worked out in dialogue with God. There is a will of God for good in that situation which is to be discerned and done. One of the major emphases that emerged from the earlier discussion on Jewish responses to the Shoah was the prime responsibility of human beings and the Jewish capacity to make a creative response to tragedy. God is silent because he wants us to make the decision. God is hidden because he wants us to act. He wants us to stand on our own feet, to be mature responsible beings. Of course this can take an atheistic form and, indeed, it is normally associated with atheism. But in Judaism it has become a significant part of what it actually means to be Jewish. Nor is this insight lacking in Christianity. It emerged particularly strongly in the letters of Dietrich Bonhoeffer which he wrote in prison.

> So our coming of age forces us to a true recognition of our situation *vis a vis* God. God is teaching us that we must live as men who can get along very well without him. The God who is with us is the God who forsakes us. (Mark 15: 34). The God who makes us live in this world without using him as a working hypothesis is the God before whom we are ever standing. Before God and with him we live without God.[10]

The distinctive response of Judaism in the face of adversity is, creatively, to choose life. As Irving Greenberg puts it:

> The classic Jewish response to catastrophe is to renew life. Every major Jewish catastrophe has led to the falling away of some Jews as they lost faith, but every major tragedy has also led to revival, as other Jews strove harder to match tragedy with hope.[11]

It was this powerful impetus which led to the founding of the State of Israel after the Shoah. As already quoted, the Chief Rabbi, Dr Jonathan Sacks, has written about the Jewish people:

> Faced with destruction, it has chosen survival. *Lo amut ki echyeh*, says the psalm: 'I will not die, but I will live.' . . . Without answers the Jewish people has its covenant with history. The people Israel lives and still bears witness to the living God.[12]

At a personal level, suffering has led some to intensify their devotion, as with a good number of Jews in the camps. Others have responded to suffering in such a way that others have seen in them an extraordinary display of courage and patience and selflessness. Yet others have offered their suffering to God in order that it might be used in some way for redemption. In the commentary on and expansion of the Mishnah known as the Tosefta we read that neither repentance alone nor the day of atonement alone can atone for desecrating the name of heaven. 'Rather, repentance and the day of atonement atone a third,

---

[10] Dietrich Bonhoeffer, *Letters and Papers from Prison* (Fontana, 1959), 122.

[11] Irving Greenberg, 'The Unfinished Business of Tisha B'Av', *Jewish Chronicle* (4 Aug. 1995).

[12] Jonathan Sacks, *Faith in the Future* (Darton, Longman and Todd, 1995), 242.

and sufferings atone a third, and the day of death cleanses along with suffering.'[13] Suffering plays a role in atonement, in redemption. We see this in everyday life. A mother with a difficult teenage son going through a period of rebellion, experimenting with drugs and so on, continues to reach out to him, to care for him and to help him through. But this cannot be done without her bearing much hurt within herself. He should be suffering the consequences of his actions. Instead, she is bearing them within herself. This is part of the price she pays for going on loving him, helping him to find himself and grow into his true self. So, when someone suffers, one response might be for them to offer that hurt for a wider redemption. In none of these instances should it be said that God has caused the suffering in order to bring about certain moral or spiritual values. Rather, suffering is an inescapable part of any kind of physical existence. But as free beings, made in the image of God, we can make a creative response as part of our response to God. Or, to put it another way, God is ceaselessly working to draw some unique good out of every situation and we can seek to discern and co-operate with this purpose.

Seeing the suffering of the Shoah as something done for the benefit of others and the redemption of the world was, understandably, not part of the main Jewish response. Jews had suffered enough and they did not want to add to the indignity of those who died by thrusting upon them any kind of meaning for their suffering which would detract from the sheer evil of what happened. Nevertheless, it is important to bear in mind that suffering on behalf of others is strongly there in the Jewish tradition and is not confined to Christianity. This has been brought out recently by three essays in *Christianity in Jewish Terms*, a book which will be discussed more fully later. A Jewish writer Leora Batnitzky points out that Isaiah 53 about the suffering servant has been just as important for the Jews as it has for Christians, only of course for Jews the suffering servant to which it refers is the people of Israel as a whole. She says, 'That there is theological and ethical value in suffering for others is basic to the Jewish tradition in its rabbinic, mediaeval and modern forms.' She finds this not only in discussions of

---

[13] David Kraemer, *Responses to Suffering in Classical Rabbinic Literature*, 68.

Isaiah 53 but also in discussions of the chosenness of the people of Israel and in commentaries on the binding of Isaac. Indeed medieval Jews quoted Isaiah explicitly to prove to Christians that the degraded status of the Jewish community was in keeping with Jewish chosenness. The same theme is there in Judah Halevi and in some nineteenth-century Jewish thought. She does, however, argue that there is a difference between Christianity and Judaism, in that the former regards suffering as of intrinsic value, whilst the latter regards it as something which can be put to good use but which is not of value in itself. Robert Gibbs, another Jewish scholar, is highly critical of the usual stereotype that Christianity tries to find a meaning in suffering and Judaism doesn't. Whilst he certainly understands why people should hold this stereotype, he argues that it is essential to Judaism, and true to its tradition that it too tries to make suffering yield meaning: 'The martyr does not will suffering but suffers for the sake of God's name. And in many strands of this theme, God suffers with the suffering Jews.'

Christian scholar John Cavadini responds sympathetically to those two essays but denies that Christianity as a whole sees an intrinsic value in suffering. In particular he looks at St Augustine's understanding of original sin. If suffering is a result of original sin, then it must be seen as evil, not as good in itself. Conformation of one's suffering to Christ is a use of suffering 'that faith in Christ permits without turning the intrinsic evil of suffering into something good or useful in itself'.[14] Whatever impressions some Christians might have given in the past, we cannot believe that suffering is good in itself. The assumption behind every parent's care for their child, every teacher's concern for the pupils they teach, everyone concerned with social welfare, is that ensuring that people are decently fed and housed, healthy, stimulated and cared for, is that physical and material well-being is the primary good. This is what God wills for people, which is why we try to ensure that people have an adequate standard of living; that so far as possible they are kept out of pain and that they are not bullied or oppressed by

[14] The three essays are in ch. 9 on 'Suffering', in Tikva Frymer-Kensky, David Novak, Peter Ochs, David Sandmel, and Michael Signer (eds.), *Christianity in Jewish Terms* (Westview Press, 2000), 203–37.

others. Nevertheless, it is open to us, as both Jews and Christians, to try to give our own human suffering—not that of others, that is up to them—some meaning. For some this has meant offering it to God for the redemption of others. St Paul wrote from prison to the Christians at Colossae:

> It is now my happiness to suffer for you. This is my way of helping to complete, in my poor human flesh, the full tale of Christ's afflictions still to be endured, for the sake of his body which is the church. (Colossians 1: 24)

The Greek word which is translated as 'afflictions still to be endured' is a technical term for the birth pangs of the Messianic age. This is also a theme which has been present in some forms of Jewish thought, even in response to the Shoah. Although it was not part of the post-war understanding, there were Jews who met their death in this spirit. Elchanan Wasserman was one of the leading Rabbis of the pre-war generation. When he visited the United States in 1938 he was dismayed by the lack of observance amongst Jews. Norman Solomon has written that those of us who tend angrily to dismiss all talk of 'punishment for sin' need to understand the feelings of dismay of people like Wasserman.

> To understand the Rabbis who spoke and even now speak in this way it is necessary to know how deeply they felt the gulf between the ideal demanded by Torah and the reality of modern secular civilisation. It was for them, in their piety and faithfulness, as if the modern way of life, adopted by many Jews through assimilation to 'The ways of the nations round about', had totally destroyed the holy world of the Jew nurtured over the centuries.[15]

Wasserman was martyred in 1941 and there is a graphic eye-witness account of what he said before he died.

> It seems that in Heaven we are regarded as *Tzadikkim* ['Righteous'. Norman Solomon comments 'He is not boasting, but expressing mild surprise at the divine compliment of having been selected for a sacred task'], for we are being asked to atone with our bodies for the sins of Israel. Now we really must do *Teshuva* (repent) in such a manner—for the time is short and we are not far

---

[15] Norman Solomon, *Jewish Responses to the Holocaust* (Centre for the Study of Judaism and Jewish–Christian Relations, Birmingham, 1988), 8.

from the ninth port—we must have in mind that we would be better sacrifices if we do *Teshuva*, and we may [save?] our American brothers and sisters. . . . We are about to fulfil the greatest *Mitzva* of all—'With fire you destroyed it, with fire you will rebuild it'—the fire which destroys our bodies is the self-same fire which will restore the Jewish people.[16]

So although the emphasis upon vicarious suffering, using one's sufferings for others and the advance of God's purpose in the world, is particularly associated with Christianity, as we have seen it is firmly embedded in the Jewish tradition. Although it was not prominent in the responses to the Shoah after World War II, the attitude of Rabbi Wasserman (and others) shows that this was still a living idea for at least some of those who were murdered.

Hope in the Face of Death

Suffering is an inescapable part of human life, arising either from our existence as vulnerable physical beings in a material world or as a result of the negligence, weakness, and malevolence of other human beings. It may be that we come to believe that there is no other way in which we could have come into existence, that these are the inescapable conditions of finite being, that we could not be on any other terms. But this acceptance, if it comes about, has gone together with one of the most deeply felt and passionate convictions of Judaism, namely God's will to overcome all evil and establish his just domain. Time and again in the Hebrew scriptures this hope breaks through. It is there in the Rabbinic writings and it has sustained millions of Jews in adversity down the ages. However long delayed, the time will come when God's Kingdom will be established. If we believe that God loves each person as though they were the only one, then it is difficult to avoid the conclusion that God's perfect kingdom must gather into it all who have ever lived; that all wrong in history will be put right and that God's faithful ones who once suffered will be revealed in all the glory and beauty of their being. Indeed some would maintain that this hope is fundamental to the retention of faith in a

---

[16] Quoted by Norman Solomon, ibid. 10.

wise and loving Creator. Although this hope grew up comparatively late in biblical times and though many Jews today sit light to it, I believe it is basic to Judaism, as to any faith in a God who is to be trusted and loved. For God is not a social engineer. He is not simply concerned to achieve a perfect society in the future for which the whole of previous history pays the price. He is no less concerned with all who have gone before.

Rabbi Dan Cohn-Sherbok in his book *Holocaust Theology* and other writings has been highly critical of other Jewish responses to the Holocaust for a variety of reasons but above all because they have not taken into account the hope of life after death. He believes that there is absolutely no way in which such evil can be squared with the existence of a loving God without taking into account the divine vindication of innocent sufferers in the hereafter. He quotes a letter allegedly discovered in a jar in the Warsaw ghetto by someone expecting death from the Nazis 'In an hour at most I will be with my wife and children and with millions of people who died, in that better world, where God rules alone.' Unfortunately that testimonial like others has been dismissed as a 'post-Holocaust invention', one of the edifying fictions or fairy tales that have become associated with that terrible time.[17] There are I think a number of reasons why the hope of an afterlife has played virtually no role in theological responses to the Holocaust. There is of course the point mentioned by Norman Solomon and referred to earlier, the general erosion of such belief in the modern world because of what we know about the unity of body, mind, and spirit and the difficulty of conceiving of a separate entity outliving the death of the physical body. But more important I think has been the moral protest against any concentration on life after death. Most famously Karl Marx criticized it as a displaced hope. People should be hoping and working for a better world, instead of resigning themselves to suffering now in the hope of a happier existence in the hereafter. The novelist Iris Murdoch once said that 'All that consoles is fake.' This lapidary statement sums up Freud's influence on so much of the twentieth century. We are so conscious of the suffering of the world and so

---

[17] The testimony is quoted in Dan Cohn-Sherbok, *Holocaust Theology* (Marshall Morgan and Scott, 1989), 126. The rejection is by Zev Ben-Shlomo, *Jewish Chronicle* (1 Sept. 1995).

suspicious of any kind of wishful thinking that we reject any kind of consolatory philosophy or theology out of hand. There is a moral dimension to this as well, in that it forces us to focus on the reality of this world, however bleak. Yet when it comes to the Holocaust I think that there is an even more fundamental reason why the thought of life after death has played no part in theological thinking. For it would be too easy for people to slip from having hope in the hereafter for those who died, into feeling unconsciously, even if it was never stated consciously, that the Holocaust was not the evil if it was. It was evil, of course it was, so the thought goes, but those who perished live forever now in God. The problem is that, however it is put, this can detract from the cruelty, degradation, suffering, and unspeakable evil of what happened. However well meant, it can seem to cheapen the lives and deaths of those who died. So the theologians were perhaps right to be silent on this point; to say nothing, rather than become the worst kind of Job's comforter.

And yet, and yet. A major theme running all through the Hebrew Bible, a theme championed equally by Jews and Christians, is that God's justice will finally prevail; in time or out of time innocent sufferers will be vindicated and divine justice will be done and shown to be done to those who have perpetrated evil. In every generation the cry goes up 'How long, O Lord, how long?' In John's vision of heaven, underneath the divine altar the souls of those who have been slaughtered for God's word and for the testimony they bore cry out (Revelation 6: 10). Christian liberation theologians have worked with the poor and spoken for the poor to bring about better conditions on this earth. Their concern is justice. But as the Vatican document which discussed liberation theology puts it:

For true justice must include everyone; it must bring the answer to the immense load of suffering borne by all the generations. In fact without the resurrection of the dead and the Lord's judgement, there is no justice in the full sense of the term. The promise of the resurrection is freely made to meet the desire for true justice dwelling in the human heart.[18]

[18] *Instruction on Christian Freedom and Liberation*, III. 60.

Personally, I do not find it possible, from either a Jewish or a Christian point of view, to retain faith that there is a wise and loving power behind this universe without also having hope for the departed, especially those whose lives have been cut short by cruelty and injustice. It may not be possible to talk much about this hope, or indeed in some circumstances to talk about it at all, because love is prior to hope and love means focusing on the other person, where they are, in all their distress. So hope may very often remain a silent hope; but it will be hope none the less, hope in the face of death and hope that God's purpose of love will finally prevail.

Suffering in the world happens and it is not directly attributable to God. But in this suffering there is the hope that God will indeed act. Amongst the Halakhic Midrashim is one which tells the parable of a cow which gets badly treated by the people to whom it is lent until the owner comes to rescue it.

Similarly, Israel, in this world, one regime comes and enslaves them and then goes, then another regime comes and enslaves them and goes . . . Tomorrow when the end time arrives, the Holy One, blessed be he, will not say to the nations, 'Thus and thus have you done to my children.' Rather, he will immediately come and break the yoke and cut the ropes.[19]

Despite all appearance to the contrary, this is God's world and in the end his justice will be established and revealed for all to see. In place of the cruelty and injustice of human regimes, there will be only God's just and gentle rule. Here, however, emerges a moral conundrum. Should we not do what is right for its own sake? And does not a system of rewards and punishments undermine any attempt to achieve that? In one of the Haggadic Midrashim there is a discussion about whether death is an evil or whether it is part of the creation which God pronounced good. The opinion of Rabbi Yonatan is that death is a proper part of life and it is right that both good and evil people should die. For if only evil people died and the good lived for ever, the wicked would be tempted to do good simply in order to stave off death, for purely prudential reasons.

[19] David Kraemer, *Responses to Suffering in Classical Rabbinic Literature*, 91.

The real reason for death, even of the righteous, is so that the wicked do not do deceitful repentance, and the wicked do not say, 'The righteous live eternally only because they store up Mitzvot and good deeds, so too will we store up Mitzvot and good deeds', and thus, their performance of these deeds will not be for their own sake but only for the purpose of receiving a reward.[20]

This opinion was not accepted but it heightens the dilemma.

For us there can be no question of death being regarded as a punishment for sin. Death belongs to the natural order.[21] We were always as destined to die as were cockroaches and flamingos. Sin had nothing to do with it. The question therefore arises as to why God creates us as mortal creatures, with only a limited lifespan. And why does he not give us a clearer picture of what might lie beyond death? It's possible to hazard a guess about this.

First, if we lived for ever as finite creatures it would be difficult if not impossible to make anything of our life; there would always be a tomorrow and therefore the possibility of endlessly putting things off. The fact that we live only for a short period forces us to choose and act; to live out what matters to us. We can compare an artist, a sculptor, for example, who always has to carve a specific piece of stone, in a specific period, even if it is a long one. He does not have endless materials and endless time. The particularity and the specificity is of the essence. So it is with the shaping of our lives. Death is the edge of the canvas, the shape of the rough stone, the three hours which audiences will bear for watching a play. Given limits we are forced to choose, to shape things in one way rather than another, to decide what is important. Secondly, if I knew that, for example, lying would lead to a specific amount of post-mortem pain, in precisely the same way that I might know the effects of certain drugs, it would be difficult to avoid being honest for purely prudential reasons. There is nothing wrong with prudential self-interest. We could do with more of it. But in order for us to appreciate the good for its own sake and pursue it because it is desirable in itself, there needs to be a degree of unknowingness about the exact relationship between doing good and good's reward. If there was an

[20] David Kraemer, *Responses to Suffering in Classical Rabbinic Literature*, 136.
[21] Ibid. 89 and 162.

exact and certain calculus available, disinterested love as we know it, could not emerge.

We can see therefore that for us to shape our lives as an artist shapes his or her materials into a work of art, we need the horizon of death, the discipline of a limited number of days. To a person of faith in God's justice, we need a hope that this will indeed be established. Yet at the same time it is important that this should not be spelt out in exact and certain detail. Otherwise we would just be like people pressing buttons on a computer, knowing that each button would have a corresponding symbol on the screen. The uncertainty and unknowingness of what will happen after death creates the conditions in which we can do good for its own sake. We could use the analogy of a developing relationship between two people. One of them wants to marry the other and hopes and believes that this will one day come about. But if they start to be kind and to give presents etc. in order to bring about that result, we would think that something was wrong. These should be done for their own sake. On the other hand, it is hardly wrong to hold out the hope that the relationship will develop to a point where marriage would be natural. This is where the relationship if it deepened would lead. Similarly, heaven is where our relationship with God leads. Hope for the establishment of God's Kingdom must be strong enough for us to retain a faith in divine justice but indistinct enough in its details for us to come to appreciate good for its own sake. And these are the conditions under which people of faith find themselves living.

Sharing our Suffering

The danger of stressing the autonomy of the world and its processes is that this could become indistinguishable from Deism. If God lets things 'be', with their own life, does he then just stand back? No: for moment by moment he holds all things in being and moment by moment he enables all things to go on being themselves. In addition God has an infinite capacity to go out of himself and enter into the context and feelings of others, to know them from within and feel them from within.

A 7-year-old girl is abducted, sexually assaulted, and murdered. Where is God here? we ask, a question humans ask a thousand times a day. In faith we believe God is present. As the girl suffers, so does God. He suffers in her for her. He suffers also because of the twisted mind of the perpetrator. He is in anguish here and elsewhere to the end of time. But he seems to do nothing, absolutely nothing. What good is a God who weeps as McNamara allegedly wept over the war in Vietnam, doing nothing to stop it, who wrings his hands or holds them up in horror?

God, we believe, lets things take their course, for that is what creation means and he himself suffers in and through all things. He is present as 'the infinitely gentle, infinitely suffering thing' and he goes down defeated, as much as that 7-year-old girl does; goes down defeated a million times a day. In a discussion in the Haggadic Midrashim the focus is on the phrase in Lamentations 2: 3: 'He hath withdrawn his right hand in the presence of the foe.' Israel is bound and helpless. Rabbi Azariah and Rabbi Abbahu say:

The Holy One, blessed be he, said: it is written, 'I will be with him in distress' (Psalm 91: 15). Yet now my children are in pain and I am in comfort?! Consequently, as though it were possible, 'He withdrew his right hand in the presence of the foe.'[22]

The thrust of this Midrash is to look for an end to the enslavement of Israel. But as that opinion indicates, for the moment God has let himself be powerless with his powerless people. He does not use his right hand of power to save them. He lets events take their appalling course and suffers with them. 'I will be with him in distress.'

There are other clear sayings that make the same point. For example:

When God remembers his children who dwell in misery among the nations of the world, he causes two tears to fall into the ocean and the sound is heard from one end of the world to the other.

In another place we read that an angel came to God, fell on his face and said:

---

[22] David Kraemer, *Responses to Suffering in Classical Rabbinic Literature*, 139.

Lord of the universe, let *me* weep! You may not weep! He said to him: If you do not let me weep, I will enter into a place which you are not free to enter, and I will weep there. Thus it is written, 'If you do not hear this, my soul will weep in a secret place.'

Again, the *Encyclopaedia Judaica* sums up the thought of Franz Rosenzweig in these words:

The descent of the Shekhinah upon man and its dwelling among men is conceived by Rosenzweig as a separation which occurs in God himself. God descends and suffers with his people, wandering with them in exile. At the end, it is God who suffers the most, and a remnant of Israel who bears his sorrow.

This insight has recently received fresh acknowledgement and endorsement from Rabbi Albert Friedlander.[23]

It is I think important to stress this aspect of Jewish thought because the belief that God shares in human suffering has too often been associated only with Christianity. It is, however, very much to the fore in the Christian faith.[24] In Jesus God shares human anguish to the uttermost. The early Fathers thought that in taking our human nature God did not simply become a particular person but he also took into himself human nature as a whole. God's suffering on the cross is a sign of God sharing in every form of human suffering. Understandably, this has been a Christian truth that has received a great deal of emphasis ever since World War I. This means that, from a Christian point of view, when Jews suffer it is also Christ in them who suffers. Or, to put it even more starkly, when down the ages Christians have persecuted Jews in the name of Christ, the Christ to whom they appealed was even then in the agony of those whom they persecuted. There is a remarkable painting by the Jewish artist Marc Chagall called *White Crucifixion* reproduced on the cover. In small scenes around the outer edge of the painting there are depictions of some of the terrible events

---

[23] Dr Albert Friedlander, 'The Concept of a Suffering God in the Jewish Tradition and its relation to Christian Teaching', *Manna*, Theology Supplement. See also Tony Bayfield and Marcus Braybrooke (eds.), *Dialogue with a Difference* (SCM, 1992), part 3.

[24] See for example the essay 'The Power of Suffering Love' by Marcus Braybrooke and the response to this by Rabbi Colin Eimer and myself in Bayfield and Braybrooke (eds.), *Dialogue with a Difference*, part 3.

of the 1930s, synagogues being burnt down and people fleeing for their lives. One image is that of a Jewish figure with a scroll of the Torah from which a great band of light goes forth. The light goes up the centre of the painting to illuminate a figure on a cross, a Jew being crucified. Christians cannot help but see in this painting a figure of Jesus suffering in his own people. What a terrible paradox, so much cruelty or cruel indifference shown by people who have been baptized as Christians towards those in whom Jesus, the Christian Christ, continues to suffer. As Franklin Littell put it:

When the body of Christ is discovered at Auschwitz, it will be raised from among the victims, not hidden among the Catholic and Protestant and Orthodox guards and administrators.[25]

Despite the tragedy and suffering of human existence it has been the unfailing conviction of Judaism that life is a blessing; that, despite everything, it is better to have lived than never to have lived at all. The fact that God foresaw the sin and suffering and still went ahead with creation, is an expression of his mercy.

Rabbi Berekhiah said: When the Holy One, blessed be he, came to create the first human God saw righteous and wicked people arising from him. God said: If I create him, the wicked will arise from him. But if I don't create him, how will the righteous arise from him? What did the Holy One, blessed be he, do? God removed the way of the wicked from before God's sight and joined the attribute of mercy to himself and created Adam.[26]

Justice, if applied too strictly, would not have allowed for the creation of human beings. All human beings are conscious of the suffering and tragedy of the world. But if we were totally burdened and broken by this, if we allowed ourselves to be overwhelmed we would be no use to anyone. It would in effect be a denial of life. For life invites, demands, us to get up and get on and, despite everything, still to find opportunity for laughter and play. Yet we can never quite forget, nor should we. We pay a visit to the grave, we keep a photo on the bureau, we erect war memorials, we have our rituals. This approach, at once life-

---

[25] Franklin Littell, *The Crucifixion of Jesus* (Mercer University Press, 1986), 131.
[26] David Kraemer, *Responses to Suffering in Classical Rabbinic Literature*, 121.

affirming and sensitive, balanced and practical, is memorably expressed in the Tosefta; talking about the destruction of the temple:

Not to mourn at all is impossible, for the decree has already been enacted, but to mourn too much is also impossible. Rather the sages said thus: a man should plaster his home with plaster, and leave a small amount unplastered in memory of the temple.[27]

We are to get on with living but not to forget.

People in the past sometimes said too much in the way of explaining and justifying suffering as sent from God. The warning of the Tosefta is pertinent:

Just as there is over-reaching in trade, so too is there oppression by words and, moreover, oppression by words is a greater wrong than oppression with money . . . if illnesses and sufferings were coming upon him, or if he buries his children who have died prematurely, one should not speak to him as Job's colleagues spoke to him.[28]

Those who suffer want those they love beside them, sharing their pain. Words justifying and explaining are not usually wanted. Yet in the shared suffering, in the deliberate reticence, in the profound silence the hope remains; a hope sometimes expressed in prayer and always looking for the appropriate practical response.

A Shared Approach

When the silence ends and it is appropriate to speak, I think that Jews and Christians will both want to make the following points. First, God wills our well-being and ordinary human flourishing. In the Hebrew scriptures God wants every aspect of life to prosper. He wants our corn and wine and oil to increase. So it is very important when focusing on the attitude to suffering we get in the New Testament, where there is certainly great emphasis upon sharing in the suffering of Christ, to remember that this is affirmed against the background of the Hebrew scriptures in which God's will is health and happiness. Suffering itself is not of intrinsic value. It is also worth noting that the earliest

[27] Ibid. 76.   [28] Ibid. 69.

Christian art, as we have it in the catacombs, focuses almost entirely on scenes of deliverance, more often than not drawn from the Hebrew scriptures. The first depiction of Christ on the cross dates from the early fifth century. Christianity, particularly Western Christianity and its medieval form, may appear to have become fixated on suffering but in the early centuries it very much shared the Jewish hope of deliverance from it.

Secondly, God does not 'send' suffering. As Rabbi Jonathan Romain has put it:

God is not the source of suffering . . . God does not intervene in the world and is not responsible for everyday affairs . . . The world is in the hands of humanity. Misfortunes happen not because of a person's guilt or because of God's will but simply because such things happen.[29]

It is certainly true, and very understandable, that the more devout a person is the more they will want to try to see suffering in terms of God's will for them. A girl once met a tragic death. Her parents said to me that they supposed that God must want her in heaven even more than they wanted her on earth. I don't think so. It is better to acknowledge evil as evil, tragedy as tragedy, and recognize that so much that happens on this earth is plain contrary to God's purpose for us. It is not God's will but opposed to God's will. Because of this the Jewish tradition of protest against God, of questioning God, is so important.

Thirdly, we must shoulder the responsibility because we do have a capacity for good as well as evil. There were righteous Gentiles, and not just those who have so far received official recognition as such. Anne Frank's diary on Saturday 15 July 1944 reads:

It's really a wonder that I haven't dropped all my ideals because they are so absurd and impossible to carry out. Yet, I keep them, because in spite of everything I still believe that people are really good at heart. . . . I see the world gradually being turned into a wilderness, I hear the ever approaching thunder, which will destroy us too . . . in the meantime, I must uphold my ideals, for perhaps the time will come when I shall be able to carry them out.

---

[29] Jonathan Romain, *Faith and Practice—A Guide to Reformed Judaism Today* (The Reformed Society of Great Britain, 1992), 35.

Fourthly, because of this, we can make a constructive response even to most appalling tragedy, as Jewish history down the ages shows. In Chaim Potok's novel *The Chosen* Ruven and his father discuss the Holocaust and the view that it has to be accepted as God's will. Ruven is not satisfied with that answer. His father says, 'I'm not satisfied with it, either, Ruven. We cannot wait for God. If there is an answer, we must make it ourselves.'[30] It is crucial at this point, however, not to slip into thinking that because human beings can sometimes wrest something good out of evil, God designed the evil in order to bring the good out of it. That is a totally fallacious step. For whatever reason, pain and anguish is part of human existence.[31] Austin Farrer gets the balance just right when he writes:

Good, even animal good, such as physical health or a moderate plenty, is a more fertile breeder of good on the whole—yes even of moral good—than distress of any kind can be. . . . Good breeds more good than evil can. It is a special revelation of God's divine power that he is able to bring some good even out of evil.[32]

Fifthly, God's purpose will finally prevail. Justice will out.

I believe that all these five affirmations are shared by both Jews and Christians. Nevertheless, it probably remains true that Judaism will emphasize some and Christianity others. It is an interesting exercise to look at those five affirmations and ask oneself which are most emphasized by Judaism and which by Christianity. In my judgement, Judaism emphasizes the first more than Christianity. The second has been emphasized equally, in the modern world, by Jews and Christians. The third has been stressed most strongly by Judaism, the fourth has been part of both traditions though it is Christianity that has stressed that when we are trying to act constructively, it is God himself who is trying to bring good out of evil and our task is to co-operate with him in that work. The fifth one probably varies a very great deal depending upon which tradition of Judaism and which tradition of Christianity one is thinking of.

[30] Chaim Potok, *The Chosen* (Penguin, 1966), 191.

[31] This wider debate I have discussed in 'Evidence for God's Love', in Richard Harries *Questioning Belief* (SPCK, 1995), ch. 3.

[32] Austin Farrer, *Love Almighty and Ills Unlimited* (Fontana, 1962), 167.

Responses to Suffering

The challenge for Jews since the Shoah has been to rebuild Jewish life both in the Diaspora and in Israel. The challenge that the Shoah poses to Christians is a double one. For it not only poses the problem of evil in its starkest form conceivable, it faces the Christian churches with the fact that this evil occurred in the heart of what might legitimately have been called the most civilized and Christian culture in the world. So Christians are faced not only with the fact that this massive suffering somehow has to be reconciled with a loving creator but that the Christian Church was significantly responsible for this suffering in the twofold sense of preparing the ground through centuries of anti-Judaic teaching and in either carrying out or at least being complicit in the attempt to exterminate Jews and Judaism. The quotation from the poet Swinburne comes to mind again. When Christ was on the cross did he reflect on all the horrors which would be perpetuated in his name? Since World War II Jews have taken upon themselves the responsibility of rebuilding Judaism. So the Christian Churches have begun to radically rethink their relationship to Judaism and rebuild it on a new more constructive basis. To this I now turn.

Forgive and Forget? 4

One of the underlying tensions between Judaism and Christianity, which erupts from time to time, is their alleged attitude to forgiveness. I say alleged, because it has to be examined whether there really is a difference and, if so, in what that difference consists. First, however, it must be stressed that for both Judaism and Christianity, the concept of forgiveness emerges in the context of relationships: our relationship with one another and our relationship with God. Sometimes the implications of some metaphors connected with forgiveness, such as 'wiping the slate clean', can imply an impersonal process. But forgiveness is always about how one person restores a relationship with another.

The *Oxford English Dictionary* includes under the heading forgive 'To give up, cease to harbour (resentment etc.) . . . to remit (a debt) . . . to give up claim to, requital for an offence or pardon for an offender'. In short, it is about continuing in relationship with another person even when you think they have hurt you or done you harm: not holding this harm against them but continuing to reach out to them. In the classic Christian picture the prodigal son wants to return home to his father and the father receives him back with rejoicing without harping on the fact that the son has blown the family money (Luke 15: 11–32).

A stereotype which has gone deep into Western culture is that Christians are willing to forgive and Jews are not. In Shakespeare's *The Merchant of Venice*, for example, Portia makes a case for mercy. In response Shylock declares

Forgive and Forget?

> My deeds upon my head! I crave the law
> the penalty and forfeit of my bond.   (IV, i. 203–4)

A little later Shylock again emphasizes:

> There is no power in the tongue of man
> to alter me. I stay here on my bond.   (IV, i. 237–8)

This stereotype is damaging: it is also false. In addition there is a sinister echo in the words 'My deeds upon my head' of the cry of the crowds in the gospel 'His blood be on us and our children' (Matthew 27: 25).

This stereotype can surface in surprising quarters. Dr Anthony Phillips is an Old Testament scholar and has been adviser to the Archbishop of Canterbury on Jewish–Christian relations. But in an article in *The Times* in 1985 he ended with the words 'In remembering the Holocaust, Jews hope to prevent its recurrence: by declining to forgive I fear that they unwittingly invite it.' This caused a double offence. First, that a Jewish unwillingness to forgive the unspeakable evil of the Holocaust would somehow bring upon them another tragedy, and, secondly, that Jews are unwilling to forgive and, in the case of the Holocaust, are to be blamed for this unwillingness.[1]

Christians tend to assume the high moral ground in their emphasis upon forgiveness. So it has to be emphasized that there is a moral case in favour of not forgiving and a moral protest to be made against what appears to be easy forgiveness. If someone murders your child you have the preciousness of that child in your mind, their value as a unique person loved and cherished by you and others. Forgiving the perpetrators of the evil deed can make it sound too easy, a cheapening of the life of the one you love. You hold their memory dear, the worth of your dead child is much more, as it seems to you, than the worth of the murderer, let alone their peace of mind. This example concerns the death of a single person. When this is magnified six million times and includes the loss not only of individual lives but of whole cultures the sense of protest against talk of forgiveness can be well understood. Not only does it seem to detract from the value of what has been lost on

---

[1] The letter by Anthony Phillips and the whole correspondence caused by this controversy is helpfully gathered together in *European Judaism*, 19/2 (Spring 1985). Also see below, n. 17, and the Appendix to this chapter.

such a gigantic scale but it detracts from a proper sense of horror at evil as evil.

There is also the question as to who has the right to forgive. Here it would be wrong to think that this question is posed only in Judaism. It is also there most powerfully in Dostoevsky. In *The Brothers Karamazov* Ivan tells some stories of horrific cruelty to children. He does not believe that God was justified in creating a world in which such things could happen. He argues that no future reconciliation or harmony could ever justify a world in which such evil occurs. He says:

I do not want a mother to embrace the torturer who had her child torn to pieces by his dogs! She has no right to forgive him! If she likes, she can forgive him for herself, she can forgive the torturer for the immeasurable suffering he has inflicted upon her as a mother; but she has no right to forgive him for the suffering of her tortured child. She has no right to forgive the torturer for that, even if her child were to forgive him! If that is so, if they have no right to forgive him, what becomes of the harmony? Is there in the whole world a being who could or would have the right to forgive? I don't want harmony. I don't want it, out of the love I bear to mankind. I want to remain with my suffering unavenged and my indignation unappeased, *even if I were wrong.*[2]

Christians tend to identify both themselves and Dostoevsky himself with Alyosha, the other brother. But Stewart Sutherland (now Lord Sutherland), when Professor of the Philosophy and History of the Christian Religion at King's College London, used to give a lecture entitled 'Will the real Mr Dostoevsky stand up?' The debate between the three brothers was a debate going on within Dostoevsky's own mind and it is a very proper debate to go on within any Christian mind. For the moment we draw the conclusion from this passage that those who are hurt, and only those who are hurt, have the moral right to forgive those who have done the hurt to them. There is a further question: whether Ivan, when he asserts 'She has no right to forgive the torturer for that, even if her child were to forgive him!' is correct. This is a question I will return to.

Both Christianity and Judaism have their basis in the Hebrew scriptures, the Christian Old Testament. There the theme of God's

---

[2] Dostoevsky, *The Brothers Karamazov* (Penguin, 1958), i. 287.

willingness to forgive his sinful people, is loud and clear. When King Solomon builds the temple and prays to God, his prayer includes the words 'Hear thou in Heaven thy dwelling and, when thou hearest, forgive' (1 Kings 8: 30). Later Solomon hears the Lord saying to him, 'If my people whom I have named my own submit and pray to me and seek me and turn back from their evil ways, I will hear from heaven and forgive their sins and heal their land' (2 Chronicles 7: 14). As the Psalmist put it:

> Thou, O Lord, art kind and forgiving,
> full of true love for all who cry to thee.   (Psalm 86: 5)

But in thee is forgiveness, and therefore thou art revered   (Psalm 130: 4)

If one aspect of forgiveness is God's willingness to restore his relationship to us the other is our willingness to restore our relationship with those who have hurt or damaged us. Anthony Harvey argues that what is so familiar to Christians, as expressed in the Lord's Prayer 'Father, forgive our sins as we forgive those who sin against us', is also there in pre-Christian Jewish tradition. Referring to Mark 11: 25 he says:

This is traditional wisdom teaching on prayer: it is succinctly expressed in Ben Sira: 'Forgive your neighbour any wrong he has done you; then, when you pray, your sins will be forgiven'.   (28: 3)[3]

This emphasis is also there in the formative period of Jewish life, as expressed in the Mishnah and the Talmud. A. Cohen, summing up the teaching of Rabbis in this period, says that two attitudes are fundamental for community harmony: first, people must be willing to admit that they have done something wrong and ask pardon for it. 'Secondly, it was the duty of the aggrieved party to accept the apology when made to him and not nurse his grievance'; 'forgive an insult done to you' (ARN xl1). Again, one particular Rabbi, on going to bed, used to offer the prayer 'Forgive whoever has caused me trouble' (Meg. 28a). Cohen says that 'To refuse to repair the breach and reject the overtures when they are made is an attitude which is censured':

---

[3] A. E. Harvey, *Strenuous Commands* (SCM, 1990), 112.

Whoever is compassionate towards his fellow creatures (and forgives wrongs done to him), compassion is shown to him from heaven; and whoever is not compassionate towards his fellow creatures, compassion is not shown to him from heaven.   (Shab. 151b)[4]

There is no doubt that an emphasis both on God's forgiveness and our obligation to forgive others is particularly strong in the teaching of Jesus. There is no reason to deny that there are features of his teaching which whilst rooted in and drawing on the great tradition of Judaism, find in him a distinctive voice. But the point is that, however much he stressed these truths, he did not invent them. Nor are they confined to Christianity but, as we have seen, they were taken up in the defining period of Judaism.

In the modern period of Judaism, again, both insights are fundamental. The mercy and forgiveness of God underlie every Jewish prayer and examples could be multiplied a million times. To take just one from the Authorised Daily Prayer Book of the United Hebrew Congregations of the British Commonwealth of Nations, the following words are said on Monday and Thursday mornings:

And he, being merciful, forgiveth iniquity and destroyeth not: yea, many a time he turneth his anger away, and doth not stir up all this wrath. Withhold not thou thy tender mercies from us, O Lord: let thy loving kindness and thy truth continually preserve us . . . If thou shouldest mark iniquities, O Lord, who could stand? But there is forgiveness with thee, that thou mayest be feared.[5]

In the prayer book of the Union of Liberal and Progressive Synagogues there is a particularly fine section on reconciliation in which we read:

For transgressions between ourselves and God, the Day of Atonement atones; but for transgressions between one human being and another, the Day of Atonement does not atone unless they have reconciled one another.

Forgive your fellow human beings the wrong they have done; that you may pray, and your sins will be pardoned.[6]

[4] A. Cohen, *Everyman's Talmud* (Schocken Books, 1975), 228 ff.

[5] *The Authorised Daily Prayer Book* of the United Hebrew Congregations of the British Commonwealth of Nations (Eyre and Spottiswoode, 1988), 60.

[6] *Siddur Lev Chadash*, Union of Liberal and Progressive Synagogues (London, 1995), 202–5.

Forgive and Forget?

Having given examples from the Orthodox and Liberal traditions it is not difficult to find many examples of teaching about God's forgiveness of us and our need to forgive others in the Reform tradition, for all traditions of Judaism are united on this theme. One of their prayer books gives for study a passage from the *Kitzur Shulchan Aruch*, which is a simplified edition of the *Shulchan Aruch* by Solomon Ganzfried (1804–86). The *Shulchan Aruch* is an authoritative code of Jewish law and practice written by Joseph Caro (1488–1575) and published in Venice in 1565. This passage reads:

The one whose forgiveness is sought should forgive with a perfect heart and not be cruel. For such is not the characteristic of an Israelite . . . It is customary for the seed of Israel to be slow of anger and easily appeased, and when the sinners ask for forgiveness he should do so wholeheartedly and with a willing soul. Even if he has been grievously wronged, he should not seek vengeance, nor bear a grudge against the other. On the contrary, if the offender does not arouse himself to come unto him to sue for forgiveness, the offended one should present himself to the offender in order that the latter may beg his pardon. If one does not let his enmity pass away, his prayers are not heard on Atonement Day, Heaven forfend, and one who is magnanimous and forgives, has all his own sins forgiven.[7]

One of the strengths of Judaism is its emphasis on the moral law which binds communities together and which alone makes living in community possible. Together with this there is an emphasis on saying sorry, penitence, to fellow Jews, other human beings, and God when that moral law has been broken. There is an emphasis on the necessity of that penitence. Jonathan Sacks argues that *teshuvah*, usually translated as penitence, in fact is better translated as returning, retracing our steps, coming home. The most characteristic sense of sin is less one of guilt than of being lost and *teshuvah* means finding your way back home again. In his essay on the meaning of Yom Kippur, the Day of Atonement, he writes:

Yom Kippur is a day of awe. Yet the Talmud calls it one of the most joyous days of the year. Rightly so, for its message is that as long as we breathe, there

    [7] *Forms of Prayer for Jewish Worship*, iii: *Prayers for the High Holy Days* (The Reform Synagogues of Great Britain, 1985), 727.

is no final verdict on our lives. . . . God has given us free will, and thus the strength to turn from bad to good. . . . There is always a chance to begin again. Although we may lose faith in God, God never loses faith in us. On this day of days we hear His voice, gently calling us to come home.

There is a proper stress in that passage and in others on our responsibility to turn from evil to good, to turn round and retrace our steps back to our true home. But the thought of God's prior mercy is never far away. This is the God who never loses faith in us. This is the God whose voice gently calls us to come home.[8]

If an emphasis on the necessity of repentance, ourselves taking the steps to come home, has been a feature of Judaism, this is no less so in Christianity and its necessity has been strongly affirmed in times of apparent laxity. Dietrich Bonhoeffer wrote some words at the time of the church struggle against the Nazis which have since become famous:

Cheap grace is the deadly enemy of our church. We are fighting today for costly grace. Cheap grace means grace sold on the market like a cheapjack's wares. The sacraments, the forgiveness of sins, the consolations of religion are thrown away at cut prices. . . . Cheap grace is the preaching of forgiveness without requiring repentance, baptism without church discipline, communion without confession, absolution without personal confession.[9]

As we have seen, the forgiveness of God and God's call to us to forgive those who have wronged us, is a fundamental feature of Judaism. Nevertheless, the emphasis on this is a distinctive feature of the teaching and life of Jesus. We are to pray, 'Father . . . forgive us the wrong we have done as we have forgiven those who wronged us' (Matthew 6: 12); (Luke 11: 4). If we forgive others God will forgive us but if we don't forgive others we ourselves will not be forgiven (Matthew 6: 14–15). This forgiveness is to be for 'seventy times seven', i.e. unlimited (Matthew 18: 21–2). This message is reinforced by a vivid parable (Matthew 18: 23–35). According to Luke's account, Jesus prayed on the cross 'Father, forgive them; they do not know what they are doing' (Luke 23: 34). Somewhat disturbingly for Christians this prayer is not in some of the

[8] Jonathan Sacks, *Faith in the Future* (Darton, Longman and Todd, 1995), 168. There is a fine section on the Jewish attitude to forgiveness in his *The Dignity of Difference*, chap. 10, (Continuum, rev. edn. 2003).
[9] Dietrich Bonhoeffer, *The Cost of Discipleship* (SCM, 1959), 35–6.

best manuscripts. An obvious explanation is that it was not in the earliest text of the Gospel but was added later. But there is another explanation. It was indeed in the earliest text of the Gospel but was erased in some later manuscripts. It has been pointed out that the prayer of Stephen in Acts 7: 60 'Lord do not hold this sin against them', which echoes the prayer of Jesus on the cross, makes it quite clear that it is the Jewish people who are being prayed for. It has been suggested therefore that some early scribe thought it inconceivable that Christ should pray for those who had crucified him. Furthermore, after the destruction of the temple in Jerusalem in the year 70, it seemed clear to him that God had not forgiven them. So the scribe left the phrase out.

In addition to the teaching and example of Jesus himself there is the implication that the Church has drawn from his death. The eucharistic prayer in the Book of Common Prayer communion service refers to the death of Christ upon the cross in the words 'Who made there (by his one oblation of himself once offered) a full, perfect, and sufficient sacrifice, oblation and satisfaction, for the sins of the whole world': because of Christ's sacrificial death there is forgiveness, as it were, ready and waiting for all human beings. How Christ's death brings about our at-one-ment with God is a mystery which the Church has explored down the ages in a variety of metaphors. The point here is that whatever metaphor has been used, people are freed from everything which might block their relationship with God. Forgiveness is offered freely and unconditionally. At the same time, people have to recognize that they have done wrong and say sorry in order to receive this forgiveness. Jesus began his mission with the words 'The time has come; the kingdom of God is upon you; repent, and believe the Gospel' (Mark 1: 15). The Greek word repentance is related to the word mind, it means to radically rethink our lives in the light of God's just and gentle rule which Jesus described in a series of penetrating parables.

One theme shared by both Judaism and Christianity is the responsibility of human beings. God is God but he has bestowed on us the dignity and responsibility of shaping our lives and the world. To be creative at all is to be given a life of our own and in us the autonomy of the created order becomes a conscious freedom of choice. On one reading of the New Testament this delegation includes forgiveness. Jesus forgave sins in the name of the Son of Man, a title whose exact meaning is not certain but which could mean simply man, or as we would say today, human. When Peter declared Jesus to be Christ, according to Matthew's account he was given authority to bind and loose, to release people from their sins or the reverse. This may date from the time of the New Testament Church, rather than the ministry of Jesus, but it takes its place there, along with other evidence, that the Church believed that Jesus had delegated to it the role, responsibility, and power to forgive sins. Forgiveness was not just something for the end of time. In Jesus it had become embodied and through him had entered the flux of history as it was exercised by his body on earth, the Church (Mark 2: 1–10; Matthew 16: 19; John 20: 22–3). As Haddon Willmer has written, 'God's forgiveness is enacted humanly. The Gospel unites God and humanity in forgiving.'[10] This means that all Christian churches have a means of assuring penitents that they are forgiven and the major churches, the Roman Catholic Church and the Orthodox Church as well as the Catholic tradition of Anglicanism, have a specific rite in which this forgiveness is not only offered but mediated.

There may be a difference here from a Jewish perspective. For in quotations from Rabbi Julia Neuberger and Dr Albert Friedlander, which will be stated later, Rabbis reject any idea that they are mediators of divine forgiveness. It is for God to forgive and him alone. Nevertheless, as we have seen, there is an imperative within Judaism as in Christianity, to forgive those who have harmed us, if they are sincerely penitent. Furthermore, there is evidence that individual Jews as well as individual Christians have been willing to take the initiative in praying to God for the forgiveness of those who have done them harm.

Within Christianity the prayer of Jesus on the cross is quickly taken up by Stephen, the first martyr, who prays to God for the forgiveness of those who are stoning him to death. In modern times such a prayer

---

[10] Haddon Willmer, 'Forgiveness', in Adrian Hastings, Alistair Mason, and Hugh Pyper (eds.), *The Oxford Companion to Christian Thought* (Oxford University Press, 2000), 245.

came from the Bishop of Iran, Dehqani-Tafti, when his son was murdered by extremists shortly after the Islamic revolution. He prayed:

O God
We remember not only our son but also his murderers.

The prayer goes on to reflect not only on the evil brought about by the murder but on the spiritual qualities which had been strengthened in those who suffered as a result of it. So the prayer ends:

O God
Our son's blood has multiplied the fruit of the Spirit and the soil of our souls;
So when his murderers stand before thee on the day of judgement
Remember the fruit of the Spirit by which they have enriched our lives.
And forgive.[11]

There is a well-known prayer written by an unknown prisoner in Ravensbrück concentration camp and left by the body of a dead child:

O Lord, remember not only the men and women of goodwill, but also those of ill will. But do not remember all the suffering they have inflicted on us; remember the fruits we have bought, thanks to this suffering—our comradeship, our loyalty, our humility, our courage, our generosity, the greatness of heart which has grown out of all this, and when they come to judgement let all the fruits which we have borne be their forgiveness.[12]

It is not known whether this prayer was written by a Jew or a Christian and it certainly makes some who have tried to use it on their visits to former concentration camps uneasy. They have not found it helpful because they realize that they had no right to pray such a prayer. If there is such a right, it belongs only to those who suffered in such camps.

There is, however, another prayer, from a Jewish source, which carries great conviction. In 1922 Walther Rathenau, the German Foreign Minister, who was Jewish, was murdered. His mother wrote to Mrs Techow, the mother of the murderer in these words:

---

[11] *The Oxford Book of Prayer*, ed., George Appleton (Oxford University Press, 1988), 135.
[12] Ibid. 112.

In my deepest grief I hold out my hand to you, you most pitiful of women. Tell your son that, in the name and the spirit of the victim, I forgive him as God may forgive him if he confesses fully and frankly before the secular court and if he repents before the divine.

Mrs Rathenau later explained how she came to write this letter. It was when she heard that Mrs Techow could not appear in public without being insulted and it was as if her son had dictated the words to her.

Think of the position of this poor woman in relation to my own position. She had lost as much as, nay even more than, I. She had to be ashamed of her son; I could be proud of mine. When my son died, I received thousands and thousands of letters and telegrams from all over the world. Frau Techow, on the other hand, receives daily as many proofs of contempt and indignation. What was more natural than for me to write to her; I was the only one who could comfort her . . .

At least two points emerge from this important, deeply compassionate approach. First of all, Mrs Rathenau saw that she had a unique position in relation to the mother of the man who had murdered her son: 'I was the only one who could comfort her'. This was not a blanket offer of comfort to unknown thousands. She held out the hand of friendship to a particular person from her own unique position as the one who had suffered. Secondly, she offers forgiveness to the murderer, not from herself but 'in the name and the spirit of the victim'. Thirdly, she does not presume on God's forgiveness of the murderer but says 'I forgive him as God may forgive him if he confesses fully and frankly before the secular court and if he repents before the divine'.

This is an appropriate point to take up the statement of Ivan Karamazov quoted earlier. Ivan says to the mother of a child who has been tortured, 'she has no right to forgive him for the suffering of her tortured child. She has no right to forgive the torturer for that, even if her child were to forgive him!' For all the sense of proper moral protest against easy forgiveness in that passage, particularly forgiveness offered by someone on behalf of someone else, we may question whether Ivan Karamazov has got it quite right. For Mrs Rathenau wanted to offer forgiveness to the person who had murdered her son 'In the name and the spirit of the victim'. She knew her son, she knew his character and what he would have wanted. Let's suppose she was correct and that the son, in some future life, did offer forgiveness to the person who had murdered him, what justification would there then be for others to withhold reconciliation? To take an ordinary family example. A mother is feeling desperately hurt by an action of her son towards her. But he says he is sorry and she forgives him. But another son in the family refuses to let go of the matter and keeps harping on it. Perhaps he does not think that his brother's sorrow goes deep enough, that the matter is much more serious than he has faced up to, that their mother has forgiven his brother too easily. All this might be true. But if the sorrow was indeed deep and the mother, fully conscious of the seriousness of the hurt, yet forgave him, the other brother's continuing to withhold forgiveness would seem to have no moral justification. Nevertheless, what this, and the letter of Mrs Rathenau bring out, is that if forgiveness is to be offered, it is the victim, or, as it were, the spirit of the victim properly understood, who has the moral right to initiate the process.

Rabbi Dr Albert Friedlander recalls how speaking at a German Kirchentag about the anguish of Auschwitz a man approached him:

> 'Rabbi, I was a guard at a concentration camp. Can you forgive me?' I looked at him. 'No' I said I cannot forgive. 'It is not the function of Rabbis to give absolution, to be pardoners. In Judaism, there is a ten day period of penitence, between the New Year and the Day of Atonement, when we try to go to any person whom we have wronged, and ask for forgiveness. But you cannot go to the six million. They are dead, and I cannot speak for them. Nor can I speak for God. But you are here at a church conference. God's forgiving grace may touch you; but I am not a mediator, pardoner, or spokesman for God.'

This morally sensitive and appropriate response brings out a number of points. First, Albert Friedlander does not rule out the possibility that the grace of God might touch that man. But, secondly, he knows that if forgiveness is to be offered it has to be offered at the human level, from the victims: and that cannot be done, for the six million are dead.

Albert Friedlander takes a Jewish view that a Rabbi is not a pardoner or absolver of human sin on behalf of God. Here we seem to have a difference with the Christian view, because as already seen,

God's forgiveness is embodied in Jesus, who delegates responsibility for forgiveness to his body on earth, the Church. Yet we might very well wonder whether a Christian priest was ever morally in a position to offer God's absolution in such a situation. God, we might say, is in a position to forgive only those hurts done to him. Does he, any more than a human being, have the right to forgive evil, terrible evil in the case of the Holocaust, inflicted on others?[13]

One example of a request for forgiveness which has become famous is recounted by Simon Wiesenthal. Wiesenthal was a young Jewish worker in an extermination camp when he was called to the bedside of a dying SS man. The Nazi had been involved in atrocities including the burning to death of a large group of Jews in a house. The Nazi was seeking peace of mind before his death and he asked the nurse to bring him a young Jew. This Jew was Wiesenthal. Although the SS man had had a Catholic upbringing he chose deliberately to ask for a Jew rather than a priest. After Wiesenthal had heard the man's confession he left without saying anything. Wiesenthal's book *The Sunflower* tells the story and the response of Christians and Jews who considered the question of what Wiesenthal should have done.[14]

Wiesenthal was right to say nothing. Only the victims who had already suffered and died could offer forgiveness. He could not stand in the place of God and even if he could God could not have offered forgiveness for the harm done to the victims without the consent of the victims themselves. But there are silences and silences. A silence that goes along with looking someone in the eyes and perhaps holding their hand can at least indicate an understood anguish, an anguish that is not yet resolvable but which is recognized, a silence which is an implicit forgiveness for the harm done to Simon Wiesenthal in his own person for himself. Who knows what that silence was, but it could not have included forgiveness offered by the murdered millions.

It is against this background that we can understand the words of Elie Wiesel, who was in Auschwitz as a child. At the unofficial cere-mony commemorating the camp's liberation he said:

[13] *European Judaism*, 19/2 (Spring 1985), 6.
[14] Simon Wiesenthal, *The Sunflower* (Schocken Books, 1976).

Although we know that God is merciful, please, God, do not have mercy on those who have created this place. God of forgiveness, do not forgive those murderers of Jewish children here.

Do not forgive the murderers and their accomplices. Those who have been here . . . Remember the nocturnal processions of children and more children and more children, frightened, quiet, so quiet and so beautiful.

If we could simply look at one, our heart would break. Did not it break the heart of the murderers? God, merciful God do not have mercy on those who had no mercy on Jewish children.

Naturally, we know that there is no collective guilt. Only the guilty were guilty. Their children are children. So children all over the world, remember the Jewish children.

And if you remember, as we try to remember, then, as you just heard, hope is possible that because of our memory, thanks to our Jewish memory, a better world might be built in which children could be happy . . . Smiling, singing, taking each other's hands and saying to each other: 'Well, another morning, another day. Another morning, another day, for human kind.'

Wiesel's concern is memory, memory of the terrible things that happened, in order that such terrible things might not happen again and children of the future might be safe. But memory also of the murdered, for their own sake, because their precious memory is worth preserving, worth preserving not only before humanity but before God. So although God is merciful, Weisel does not want God to forgive the perpetrators of such terrible deeds.

Only the victims can offer forgiveness. Their forgiveness assumes profound repentance and is not to be taken for granted, is not to be presumed. There is also something surprising about genuine forgiveness, it is sheer grace. It could be that the victims, or some of them, would be willing to forgive. Who knows? But until the victims have indicated their willingness to forgive can even God offer forgiveness? Is not his forgiveness dependent upon human forgiveness having first been offered? So Wiesel keeps alive the memory of those who have suffered so much, whose loss is so devastating, whose memory is so precious. He keeps their memory alive even before God and refuses any premature closure of their story, of their hurt. His voice is a profoundly moral protest not just against easy forgiveness, not just against the immoral idea that we can forgive sins inflicted on others, but against even God, the idea that God can forgive hurt done to victims before the victims themselves have forgiven those who have inflicted the hurt.

What God does have the right to do, if we can put it like that, is forgive us for the hurt we have done to him, and this forgiveness can soften our hardened hearts. His forgiveness can make us more aware of the hurt we have done not only to him but to others and make us more truly sorry. It can lead us to seek the forgiveness of other people. ⁊ᴏᴊ God's forgiveness breaks down the barriers of our pride, our self image of someone who is in the right. Furthermore, God's forgiveness can lead us to offer forgiveness to those who have hurt us in some way. It breaks the cycle of resentment and mutual recrimination. As Albert Freidlander said to the SS guard who approached him, it may be that God's grace would touch his heart. God's grace can and does touch our hearts. But of its very nature, it cannot bring forgiveness for damage we have done to others. For they and they alone can offer such forgiveness, if they are so minded.

Julia Neuberger has written in relation to debates in the House of Lords about whether to try Nazi war criminals living in Britain:

One of the themes that has recurred is the Jewish desire for revenge. Many people think that it is now time to forgive and forget. Yet Jews as a *whole* cannot ever forgive anybody. Only the *victims* can forgive the perpetrators, and most of them are dead. Otherwise forgiveness is for God, and not for man—a Jewish view is very different from that of Christianity. Nor do I personally think we should ever forget, nor can we, for the memory of the people who died is still very much alive in our minds.[15]

What this chapter has shown is that the so-called Jewish desire for revenge is a stereotype that is both false and damaging: unfortunately it is one that recurs today in the same way that it did in Shakespeare's Shylock. In reality the emphasis on forgiveness is present in Judaism as it is in Christianity. Furthermore, Julia Neuberger is quite right in

---

[15] Julia Neuberger, *On Being Jewish* (Heinemann, 1995), 43. Rabbi Rachel Montagu has also written in a letter to the author, 'On more than one occasion in dialogue, I have been asked as a Jew to forgive Christians for the holocaust and obviously not been understood when I explained why not. It does seem a sort of cheap psychodrama for Christians who weren't perpetrators to want to be forgiven by a Jew who wasn't there and this needs to be guarded against in the clearest possible language.'

emphasizing that only the victims can forgive the perpetrators. Indeed, this chapter has gone beyond that and suggested that God himself, as it were, awaits forgiveness offered by the victims before he himself is in a position to offer forgiveness.

She is right in saying that the Jewish view is different from Christianity in that priests claim to absolve in the name of Christ in a way that Rabbis do not. But that apart, it has been argued that Jewish and Christian views are not so very different. Sometimes there are differences of emphasis and sometimes there is a very proper moral protest by Judaism against the failure to take evil seriously.

One question which has been raised in stark form by the Shoah is how far it is morally legitimate for an institution to express sorrow for the wrongdoings of its past members. In some ways this might be thought too easy and cheap a thing to do. After all it was people in the past who suffered and people in the past who perpetrated their crimes. Nevertheless, if we do not take an individualist, atomistic view of human society, then institutions do have a key role and representative leaders of those institutions can articulate on behalf of the institution certain views and attitudes. Edmund Burke argued that society was a partnership and a partnership not just between the living but between the departed, the living, and those who are yet to be born. If this is true of society as a whole it is even more true of the Christian Church, which feels itself bound up with all those in the body of Christ in space and time and beyond space and time. There is also no doubt that when leaders of an institution express contrition, such action can have a healing effect. This occurred in South Africa when some of the leading pastors of the Dutch Reformed Church expressed penitence for the Church's justification of apartheid.

The Roman Catholic Church has a central authority representing the Church through space and time. Because of this when the Vatican expresses penitence on behalf of church members in the past this is an act which can have great potential for healing. In March 1998 the Vatican promulgated its important document *We Remember: A Reflection on the Shoah*. It took full cognizance of the terrible suffering experienced by the Jewish community in World War II and in previous centuries. It argued that antisemitism was essentially a pagan movement but it did ask 'the question of the relation between the Nazi persecution and the attitudes down the centuries of the Christians towards the Jews'. In answering that question it pointed to erroneous and unjust interpretations of the New Testament regarding the Jewish people and the anti-Judaism taught in some quarters. So although the Nazi persecution of the Jews was driven by non-Christian considerations, 'It may be asked whether the Nazi persecution of the Jews was not made easier by the anti-Jewish prejudices embedded in some Christians' minds and hearts. Did anti-Jewish sentiment among Christians make them less sensitive, or even indifferent, to the persecutions launched against the Jews by national socialism when it reached power?' The document recognizes the many heroic Christian lives but also points to the many Christians who

were not strong enough to raise their voices in protest. For Christians, this heavy burden of conscience of their brothers and sisters during the second world war must be a call to penitence.

We deeply regret the errors and failures of those sons and daughters of the church.

In short, 'The Catholic church desires to express a deep sorrow for the failures of her sons and daughters in every age. This is an act of repentance (*Teshuva*) since, as members of the church, we are linked to the sins as well as the merits of all her children.'

There was controversy about the failure in this document to properly name the ineffectiveness, as it is seen by most in the Jewish community, of Pope Pius XII. However, more searching questions might be asked of this document, even if there is no definitive answer. The document expresses sorrow and regret for the Church's sons and daughters in every age and calls for repentance. This is quite right in one crucial respect, in that it is individuals who are responsible for their actions and therefore it is individuals who must express sorrow and repent. On the other hand, the Church is an institution with a magisterium, with official teaching. It has been the official teaching of the Church itself down the ages which has been at fault and which has led the Church's sons and daughters astray. The tendency of a document like this is to let the Church, in an official capacity, as it were float above its sinful sons and daughters. Yet it might be asked whether it is not the Church itself, as an institution, which is above all called to express sorrow for its teaching down the ages and which now needs to repent, that is radically rethink its whole outlook.

The issues in this chapter raise not only questions of day-to-day living but ultimate questions. In particular it brings to the fore Ivan Karamazov's question about whether God was justified in creating the universe in the first place and if so under what terms.

It is possible to image an ultimate reconciliation, with all those who have been tortured and murdered offering forgiveness to their torturers and murderers. In such a community, held together on the basis of a mutual forgiveness grounded in the forgiveness of God, it might be possible for all, whatever agonies they have been through, to bless God for the fact that they had once lived. We might term this restorative justice on a cosmic scale. Restorative justice, which in the British context has been pioneered by the Thames Valley Police, seeks to bring together victim and perpetrator of the crime in a face-to-face relationship. The criminal is forced to face up to the hurt he or she has inflicted. Yet here one might utter a protest about even writing about a subject which is in practice so utterly painful. A few years ago I was asked to lead a seminar at Grendon Underwood Prison for inmates on the subject of forgiveness. Of the twenty or so people who took part the majority were murderers. Of those, the majority were racked by what they had done and did not find it possible to forgive themselves.

More recently I again visited Grendon Underwood to lead a seminar and once again the question of forgiveness came up. One of the inmates shared a desperately painful story of how he had hated his father for what he had done to his mother, how he had tried to murder his father and how through much painful agonizing he had now worked his way through to the point where he could offer forgiveness. Words are easy, but the reality is suffering and sometimes torture or death.

The traditional picture of the end of all things includes the triumph of God's justice through the eternal punishment of evildoers. This traditional picture can be softened in a number of ways. For example, we need not image God actually sentencing people to hell. Rather, people are capable of creating their own hell in the midst of heaven as they are on earth. God's love, we might believe, continues to reach out to people, trying to break down their barriers of pride and hate but if a person continues to lock themselves away in self-pity, resentment, and malice, that is hell wherever it is to be found. The question at issue here is not whether that kind of scenario is compatible with a loving God, but whether it is compatible with a belief in the ultimate triumph of God's purpose, and therefore his justification of having created the world in the first place despite all the pain and travail along the way. It could be argued that such a picture, though much less harsh and more morally acceptable than the traditional one, still leaves those in heaven—presumably—aware that not all have been won over to God's love, not all evil has been assuaged, so it is difficult to see how it could be called heaven.

Another modern way of looking at the matter is to think that those who are evil will simply be annihilated, they will cease to exist, so they have no continuing place in any afterlife. This means that the redeemed will not be aware of their existence and their memories will be healed and transformed, as everything must be if heaven is to be heaven at all.

There is no certain way in which we can choose between these three scenarios. The purpose of putting them forward at this point is to suggest that the first one, in which all are bound together in a community of mutual forgiveness that is grounded in the forgiveness of God is one possible way of thinking about the future. But this picture is based upon some fundamental convictions. First, only the victims themselves can forgive, and even God, in a profound sense, waits upon that forgiveness. Secondly, that forgiveness cannot be either presumed or expected. It is a free choice and is sheer grace. Thirdly, if the victims were willing to forgive then that would initiate a process in which others would find it morally difficult to continue to withhold forgiveness.

One of the most profound novels to come out of World War II was R. C. Hutchinson's *Johanna at Daybreak*. Johanna is in a home for refugees in Holland suffering from severe amnesia. She goes on a journey across Germany but, more importantly, an inward journey to the recovery of memory. She had betrayed her Jewish husband to the

Nazis and abandoned her children. As a result of that abandonment one of the children had become mentally defective. As she struggles to resist this dawning memory, she is presented with the choice of committing suicide or going further into the painful truth. Eventually she meets her daughter.

Side by side—our hands still touching—we went into the house, to be greeted by the fumes from a pan of milk which someone had let boil over and by the pervasive bickering of children. Enveloped in that orchestra of inveterate sounds and smells, I realised I was back on the painful course I could never finally escape from—itself my one escape from the despotism of the past; the only course which could lead towards an ultimate tranquility; the harsh, acceptable, exalting road.[16]

There is nothing sentimental about the novel, no glossing over the terrible evil that has been done. The truth has to be faced. But facing that truth does not exclude reconciliation with those who have been desperately damaged. But that's only a novel. We cannot presume on its reality. And if Jewish voices protest, morally protest, against any downplaying of the enormity of the evil, any diminution of the dignity of the victims, then that voice must be heard to the end of time, and beyond time.[17]

Appendix: Rabbi Jonathan Gorsky's Response to Anthony Phillips

Dr Anthony Phillips' critique of the Jewish perception of forgiveness was based on three assumptions:

1. That in responding to hurt, the alternatives are either forgiveness or being gradually consumed by anger and hatred.
2. That in the landscape of reparation, forgiveness is the only salient feature.
3. That in the aftermath of catastrophic trauma (the Holocaust), people will be preoccupied by vengefulness unless they pursue forgiveness.

[16] R. C. Hutchinson, *Johanna at Daybreak* (Michael Joseph, 1969), 314.

[17] Rabbi Jonathan Gorsky in a letter to me has written a response to Anthony Phillips which I quote in full in the Appendix which follows. Whilst it does not contradict my discussion of forgiveness in this chapter, it is valuable in indicating the wider, morally sophisticated context in which Judaism considers this issue.

In my opinion, the three assumptions are incorrect.

1. Traditional Jewish culture addresses separately issues of bearing grudges, seeking revenge, coping with anger, jealousy, hatred and forgiveness. The forgiveness debate understandably focuses on sources pertaining to 'forgiveness', and did not place them in the larger context of the other issues: for Phillips, all of the above are aspects of 'forgiveness'; in the traditional Jewish vocabulary, forgiveness has a narrower remit, focused exclusively on the act of pardon.

The issue is clarified in the medieval ethical treatise *Orchot Tzaddikim*—the Ways of the Righteous. The anonymous author, having noted that we must forgive anyone who seeks our forgiveness, proceeds as follows; 'And even if the offender does not seek forgiveness, we should not hate him, but conduct ourselves with him in a loving way, so that eventually he will come to make reparation'. Forgiveness is identified with the act of pardon, and, for the *Orchot Tzaddikim* author, is granted only when it is sought in a penitent spirit. But even when the offender is not 'forgiven' (s)he is not to be hated—a term which need not be as strong as the English equivalent as it can only imply a keeping of distance and need not entail destructive animosity—and our response must be a loving pursuit of ultimate reparation.

Also, in this perspective, forgiveness is relational. For the *Orchot Tzaddikim* version, forgiveness is rooted in a mutual pursuit of reparation engaging both parties, the offender and the person who has been hurt. In the absence of this mutuality, the author does not speak of forgiveness, but nevertheless advocates a loving response to the person who has given offence.

2. In terms of the landscape of reparation, one locus classicus is Exodus 23: 5 about helping the ass of one who hates you when it is staggering beneath its burden. This is about transforming enmity by an act of creative reparation that will dissolve hatred and restore fraternal relations. It is different from seeking forgiveness and deserves further elaboration, which it receives in a number of rabbinic comments. It clearly implies that there are reparatory responses even in situations where forgiveness does not appear to be attainable.

3. With respect to the Holocaust and the aftermath of catastrophic trauma, there have indeed been very powerful problems for many of the survivors, but they have not generally been a consequence of frustrated desires for vengeance. Rather, for many survivors, albeit by no means all, perceptions of life have been overwhelmed by the power of the evil they experienced, by comparison with which goodness appears to be negligible and evanescent. Tadeus Borowski, a Catholic Polish survivor of Auschwitz, wrote simply that

Forgive and Forget?

Auschwitz was the world, implying that it was the ultimate reality of human society. The Holocaust, for many, was the destruction of any sense of hope or prospective triumph of goodness, and the world is seen in terms of the overwhelming capacity of the powers of darkness. People have described this in terms of ontological insecurity; their ultimate sense of being has been shaken to the foundations; forgiveness implies a reparatory prospect, but in the world of some survivors, this prospect is inconceivable, and the degradation that they experienced left them devoid of any sense of human worth—hopelessness, in other words, touched them at the very depths of their personhood.

The one difficulty is that forgiveness is a response to the injured party, rather than surrogates claiming to act on his/her behalf. I was not involved in the Holocaust and it is unclear that my 'forgiveness' of the perpetrators could be in any way significant. It might refer to my personal commitment in respect of my own subjective response, but it would in no way represent the victims or the survivors or repair their relationship with perpetrators, whose burden of guilt would likewise be unaffected, particularly in the case of those, who, unlike the Wiesenthal example, are quite explicitly unrepentant.

Nevertheless, it might be argued that such a conclusion is not wholly satisfactory. Clearly, future generations of Jews will respond to the Holocaust and future generations of Germans might experience guilt, as participants in the national culture or profound remorse for the acts of their immediate forebears. The Jews in question are not victims, and the Germans are not perpetrators of events that took place before they were born, but the shadow of the past will powerfully affect all of them.

There are young Jews, who like some survivors, see the world in very dark terms, and respond accordingly, particularly with regard to Israel and its conflict with the Palestinians. There are young Germans whose sense of national identity is damaged almost beyond repair, or whose guilt admits neither resolution nor closure, as they cannot atone for crimes that they did not commit, or discharge the great burden that has fallen upon them.

Even if forgiveness cannot be formally enacted in this context, it does not follow that its reparatory purpose must also be set aside. Reparation in a spirit of mutuality, with new generations setting out to help each other come to terms with the past, is supremely important.

It is at this point that I have difficulty with Elie Wiesel's focused insistence that God should not forgive the perpetrators: when it is translated into the human relationship it seems to foreclose on any form of reparation: the landscape will be dominated for all eternity by an image of God in unremitting confrontation with the perpetrators which will overshadow every reparatory endeavour in future generations.

Like Wiesel, I have the greatest difficulty in envisaging forgiveness for calculated acts of absolute brutality, even granting that forgiveness is relational and does not entail either overlooking or forgetting the evil that has been committed or foreclosing on justice for the perpetrators. It is possible to conceive of the souls of the perpetrators being transformed by their encounter with the Divine, but even if this is not admitted, we trust in God's wisdom, and to create a prayer for non-forgiveness is quite problematic.

The Covenant with Humanity

5

One Covenant and Different, Distinctive Voices

Dr Jonathan Sacks, the Chief Rabbi, has stated simply and elegantly what is the heart of the idea of covenant. 'God gives his word to man and man gives his word to God.' We might want to go beyond that and talk about a special relationship, or a solemn, vowed pledge of mutual faithfulness but Dr Sacks's definition brings out the essence of the idea.[1] In the Hebrew scriptures the concept of covenant occurs in a number of different traditions, referring to relationships between human beings and different aspects of their relationship between the people of Israel and God. Sometimes God's promise refers to land and sometimes to descendants. But the core idea is of a word spoken by God and that word heard and responded to by man. Because God is faithful, his word to man is inseparably bound up with undeviating commitment to human well-being. And because the human response is a response to that promise, it also involves persevering loyalty.

In recent decades there has been a debate in Christian circles, and to a lesser extent in Jewish circles, about whether we are to think of one

5

---

[1] The phrase comes from *Radical Then, Radical Now: The Legacy of the World's Oldest Religion* (HarperCollins, 2000). Jonathan Sacks has also written on covenant in *The Politics of Hope* (Jonathan Cape, 1997), 61–4, and *Crisis and Covenant* (Manchester University Press, 1992).

covenant or two covenants. Some have argued that there is only one, primal covenant, that between God and the people of Israel. Through Christ, Christians have been taken into that relationship and share its blessings. Others, on the other hand, argue for two different covenants, one with Judaism which is primarily concerned with the corporate life of the people, and one with Christians, in which people are summoned as individuals to follow Christ. These ideas will be discussed more fully shortly but at this point we must pose a simple question. What about the rest of humanity? Although statistics suggest that Christianity has the largest number of adherents on earth, it could still be argued that the majority of human beings in history have been neither Jews nor Christians. Where are they within the providence of God? It is an elementary sense of fairness that poses such a question, a sense of fairness that needs to be taken seriously and which any religion ignores at its peril. Furthermore, the Bible itself in its better moments has this dimension in mind.

It was not because you were more numerous than any other nation that the Lord cared for you and chose you, for you were the smallest of all nations; it was because the Lord loved you and stood by his oath to your forefathers, that he brought you out with a strong hand and redeemed you from the land of slavery.   (Deuteronomy 7: 7)

Although this does not directly refer to God's love of other nations, it is at least implicit. For on the Hebrew view, a large population was a sign of divine blessing, as was wealth and strength. Then there is Amos 9: 7:

> 'Are you not like the Ethiopians to me,
> O people of Israel?' says the Lord.
> 'Did I not bring up Israel from the land of Egypt
> and the Philistines from Caphtor and the Syrians from Kir?'

The meaning of this passage has been disputed but the implication is that the care that God has for Israel is also shown in his care for the Ethiopians, the Philistines, and the Syrians. Then there is the book of Jonah and Jonah's resentment that God did not destroy Nineveh. God says to Jonah:

The Covenant with Humanity

Should not I pity Nineveh, that great city, in which there are more than 120,000 persons who do not know their right hand from their left, and also much cattle?

In the light of this let us assert that the primal covenant is with neither Jews nor Christians but with humanity as a whole. After the flood God made a covenant with humanity, symbolized by the rainbow about which he said:

This is the sign of the covenant which I establish between myself and you and every living creature with you, to endless generations:

> My bow I set in the cloud,
> sign of the covenant
> between myself and earth.
> When I cloud the sky over the earth,
> the bow shall be seen in the cloud.

Then will I remember the covenant which I have made between myself and you and living things of every kind.   (Genesis 9: 12–15)

> While the earth lasts
> seed time and harvest, cold and heat
> summer and winter, day and night,
> shall never cease.   (Genesis 8: 22)

The most basic way in which God expresses his love for every single human being, in every culture, of every religion, is through the gift of life and through sustaining the conditions which make life possible: seed time and harvest. In and through this bounty of nature God may be discerned. As St Paul put it:

For all that may be known of God by men lies plain before their eyes; indeed God himself has disclosed it to them. His invisible attributes, that is to say his everlasting power and deity, have been visible, ever since the world began, to the eye of reason, in the things he has made.   (Romans 1: 19–20)

This is of course a Christian way of looking at things. A difficulty immediately arises when we remember that Hinduism and Buddhism, for example, have a very different understanding of God and the Gods. The central tradition of the main forms of Hinduism and Buddhism looks to go beyond words, beyond all forms of dualism, to

90

that which cannot be spoken. If the idea of a creator God has a place, it is in a subordinate capacity. The human pilgrimage is to grow beyond attachment, including attachment to the concept of an enduring self. In inter-religious dialogue the partners' way of defining themselves and stating things has to be taken with the utmost seriousness. Hindus and Buddhists, for example, will talk about experience in their language from their perspective. But this is a work of Christian theology, whose purpose is to set out a coherent and consistent view of the universe on a Christian basis, in Christian language from a Christian perspective. Any world-view seeking coherence and consistency would need to do that. It is not in itself an act of hubris or linguistic imperialism and, in inter-religious dialogue, the perspectives of the two partners are treated equally and their differences recognized.

From a Christian perspective, however, a perspective in which God is the God of the universe, of all peoples and cultures and religions it is inconceivable to think that he would be unwilling to make himself known to everyone and equally inconceivable that in some way, in however faltering and stumbling a manner, they would not have responded. At the very least, through nature and the conditions which sustain life, God unceasingly gives his word to humanity and in every culture, in one form or another, humanity has responded by giving its word to God. Furthermore, the sharpness of the contrast between the monotheistic religions and the religions of Asia is softened by bearing in mind two points. As Keith Ward has shown in detail, there is a similar structure to all the great religions of the world.[2] They want to assert both that ultimate reality is beyond anything that can be said about it in human words and at the same time this reality seeks to communicate to us in an intimate and accessible way. So whilst Christianity, in particular, might want to emphasize God's accessibility to us in Jesus Christ, Christianity has always been no less insistent that God in himself is ultimate mystery. As John of Damascus, a theologian who is the benchmark of orthodoxy for the Orthodox family of churches put it in the eighth century, 'It is plain, then, that there is a God. But what he is in his essence and nature is absolutely incomprehensible

[2] Keith Ward, *Images of Eternity* (Darton, Longman and Todd, 1987).

and unknowable.'[3] Conversely, whilst the religions that originated in India emphasize the unknowableness of ultimate reality, as those religions have developed people have found ways of responding to that reality in personal terms.

So the first, fundamental fact is that there is a covenant between God and humanity. Everything else that is said about covenants between God and the Jewish people, or with Christians, or with any other group is subordinate to this prior, underlying reality. This reality concerns the whole of creation. As the Chief Rabbi and Dayan Chanoch Ehrentreu, senior judge of the court of the Chief Rabbi, said in their evidence to the House of Lords Select Committee on Stem Cell Research, 'We are part of a covenant between God and humanity and are therefore responsible for the legacy, physical, moral and spiritual, that we bequeath to future generations.'

Traditionally, Christianity has made a distinction between general revelation, as a result of which something of God can be known by all people in all cultures through reflection on nature and the universal working of the Holy Spirit, and special revelation, in which God gives a definitive disclosure of himself. One analogy which has been used compares this distinction to someone who is unfailingly kind and helpful to everyone they meet but who, in some particular act, rescuing a child from drowning in the sea, reveals qualities of courage, say, that could only emerge in some such particular circumstances. Or, to take another example, a woman of great resilience and courage, who has had to cope with a difficult life meets someone who has also had to struggle against adversity. Their common experience results in an intimacy that was potentially there with a whole range of people but which needed one particular person to bring it about.

One implication of these analogies is that revelation, of its nature, has an element of particularity about it. Not everything that is revealed has to be particular but the more profound, intimate elements are inescapably particular.

Both Jews and Christians have traditionally regarded themselves as chosen people, the recipients of particular revelation and this immedi-

---

[3] John of Damascus, 'Exposition of the Orthodox Faith', I. 4, *Nicene and Post-Nicene Fathers* (Eerdmans, 1983), vol. iv.

ately poses a dilemma for those who are conscious of the billions of human beings in history and today who are neither Jews nor Christians. One way this dilemma has been softened is by the emphasis within the scriptures on the chosenness being for responsibility, not privilege; in particular the responsibility of sharing what is revealed with others.

> I, the Lord, have called you with righteous purpose and taken
>   you by the hand;
> I have formed you, and appointed you to be a light to all peoples
> a beacon for the nations, to open eyes that are blind
>
> (Isaiah 42: 6)

> It is too slight a task for you, as my servant
> to restore the tribes of Jacob, to bring back the descendants of Israel:
> I will make you a light to the nations,
> to be my salvation to earth's furthest bounds.
>
> (Isaiah 49: 6)

Light shines through, as it were, at one particular point in order that it might illuminate the whole landscape. However, there are still difficulties with this approach. We also need other analogies taken from the world of the arts. In poetry, for example, it is not a useful exercise to argue that, for example, W. H. Auden was a greater, or lesser poet than Gerard Manley Hopkins. They each have a very distinctive voice, their own voice, and each, as it happens, was a Christian who conveyed a Christian view of the world but in very different terms. People who appreciate poetry are enriched by reading them both and they both affect the way we feel about the world though they see the world in different ways. There is no question of overall superiority or inferiority. This analogy, like all analogies, ultimately fails. For religions make truth claims and those truth claims are sometimes incompatible with claims made by other religious traditions. Poets, though engaged in the struggle for truth in all its forms, nevertheless do not make truth claims in that kind of way. What we can take out of the analogy, however, is the idea of a distinctive voice, a voice that will enrich anyone who is prepared to hear it and be drawn into its way of looking at the world. From a theological point of view there is no reason to reject the idea that behind such distinctive voices there is a good God who wants human beings to be enriched in this kind of way. So in discussing the senses in which Jews and Christians claim to be in a covenantal relationship with God I would stress two points. First, the prior, underlying covenant is with humanity as a whole. Secondly, the concept of a special revelation in Judaism or Christianity needs to be taken with the idea of distinctive voices as part of God's purpose for humanity as a whole, distinctive voices which can be mutually enriching.

In the millennium year a number of distinguished Roman Catholic and Jewish scholars came together on the basis of prepared papers to discuss their relationship in terms of partnership. Key themes were those of covenant and election. Elliot Dorff, an American Rabbi and scholar, argues that other religions, that is for him religions other than Judaism, are what God wants. This does not mean giving up his commitment to Judaism or trying to evaluate the strengths and weaknesses of other religions as well as his own. It means holding to the truth of one's own religion, in so far as one can understand and grasp it, but doing so with a sense that 'We can never know, as God does, what is ultimately true and good.' So we hold our own beliefs with a certain humility and willingness to learn from others. Both reality and moral norms are objective but we can only know them from our own perspective.[4]

Dorff's position is open to further development and refinement. Nevertheless, I believe that anyone who is seriously wrestling with the issues of truth in religion today will be conscious of the kind of tension that he is articulating there. The tension between recognizing truth in religions other than one's own, and therefore their place within God's providence, together with loyalty to one's own tradition because one has discerned the fullness of truth there: and doing this whilst still holding to the objectivity of truth and the capacity of the human mind to have some understanding of it. My own position goes beyond that of Dorff in wanting to begin from the affirmation, which again I must emphasize is from a Christian point of view, that through the union of

[4] Elliot Dorff, 'Understanding Election', in Tony Bayfield, Sidney Brichto, and Eugene Fisher (eds.), *He Kissed Him and They Wept* (SCM, 2001), 73–6.

the divine and the human in Christ there is a covenant with the whole of humanity; in him all humanity is included. So although the different religions can sometimes seem very different from one another, they are in fact different voices and different songs which ought, from a Christian point of view, to be able to deepen our understanding and grasp of that fundamental bond between all that is human with its ground and goal.

Can Supersessionism be Overcome? The Work of van Buren, Pawlikowski, and Haas

I now look in more detail at the three-volume work by Paul van Buren, who has sought to pioneer, in a systematic way, a new theological understanding of the relationship between Christianity and Judaism. Some of his main points are:

Both Judaism and Christianity are primarily concerned with right living rather than right believing. Van Buren's first volume is called *Discerning the Way*, for he believes that both religions are a way in which we should walk. Indeed Christianity was first of all called 'the way' (Acts 9: 2; 19: 9; and 22: 4). Historically of course Christianity has been very much concerned with right believing and the emphasis of Judaism has been on obedience to the Torah. But there is certainly enough in the scriptures, not least in St John's Gospel, to affirm the way as a fundamental category for both Judaism and Christianity, provided that the issue of religious truth is not neglected. For the way we walk in will depend upon a prior understanding of what that way is and that opens up all the familiar issues of religious truth.

According to van Buren, there is only one God, the God of Israel: 'The church adores Israel's Lord as its God.'[5] Again, this is a statement that can be affirmed, even though it needs to be glossed by saying that the God of Israel is the God and Father of our Lord Jesus Christ. The risen Christ told Mary Magdalene to go and tell his brothers, 'I am ascending to my Father and your Father, my God and your God'

[5] Paul van Buren, *A Theology of the Jewish–Christian Reality*, i: *Discerning the Way* (Harper and Row, 1980), 33.

(John 20: 17). The brothers to whom Mary Magdalene was to go were Jews who believed in the God of Israel. But that God was the God and Father of Jesus.

Van Buren decisively rejects any notion that Christianity has replaced Judaism. He regards such a notion as fundamentally incoherent. 'No other mark of incoherence can match that of our trusting in our love of the God of the Jews while at the same time denying God's faithfulness to his people.'[6]

Van Buren does not hesitate to discuss and affirm, in his terms, the strict Christian understanding of God as trinity in relation to Judaism. God is indeed Father. He is also spirit, because the spirit of the God of Israel is the one who draws Christians to believe. Nor is the concept of sonship alien because Israel itself is called to be the son of God in a loving relationship to God the Father.

Israel remains today the foundation of the church's claim to sonship for, if Israel were to cease to be, then the historical embodied reality of divine sonship would have died. If God were to abandon his sons and daughters, what value would sonship be? When the church calls Jesus the Son of God, therefore, it must also confess Israel to be God's sons and daughters. Because this one son has claimed and loves us Gentiles as his younger brothers and sisters, so we are called to love the Jews as also our elder brothers and sisters.[7]

Through Jesus Gentiles are called into relationship with God the Father. He is for Christians the word of God, the Lord who gives access to the God of the Jews. Nevertheless for van Buren Jesus is a man. 'He was and is a man, a Jew, not a second God, heaven forbid, not a deified man, just a man.'[8]

The critical questioning of van Buren's approach must become more searching. For, it may be doubted whether Jesus can be seen solely in terms of the one who brings Gentiles into relationship with Israel's God. That he certainly does, but his role is not limited to that. Further, and even more crucially, if Jesus is simply a man then historic Christianity has been cut down at its roots. This is an issue which will be discussed later.

---

[6] Paul van Buren, *A Theology of the Jewish–Christian Reality*, i: *Discerning the Way* (Harper and Row, 1980), 51.

[7] Ibid. 80–1.   [8] Ibid. 85.

Van Buren affirms that the goal of creation is shared by both Jews and Christians. 'We need to say afresh to ourselves, then, that our hope is just the Jewish hope into which we have access through Jesus Christ our Lord.'[9] This hope for Jews and Christians is a hope for the whole of creation, for its renewal and completion. St Paul in his vision of the end in 1 Corinthians 15 and Romans 11: 25–36 describes this hope in thoroughly Jewish terms. However, whatever Christians may believe, the Messianic age has not come in its fullness. Two points arise here. First, it can be readily agreed that Jews and Christians share a common hope, a vision of the purpose of God in creation which one day will come to its consummation. Furthermore, whilst Christians will certainly want to continue to believe that in some decisive sense the end, that is the telos, or goal of creation has been anticipated and embodied in Jesus, we have to acknowledge that the Messianic age for which the Hebrew scriptures long has clearly not come in any discernible sense. The world continues to be racked by pain and sin, suffering and evil.

It follows from all this that van Buren rejects the idea of Judaism's promise being fulfilled in Christianity. Instead, he argues, it is better to speak of promise and confirmation of that promise. The covenant with Judaism is confirmed and renewed in Christ, as well as being extended to the Gentiles. Israel's covenant originated with the Exodus experience and the giving of the Torah and the promise of the land is paralleled for Christianity in Jesus. The Torah is a joy not a burden. The Gentile church has been called to the services of God not directly through the Torah but through Jesus Christ, who was himself faithful to it. Jesus Christ recapitulates and embodies Israel's reality, its relationship to God, and its calling to be a light for the Gentiles. This means that the idea of a mission to the Jews is fundamentally misconceived. The Church is the Jewish mission to the Gentiles. Indeed the Church has a duty to serve Israel both in itself and through bringing the knowledge of God to the Gentile world. 'The church exists both as an extension of the work which God has begun with his people, and as a

---

[9] Ibid. 19.

confirmation of that work.'[10] Here too a number of controversial points need to be reflected on. Even if we reject the old paradigm of promise and fulfilment, we can ask whether promise and confirmation by itself does full justice to the New Testament. Furthermore, whilst the idea of a Church as it were shouldering Israel's responsibility to bring the knowledge of God to the Gentile world is certainly part of the truth, it is doubtful whether it is the whole truth.

When it comes to Christology Paul van Buren asserts two basic principles which run through the third volume of his work. First, every proper Christological statement, however high, will make clear that it gives the glory to God the Father. Secondly, every proper Christological statement will make it clear that it is an affirmation of the covenant between God and Israel. The inescapable context for all Christology today is the abiding covenant between God and the people of Israel. The covenant is not abrogated and every Christian way of talking about Jesus Christ must make this clear and not deny it by any kind of assumption or implication. In principle both van Buren's criteria can be accepted. Certainly in the New Testament there is no problem about asserting that all Christology should give glory to God the Father. This is a theme that runs through both St Paul and the fourth Gospel. It is very strongly safeguarded by a fully Trinitarian understanding of God and is only compromised when Christianity is presented as some kind of Jesus cult, which it is not. Similarly, although a fuller discussion of this will come later, it is surely right to affirm that God's covenant with Israel remains irrevocable, 'For the gracious gifts of God and his calling are irrevocable' (Romans 11: 29). Van Buren says that the Glory of Christ, as Philippians 2: 9–11 makes clear, lies in his humility before God. Otherwise 'It turns him into the God-man of the anti-Judaic, proud, and patriarchal church of the past.'[11] This quotation begs a lot of questions. It is indeed true that what characterizes Jesus in his historic ministry and in that ministry as a disclosure of the eternal life of the

[10] Paul van Buren, *A Theology of the Jewish–Christian Reality*, ii: *A Christian Theology of the People of Israel* (Harper and Row, 1983), 331.

[11] Paul Van Buren, *A Theology of Jewish–Christian Reality*, iii: *Christ in Context* (Harper and Row, 1988), 92.

Godhead, is his total self-abnegation, his complete giving of himself to his Father, hence his perfect humility. But it is this which makes him totally transparent to the Father and which reveals the Father's glory. At the same time, this is the glory of the son. Rosemary Radford Ruether argued in an influential book that Christology is the right hand of anti-Judaism. In other words, a high Christology, viewing Jesus as traditionally the Church has viewed him, inevitably denies the validity of Judaism and leads to anti-Judaism and antisemitism.[12] Paul van Buren is clearly wrestling with this issue. It is an issue for any Christian who wishes to remain at once a faithful follower of Jesus Christ within the community of the universal Church and build a new, constructive relationship with Judaism freed of anti-Judaic assumptions and implications. However, as was indicated above, van Buren's approach fells the tree of historic Christianity. Whether historic Christianity can be stated in such a way that Judaism is also respected and affirmed as a living religion, remains to be seen and is in part the purpose of this book.

Van Buren argues that there are three stages in the relationship between the Church and Israel. First the Church within Israel, then the Church against Israel and now, the third stage, the Church with Israel. This is surely right. As Karl Barth said to the Vatican Secretariat for Christian Unity in 1966, 'There is finally only one really great ecumenical question: Our relations with the Jewish people.' It is also highly significant that the Vatican places relationships with Judaism within the Secretariat for Unity, not the department dealing with other faiths. Roy Eckardt argued that any orthodox Christian presentation of the resurrection of Jesus inevitably undermines Judaism. He did not believe it is possible at one and the same time to affirm the resurrection of Jesus and to affirm Judaism as a living religion. I do not believe this to be true, nor does van Buren. For about the resurrection van Buren writes that it confirms not only Jesus but also the covenant. 'Jesus so confirmed, however, is the same Jesus whom the disciples understood to have been authorised by God to call them as Jews into a renewal of the covenant.' Jesus was sent to the lost sheep of the House of Israel.

---

[12] Rosemary Radford Ruether, *Faith and Fratricide* (New York, 1974).

In raising him from the dead God confirms him in this role. 'The cause of the crucified one was the cause of the God of Israel. So the Church has every ground to rejoice that the God of Israel, Sinai, and Easter is a persistent God who does not give up on his cause and does not ultimately abandon those to whom he entrusts that cause.'[13]

John Pawlikowski in *Christ in the Light of the Christian–Jewish Dialogue* offers a critique of the major thinkers in the field of Jewish–Christian relations as well as some major Christian theologians and offers his own Christology.[14] He argues that history is a continuing source of revelation and in particular the Shoah has brought about and must continue to bring about a radical reappraisal of Christianity's relation to Judaism. I would argue that it is dangerous to talk of history being a continuing source of revelation, if new revelation is meant. However, there can be no objection to thinking of history as drawing out implications which lie latent in the New Testament. This was certainly what happened in the nineteenth century when Christians began to see that slavery was incompatible with the deeper truths of the New Testament. Similarly in our time Christians have begun to realize that the traditional subjugated status of women is incompatible with a life of equality in Christ. In a similar way, the Shoah has brought to light the long terrible history of anti-Judaic teaching and has discerned its source in the New Testament itself. This has begun to bring about and must continue to bring out a fundamental reappraisal, in the proper sense of the word, repentance, or radical rethinking of Christianity's relationship to Judaism. So, whilst rejecting the idea that history can be a source of new revelation, what Pawlikowski says about history, and our new understanding of history needing to bring about a fundamental change of outlook, certainly needs to be stressed.

Pawlikowski categorizes the approaches to this question as one-covenant or two-covenant theologies. He criticizes those who fall into the category of a one-covenant theology, such as Paul van Buren, for simply offering what he terms a Judaism for the Gentiles. In

[13] Van Buren, *Christ in Context*, 126.
[14] John Pawlikowski, *Christ in the Light of the Christian–Jewish Dialogue* (Paulist Press, 1982).

Pawlikowski's view, if this was all that Christianity was it would not have emerged as a separate religion and would not have been able to maintain its identity in the world. Believers would simply have joined the synagogue, as we know a good number of God-fearers did in the first centuries. So Pawlikowski prefers to think of Judaism and Christianity as two separate, complementary religions that need to live in dialogue with one another. Drawing substantially on the works of James Parkes, the pioneering Anglican theologian in this field, he sees Judaism as providing religious and ethical guidance for the building up of community. This is the essence of the revelation of Torah. Christianity, on the other hand, focuses on the individual and sees each individual as an end in themselves. Christianity needs Judaism because without it it is likely to forget the communal aspect. Furthermore, there is in Christianity a tendency to spiritualize and privatize religion. This needs continuously to be brought down to earth by the Jewish sense of the practical and historical. Furthermore, there is a tendency in Christianity to offer broad generalizations and to float off into abstract concepts. This needs to live in tension with the Torah, which gives detailed guidance for making such broad principles a practical reality in the details of everyday life. Nevertheless according to Pawlikowski Christianity does offer something unique and distinctive. This is what he calls incarnation. But by incarnation he does not seem to mean *the* incarnation, the unique embodiment in a human person of the eternal Son of God, the word made flesh. Rather he sees incarnation as a general principle of God being intimately in communion with humanity and revealing himself through humanity as a result of that closeness. Moreover, he roots this in the soil of Judaism. He sees its seed in Pharisaism, the Judaic context where he places Jesus.

Pawlikowski has a high estimate of Pharisaism, which he regards as a highly creative movement. The Pharisees had a sense of the fatherhood of God and of the worth of each individual. They began to internalize the Torah, making it a matter of personal and inward response. Moreover, their distinctive institutions, the oral Torah, the Rabbinate, the synagogue, and their emphasis upon table fellowship in the home led, even before the destruction of the temple, to a religious way of life of great vitality. It is in this tradition, according to Pawlikowski, that Jesus should be placed. Although Jesus disagreed with some Pharisees on some points, he belonged within their world. Nevertheless, there are some points where there is a stronger emphasis than in Pharisaism, for example on the closeness of God the Father and on the call to love our enemies. However, what Jesus really brought about was the sense, experienced in and through him, of God and humanity in intimate communion, of incarnation. Even this did not emerge totally new, for in Pharisaism too there was a developing sense of the indwelling of God with his people expressed through such concepts as the *Shekinah*. But as a result of the impact of Jesus this became the central insight of Christianity.

Pawlikowski does not agree that the resurrection of Christ has to be rejected, as urged by Roy Eckardt, for after all, the resurrection was a characteristically Pharisaic notion, championed by them in opposition to other groups at the time. Furthermore, according to Pawlikowski, the resurrection is a secondary notion to that of the incarnation. Its purpose is to safeguard the intimate communion of God and humanity even through death.

Two points might be raised about Pawlikowski's approach at this stage. First, in placing Jesus within the context of first-century Pharisaism he virtually ignores, as do a number of writers who want to bring Christianity closer to Judaism, the teaching of Jesus about the Kingdom of God. Ever since Schweitzer in the nineteenth century it has generally been acknowledged that the concept of the Kingdom of God was central to the teaching of Jesus and that his use of it had an inescapable eschatological dimension. With all the changes of fashion in New Testament scholarship over the last 150 years the centrality of the notion of the rule of God in human affairs that Jesus both taught and sought to live out, has remained. Moreover, whether his prime thrust was in relation to the future or the present, it is clear from the New Testament that in his message and mission there is a crisis, in the Greek sense of the word, a time when a crucial decision, a judgement, had to be made.

Even more crucially, however attractive Pawlikowski's understanding of incarnation, what he is in fact talking about has tradition-

ally been termed immanence and in more modern theology has sometimes been termed panentheism. For it is mainstream Christian orthodoxy that God is not only utterly transcendent but he dwells in all
things and that in relation to human beings in particular, he dwells
within them in intimate communion. But this is different from a traditional Christian understanding of the incarnation of God in Jesus. It is
true as the early Church Fathers liked to say that God became human
in order that humans might become divine. It is also true that the
process of theosis, or divinization, though championed more by the
Eastern than the Western Church, is fully congruous with Christian
orthodoxy. Christian orthodoxy has always wanted to assert that this
process is possible, and only possible, because of the unique incarnation of God in Jesus who takes us into the same relationship with God
the Father that he himself eternally enjoys.

At this point it might be worth checking on a Jewish reaction to the
works of van Buren and Pawlikowski. Peter Haas finds the whole
exercise odd and distasteful. 'Jews must face the odd phenomenon of
having their religious convictions be the subject of Christian theological reflection.'[15] He doubts whether there could ever be a Christian
theology of Judaism that could be satisfactory to a Jew, no matter how
well-meaning. The ideal, he argues, is to describe Judaism as it is lived
by Jews and in its own terms. This is certainly what is needed in interfaith dialogue. However, both Christianity and Judaism, if they are to
provide, in their different ways, a coherent and consistent view of
human existence, including the place of religions other than their
own within the providence of God, must inevitably have an all-
encompassing theology. Christians would look to Jews to have one, as
they would look to Muslims, however unpalatable such a theology
might in the end prove to be.

Haas is on stronger grounds when he argues that 'Theology has
never been a favoured discourse among Jews, and so its results ought

---

[15] Peter Haas, 'Recent Theologies of Jewish–Christian Relations', *Religious Studies
Review*, 16/4 (Oct. 1990). Rabbi Jonathan Gorsky believes that the work of John
Pawlikowski is more substantial than Peter Haas indicates. In particular he does not think
that Pawlikowski's understanding of the Pharisees is 'idiosyncratic'.

never to be regarded as normative or descriptive.' This is true and therefore it means that Christians will always be more strongly motivated to have a theology of Judaism than will Jews to have a Jewish theology of Christianity. Furthermore, he criticizes van Buren for inevitably recasting Judaism to fit the needs of Christian theology and therefore inevitably distorting Judaism as actually lived by Jews. The Judaism he (and others) discuss will inevitably be either an idealized version or the Judaism of a particular community that the author has encountered. This is, I think, too pessimistic. Despite the hugely variegated forms of Christianity, one could trust a good and well-meaning Jewish scholar to identify the lineaments, as it were, of Christianity which she or he wanted to relate to Judaism. Similarly, despite the variety of forms of Judaism both in history and today, there are certain things that can be said about it, or about particular traditions within it.

Haas is even more pessimistic when it comes to overcoming supersessionism. He acknowledges that van Buren and Pawlikowski amongst other authors have dedicated themselves to rethinking Christian theology precisely and in order to overcome the supersessionisms of the past.

I find it disheartening, then, but not surprising, that none has finally succeeded. The problem is that the very nature of Christianity makes the avoidance of supersessionism (on a theological level) impossible. It seems that if the 'Christ event' adds nothing to what Judaism already has to offer, then the theologians here find Christianity to be in the end unnecessary. But if they maintain, as I suppose they must, Christianity does have something new or different to say, something that Judaism has (by definition?) not recognised or acknowledged, then their theologies are by definition supersessionist, no matter how tactfully stated.

This is a sharp challenge. I do believe that Christianity has something new and different to say. It remains open at this stage whether that new and different thing can be said without supersessionism.

Peter Haas rejects van Buren's view that Jesus opens up Judaism for Gentiles. For he believes that if this is all that Christianity offers, then Gentiles should simply have become Jews. According to van Buren, Jesus has 'renewed' the covenant for the Church. Such a renewal is

104

necessary because without it Gentiles would be without hope and without God. 'As a Jew, I find this insulting. It is as if van Buren is saying that Judaism is good enough for Jews, but you cannot really expect Gentiles to find God or hope in it. I want to know why not.' It should also perhaps be pointed out that Haas is sympathetic to what van Buren is trying to do and very affirmative of much of what he says, particularly about Judaism.

Haas is also sympathetic to the work of Pawlikowski but is critical both of his understanding of Pharisaism and the use he makes of it. He finds the understanding of Pharisaism very attractive but 'an idiosyncratic historical reconstruction'. More crucially, he does not think that an understanding of Pharisaism is an adequate preparation for understanding modern Judaism. 'Talking about contemporary Jewish–Christian relations through the surrogates of Jesus and the Pharisees is, at least as regards modern Jews, utter gibberish.' Nor does Haas like the idea that Judaism has 'seeded' Christianity, with the implication that the plant that has grown as a result of the seeding is somehow superior to the original seed. With this image he believes 'a supersessionist conclusion is almost unavoidable'.

In contrast to van Buren, I have maintained that Christianity is not just Judaism for Gentiles. Jesus brought something distinctively new into the world. There is, however, some truth in the plea by a number of Jewish scholars to see Judaism and Christianity as two different religions. If we are to talk in this way I would characterize Judaism as a religion of the Torah and Christianity as a religion of participation.

A Religion of Torah and a Religion of Participation

Christians have often held unhelpful stereotypes of Judaism as a religion of law. It has brought to mind something legalistic rather than spiritual, something rigid rather than sensitive to human need, and so on. From this point of view law is seen as something oppressive, a burden. But for Jews Torah is not so much a law as a way of life. It is not a burden but a delight. Furthermore, in contrast to what is seen as Christianity's overemphasis upon theology and abstract concepts,

Judaism gives specific guidance for day-by-day living. It is therefore specific and practical and this is in character with Judaism's understanding of itself as being less interested in theology than it is in observance of God's revealed will.

Christianity as a religion of participation has, as its defining rite of initiation, baptism. New Testament writers see baptism as a mystical participation in the dying and rising of Christ. Christians become one with Christ in his death and his resurrection. This Christian insight is explored in a number of different ways in a variety of images. For example, the great prayer in the letter to the Ephesians ends with the words 'that you may be filled with all the fullness of God' (Ephesians 3: 19). In St John's Gospel Jesus tells his followers that those who love him will keep his command and his command is that they love one another. If they love one another then God himself will come to dwell within them. The theme of baptism and our participation in God is brought together in the statement: 'I repeat, you died; and now your life lies hidden with Christ in God. When Christ, who is our life, is manifested, then you too will be manifested with him in glory' (Colossians 3: 3–4). The Christian understanding of God as trinity should likewise be seen in terms of human participation in the life of God. Jesus lived his life in response to the one he called Father. He did this, conscious of living out an intimate relationship of sonship to this Father. He was able to do this because the Holy Spirit filled him. This is depicted in iconic form in his baptism (Mark 1: 9–11). Christians through their faith and baptism are taken into the same relationship with God that Jesus eternally enjoys. They too call God Father. They too are God's daughters and sons. They too are filled with the Holy Spirit. They are taken into the very life of the Godhead, for God dwells in them and they participate in the life of God. This way of looking at things received particular emphasis in the theme of theosis or deification. Athanasius said that 'The word became flesh that we, partakers of his spirit, might be deified.' Again, 'He became man that we might become divine.'

Both religions see themselves as called to reveal the light and truth of God to the world. Both religions are necessary to one another and as they have evolved in history they live in dialectical relationship with one another. Christianity needs Judaism in order to be continually reminded that there is no participation in the life of God without obedience to God's revealed purpose. Christianity would want to say to Judaism that faithful obedience to the Torah is also participation in the life of God, a life which is nothing less than personal.

In chapters 9 to 11 in his letter to the Romans Paul wrestles with the issue of the relationship between Judaism and Christianity. Indeed, he does more than wrestle, he agonizes. He knew that God had called the people of Israel into existence and given them so much. 'They were made God's sons; theirs is the splendour of the divine presence, theirs the covenants, the law, the temple worship and the promises' (Romans 9: 4). Yet he had to face the fact that the majority of Jews did not follow Jesus and in his own mission work only a minority came to believe. As a Jew then, like Muslims today, Paul believed that everything was in the hand of God and nothing happened that was not willed by God. The lack of response by the Jewish people was therefore within the divine purpose. After all, it was only by a supreme supernatural act that he himself, the most destructive of the opponents of Christianity, had come to believe in Christ. As Robert Morgan has written:

Considering what it took to persuade Paul himself that Jesus is the messiah he cannot have been surprised by the common Jewish rejection of the Gospel. It must have been all part of God's plan.[16]

'I ask then, has God rejected his people? I cannot believe it!' (Romans 11: 1). Paul then uses the analogy of an olive tree. Gentile Christians were like a cutting from a wild olive that had been grafted onto a cultivated one. If God was able to do that, how much more would he be willing to graft back on natural olive branches. So he looked to a time when this will happen.

This partial blindness has come upon Israel only until the Gentiles have been admitted in full strength; when that has happened, the whole of Israel will be saved. (Romans 11: 25–6)

---

[16] Robert Morgan, *Romans* (Sheffield Academic Press, 1995), 56.

This time will be when 'the Deliverer' comes from Zion. So

> God's choice stands, and they are his friends for the sake of the patriarchs. For
> the gracious gifts of God and his calling are irrevocable . . . For in making all
> mankind prisoners to disobedience, God's purpose was to show mercy to all
> mankind.   (Romans 11: 28–32)

In this passage Paul is trying to understand or read history in the light
of his belief in the overriding providence of God. He believed that
God's purpose will finally prevail, despite human blindness and unbe-
lief. We too have to read history as best we can. The history we have to
come to terms with is 1,500 years of Christian teaching about supersessionism and contempt for Judaism, with all the disastrous consequences that have followed from this. Furthermore, we have to come
to terms with the fact that the Jewish people have, against all the odds,
survived and Judaism is a living religion in the contemporary world. It
is through an understanding of this history that God is calling us into
a new relationship with Judaism. Nevertheless, as Paul puts it in his
wonderful ending, the purposes of God are ultimately mysterious to us
and before that mystery there is a proper sense of creaturely humility:

> O depth of wealth, wisdom and knowledge in God! How unsearchable his
> judgements, how untraceable his ways! Who knows the mind of the Lord?
> Who has been his counsellor? Who has ever made a gift to him, to receive a gift
> in return? Source, Guide, and Goal of all that is—to him be glory forever!
> Amen.   (Romans 11: 33–6)

To this we might add a point which was stressed by Karl Barth and
which is referred to in a quotation from him in the next chapter,
namely Paul's emphasis on our responsibility to live a truly Christian
life, such a life that Jews will be able to see the glory of God in it. Paul
tells his readers not to be complacent, not to be full of pride, for it is
only through the mercy of God that they, cuttings from a wild olive,
have been grafted onto a cultivated one. They are to act in such a way
as 'to stir Israel to emulation'. He himself says that he is a missionary
to the Gentiles and gives all he is to that ministry: 'I try to stir emulation in the men of my own race'. (Romans 11: 11 and 14).

In this passage St Paul is clearly looking to the end of all things when
the mystery of God's purpose will be clearly revealed. Indeed as he

says elsewhere, 'Now we see only puzzling reflections in a mirror but then we shall see face to face. My knowledge now is partial; then it will be whole, like God's knowledge of me' (1 Corinthians 13: 12). It is only at the end when the purpose of the whole can be seen and therefore the meaning of every individual part that makes up that whole. Now we are on a journey:

> And what you thought you came for
> Is only a shell, a husk of meaning
> From which the purpose breaks only when it is fulfilled
> If at all. Either you had no purpose
> Or the purpose is beyond the end you figured
> And is altered in fulfilment.[17]

Those words of T. S. Eliot are true of the human journey towards its consummation in God at the end of all things, true for all of us. Nevertheless, both Jews and Christians believe that they have been granted an anticipatory sense of that final goal. For Christians that anticipation of the end is given in Christ, in whom heaven and earth, God and humanity are joined never to be unjoined and through whom we are taken into that unbreakable union with God, into a love from which nothing, not even death itself, can separate us. That is the faith on the basis of which we live. But Jews too have their anticipatory sense of the end and when the end comes for both of us the purpose will be beyond the end we figured and will be altered in fulfilment.

The preceding paragraphs have explored the relationship between Judaism and Christianity. Nevertheless, as was stated right at the beginning, this has to be seen against the background of a primal relationship between God and the whole of humanity. Van Buren's first three volumes were criticized as being too concerned with Judaism and Christianity at the expense of the other religions of the world. Nor is a preoccupation with the revelation of God on Mount Sinai, shared with Gentiles through Jesus Christ, true to the New Testament. The New Testament had no difficulty relating God's light in Jesus Christ with the light of spiritual truth in the Graeco-Roman world. In the

---

[17] T. S. Eliot, 'Little Gidding', lines 30–5 in *Four Quartets*.

prologue to St John's Gospel the *logos* is not only the Hebrew *dabar* who creates the world and speaks so forcefully through the prophets. He is also the light of reason and spiritual insight that a range of schools of Greek philosophers believed in different ways dwelt in the human mind. In recent decades theologians have seen that same *logos* at work in the religions of the Indian sub-continent.

Van Buren delivered a fourth volume, published posthumously, but this according to Pawlikowski, began to step away from his bolder assertions in the first three volumes. Nevertheless in a lecture towards the end of his life van Buren came to talk of 'covenantal pluralism'. He argued that at its heart for both Judaism and Christianity election is 'the code name for immediacy, intimacy and singularity'. This singularity is not to be dissolved into some general image of the divine–human relationship but it is meant to open us to the possibility of God's way for others being different.

It is an important feature of Israel's covenantal story that it does not require that there be no stories except this one. On the contrary, the biblical story implies that there will be other stories as well, for it is the story of a God of the whole earth. The very singularity of its story would be lost if others did not have their stories too. We are to discover the incredible richness of a God who can love all creation and relate to the multiplicity of creatures in multiple ways. It is a matter of both joy and wonder that God may be God to quite different human communities in quite different ways. Covenantal thinking will be open to a plurality in God's reality.[18]

To use the analogy suggested earlier, there will be different voices and different languages in the divine–human encounter. From a biblical point of view this is all underwritten in the promise given by God to Noah after the flood that seed time and harvest time shall not fail. God will continue to maintain life and the conditions which make life possible. Through this people experience and may consciously know God's loving kindness towards them. From a Christian point of view this relationship is undergirded and validated in Christ in whom heaven and earth, God and man are joined never to be unjoined. For

---

[18] Paul van Buren, *Covenantal Pluralism?*, Lecture delivered at the Harvard Divinity School on 20 Mar. 1990 at a presentation of the Sir Sigmund Sternberg Award.

the Church has always insisted that Jesus is not just a human being but in him all humanity is included. Of course, as has been stressed in the Introduction and elsewhere, every religion will have its own way of talking and this needs to be understood and grasped in its own terms. At the same time, any religion which is seeking a consistent and coherent world-view will have an account of other religions in its own terms. From a Christian point of view that account will include the work of the Holy Spirit in every human heart and the presence of Christ in every human being. Gerard Manley Hopkins has a wonderful poem in which he sees everything in nature, as we would say, doing its own thing. Everything in nature cries, 'What I do is me: For that I came.' He then goes on to say that when human beings act with justice and grace then that person

> Acts in God's eye what in God's eye he is—
> Christ. For Christ plays in ten thousand places,
> Lovely in limbs, and lovely in eyes not his
> To the Father through the features of men's faces.[19]

When a person acts justly and with grace in whatever culture they live, or whatever religion they follow, it is Christ within them reaching out to God the Father. Or, to use another analogy, one much liked by John Henry Newman, Christ in his incarnation came to gather all the fragments of divine glory scattered about the world and unite them in himself before the Father.

When it comes to specific beliefs and doctrines it is first of all important to identify the common ground. For what unites us is far more than what divides us. I do not in any way underestimate the differences between Judaism and Christianity, differences brought about above all by the Church's faith in Jesus Christ. But those differences have to be set against the foundation and fundamental framework that we hold in common. This has first of course to do with God himself, the one God, creator of all that is, both seen and unseen. This God brings into being a creation, that is a universe with a life of its own, not

---

[19] Gerard Manley Hopkins, 'As Kingfishers Catch Fire . . .', in *The Poems of Gerard Manley Hopkins*, ed. W. H. Gardner and N. H. MacKenzie (Oxford University Press, 1967), 90.

simply an emanation of himself. Christians and Jews know that we are creatures before a creator. We believe that this creator is characterized above all by *hesed*, loving kindness, that he is undeviating in his goodwill towards humanity; that he calls people into a special relationship to himself for a particular purpose, not of privilege but of service. We believe together what a rather surprising person, D. H. Lawrence once said, namely, 'All that matters is to be at one with the living God.' It is because of this that the first priority in Judaism is that God's name be sanctified, or held holy. It is because of this that the first petition in the Christian Lord's prayer begins 'Our Father in heaven, hallowed be your name'.

Fundamental also to Judaism and Christianity is a belief in God's kingly rule, a kingly rule which can take effect in the human heart now and which one day will embrace all things. So Christians pray 'Your kingdom come, your will be done on earth as in heaven', a petition which again is Jewish through and through. It is true that Christians believe that this kingly rule of God on earth has in some decisive sense been inaugurated in the life, death, and resurrection of Jesus Christ. Nevertheless the history of the world goes on apparently much as before, characterized by strife and killing, torture and cruelty, poverty and injustice. When Jews say that the Messianic age has not yet come, every page of history seems to bear out the truth of what they are saying. So both Jews and Christians look to the fullness of time, and beyond time, when all will be changed, utterly changed. So believing in one God and sharing one hope we both seek to make that hope a reality now through enacting God's purpose for humanity by justice and mercy. Clearly there are differences. One concerns the person of Jesus and that is explored in another chapter. Here we simply note in anticipation that two doctrines fundamental to Christianity, a belief in the incarnation and a belief in God as Holy Trinity, though they seem to separate Christianity very sharply from Judaism, have counterparts in Judaism and that they are not so alien as is often supposed.

The Christian belief is that 'the Word became flesh' (John 1: 14): that in Christ 'the complete being of the Godhead dwells embodied' (Colossians 2: 9) or again, 'For the divine nature was his from the first; yet he did not think to snatch at equality with God, but made himself nothing, assuming the nature of a slave' (Philippians 2: 6–7). This kind of language has always seemed particularly alien to Judaism, which has wanted to stress the utter transcendence of God, the great abyss between the uncreated and the created. But there are at least counterparts to this belief in Judaism. First in the idea of the *Shekinah*, the divine presence: God is close to his people, closer than their breathing. More than this, however, the obedient life of the community of Israel is to reveal the glory of God. Through obedience to the Torah God is not only present with his people but he is, as it were, embodied in them and their just dealing. The embodiment of God in Jesus does not, as it were, come out of the blue. God is already embodied in his people in so far as they are faithful. That correspondence does not take one all the way to understanding the Christian doctrine of the incarnation. But no analogy can. We can only understand anything in religion on the basis of human analogies. But in the end every human analogy breaks down because the Church has always claimed that the incarnation is not just one more example of what can be fitted into a human category but that which lies outside every category. Therefore to talk about correspondences between the embodiment of God's presence in his people Israel as they are faithful to the Torah and the embodiment of God as the focus of Israel in the faithfulness of Jesus, is to do what every attempt to understand the incarnation does and it fails in just the same way. The Graeco-Roman world was full of gods walking about disguised as human beings. Indeed Paul and Barnabas were taken for such gods after they had healed someone. Judaism has always quite rightly reacted strongly against this kind of belief. The Christian doctrine of the incarnation is to be seen not against the background of such notions but against the background of God's dealing with his people Israel. Against that background it still may not be believable, but at least it should not seem so utterly alien.

Then there is the Christian belief in God as Holy Trinity, which again has seemed totally alien to Judaism with its stress on the unity of the one God. But within Judaism God is known as Father, the people of Israel themselves are called into a relationship of sonship to that Father, and this relationship is made possible by the leading and empowering of God's spirit. It is this, Christians believe, which comes to a focus in Jesus. The Christian doctrine of the Holy Trinity says it is not simply a question of God relating to us or making himself known to us in three different ways but that he is in his essential being Father, Son, and Holy Spirit. But again this belief is not necessarily totally alien to Judaism. For Judaism stresses the free call and grace of God who calls his people Israel into existence and gives them their mandate. They have a responsibility and capacity to live out the Torah but that responsibility and capacity is itself the gift of the one gracious God and it is he who makes this possible. In living out this vocation the people of Israel is God's son responding to the Father and being guided by his wisdom or Holy Spirit. If the matter is seen in this way then God is at one and the same time Father, Son, and Holy Spirit, not just three ways of relating or three aspects of God. I am not of course arguing that Judaism has a fully developed belief in God as Holy Trinity nor am I trying to impose such a belief when it is not there. I am simply suggesting that the concept has more affinities with Judaism than is sometimes allowed.

I have argued that the primal covenant is between God and humanity. Within that there are a number of voices and languages and amongst them Judaism and Christianity are intertwined. Christianity does bring something new into the world, participation in the life of God through Jesus Christ, but this does not supersede Judaism. On the contrary, Judaism and Christianity live in dialectical relationship with one another, Judaism calling Christianity to practical, detailed obedience to God and Christianity holding out the possibility to Judaism that faithfulness to the Torah is also participation in the life of God. From a Christian point of view that faithfulness to God is the faithfulness of Jesus Christ to his Heavenly Father in and through his ancient people. As St Paul said about the people of Israel in the wilderness:

They all ate the same supernatural food, and all drank the same supernatural drink; I mean they all drank from the supernatural rock that accompanied their travels—and that rock was Christ. (1 Corinthians 10: 4)

Sister Margaret Shepherd has criticized the argument in the immediately preceding pages. She writes, in a letter to me:

You do not concede that a statement such as 'The presence of Christ in every human being' and quoting Hopkins on this would be abhorrent to Jews. . . . A Jew could justifiably protest: When I as a Jew 'act with justice' am I then, according to Hopkins and presumably to you, 'Christ'? Do you think that . . . any of your Jewish friends and colleagues—will accept that when they (or those of any other faith) 'act justly and with grace' that it is, whether they know it or not 'Christ within them reaching out to God the Father'? If I were them I would feel insulted and deeply hurt.

I can hear Haas saying in your response to your proposal of 'Christianity holding out the possibility to Judaism that faithfulness to the Torah is also participation in the life of God', 'Thank you, but we are already aware of that' and don't need Christianity to point it out to us. Even the suggestion, though kindly meant, is impertinent and of itself smacks of the supersessionism you are trying to deny.

I take this criticism seriously. Nevertheless, as I have suggested earlier, I think that it is necessary for all religions, not just Christianity, to combine two approaches. First, there is the approach of dialogue, in which we listen to the partner speaking in their terms, with their perspective. It would indeed be impertinent in such an encounter to impose Christian language on a Jewish experience described in Jewish terms.

Yet dialogue itself can move beyond this mutual respect for one another's languages without losing the fundamental respect which makes such dialogue possible in the first place. For the fact is that any religion worth its name will seek to have a coherent and consistent view of the whole universe, including the place of other religions within it. The God in whom Christians believe is not just a God for Christians. The God in whom Jews believe is not just a God for Jews. We both believe that this God is the creator of heaven and earth with a purpose for every human being. It is therefore not only inevitable but absolutely right that both Judaism and Christianity will have a perspective and a language which includes the other in their own terms. This will of its nature be jarring to the other, which is why the sharing of such perspectives will only be appropriate when the relationship of dialogue has reached a certain depth. But when that level has been reached, it is imperative that uncomfortable truths are shared as well as the mutually affirming ones. So Judaism looking at Christianity from a Jewish point of view will state what are believed to be truths which Christians will find unpalatable, however sensitive that Jewish perspective is trying to be. Some examples of this will be discussed in the chapter 'Jewish Attitudes towards Christianity'. There, one position taken is that Christianity is God's way of bringing the light and truth revealed in Judaism to the Gentile world. But what it brings is a Jewish truth, therefore what is authentic and of continuing validity about Christianity is what it has preserved of Judaism. Along the way it has attracted to itself various unhelpful extraneous beliefs which should be jettisoned. In a precisely similar way though from a very different perspective, Christianity will want to have an inclusive understanding of Judaism, in Christian terms. However inclusive and affirmative this is, it will inevitably have a jarring element about it. The real difficulty is not this exercise in itself but the fact that for so much of human history it was carried on by one religion that had all the power, a power which it used in an oppressive manner. That is why as Christians we need to be particularly sensitive about engaging in this second level of dialogue at all. But this book has come out of the grateful experience of having participated in dialogue at that level.

Should Christians Try to Convert Jews?   6

Mission is fundamental to the life of the Christian Church. Indeed, as the old cliché has it, the Church is mission. However, mission is not to be equated with Evangelism or even with Evangelization, the preferred term of the Roman Catholic Church. Evangelism is an aspect of mission but not its entirety. Mission begins in the heart of God. It is God going out in love to create a universe in the first place, to bring into being a world that is not himself, which is free to be itself, a freedom which becomes conscious in us human beings. The same love which goes out to create the cosmos, goes out to each individual in perfect understanding and desire for their well-being. Because mission begins in the heart of God and indeed is God himself going out to humanity in love, mission is inseparable from prayer, for it is prayer alone that enables us to enter into that heart and mind. For Christians, that heart and mind has gone out to humanity in a decisive way in Jesus Christ and Jesus Christ mandated his followers similarly to go out to others. According to St John's Gospel, the Risen Christ appeared to his followers and said, 'As the Father sent me, so I send you'; he then breathed on them, saying, 'Receive the Holy Spirit' for it is the Holy Spirit that enables us, through prayer, to enter into the heart and mind of God and to go out at one with his purpose (John 20: 21–2).

It has been argued that Judaism was once a missionary religion and indeed for a period seemed as successful as Christianity. Nevertheless, in the modern world, most Jews are at pains to say that Judaism is not a missionary religion and in practice it is very arduous for anyone to convert to Judaism. Judaism today finds the Christian emphasis on mission alien and unpalatable. However, it is a fundamental feature of Christianity which it would be false not to bring into the dialogue with Judaism in the same way that the state of Israel today is a fundamental feature of Judaism which cannot be left out of consideration in any meaningful relationship between Jews and Christians. The 1988 Lambeth Conference and subsequent meeting of the Anglican Consultative Council set out the five marks or strands of mission as follows:

To proclaim the good news of the Kingdom;
To teach, baptize and nurture new believers;
To respond to human need by loving service;
To seek to transform unjust structures of society;
To strive to safeguard the integrity of creation and sustain and renew the life of the earth.

This holistic way of looking at mission is important and a healthy safeguard against stressing social justice concerns at the expense of proclaiming the good news of the Kingdom or emphasizing the latter at the expense of the former. For some the Evangelistic side of mission is crucial. A key text occurs at the end of St Matthew's Gospel when the Risen Christ says to his disciples:

Full authority in heaven and on earth has been committed to me. Go forth therefore and make all nations my disciples; baptize men everywhere in the name of the Father and the Son and the Holy Spirit, and teach them to observe all that I have commanded you. And be assured, I am with you always, to the end of time.   (Matthew 28: 18–20)

This emphasis is of importance to four groups of people in particular. First, those who define themselves as Evangelicals. As the name indicates, they see it as an essential part of their Christian duty to help other people put their trust in Jesus Christ. Any downplaying of this aspect of Christian life they would regard as a denial of an essential aspect of the faith. Secondly, there are those organizations that have a specific role in relation to the Jewish people. The best known one amongst Anglicans is the Church's Ministry among the Jewish people, which was founded in 1809 as the 'London society for promoting Christianity amongst the Jews'. It was at its peak in terms of the amount of missionary activity in 1914 when it had a mission staff of around 280, of whom a third were of Jewish descent. Part of their work is to help Christians rediscover the Jewish roots of their faith. But they also see it as an essential part of their task to bring Jews to Christian faith. Thirdly, there is Jews for Jesus or, more generally, Messianic Judaism. This is a movement of people often of Jewish background who have come to believe that Jesus is the expected Jewish messiah and who wish to follow him whilst at the same time retaining their Jewish religious and cultural heritage. They often have congregations independent of other churches and specifically target Jews for conversion to their form of Christianity. Fourthly, there is a smaller group of people who would not necessarily regard themselves as belonging to any of the three aforementioned categories but who have converted to Christianity, the best known person in our time being Hugh Montefiore, the former Bishop of Birmingham.

Over the last decade or so issues have arisen that have affected all or some of those groups. As indicated in the introduction, I was asked to convene and chair a small group of people to produce some 'Jewish–Christian guidelines for the Anglican Communion'.[1] Section 8 of the document, entitled 'The one mission and the mutual witness', reads as follows:

The people of God, which includes both Jews and Christians, have one mission. This mission is the sanctification or hallowing of God's name in the world. The sanctification of God's name, that is, so acting with justice and holiness, that his reality is acknowledged and honoured, is fundamental to Judaism. It is, of course, the very first petition in the prayer which Jesus taught his followers. 'Our Father in heaven, hallowed be your name'.

The mission of Jesus was first and foremost to his own people. The Christian church began as a community within Judaism and it preached the

---

[1] Members of this group, in addition to myself, were the Revd John Bowden, the Revd Marcus Braybrooke, the Rt Revd Michael Nazir-Ali, Sister Margaret Shepherd, Rabbi Dr Norman Solomon, and the Revd Dr William Weiler, with Vanessa Wilde from the Anglican Consultative Council in attendance.

Should Christians Try to Convert Jews?

Gospel first to Jewish people. The mission to non-Jews came later and the first crucial question that the Christian church had to decide was whether non-Jews could be admitted to the fellowship and if so, on what terms. So the church, in being true to itself and its Lord cannot escape a proper concern for the Jewish people.

However, the form that this concern takes is different from age to age and will certainly be very different today from what it has often been in the past. Today, it will firmly reject any form of proselytising, which attempts to convert individual Jews to Christianity.

Mission, which is essential to the being of the church, is nothing less than a sharing in the out-reaching love of God. It belongs in and is rooted in prayer, which is the most fundamental of all forms of sharing in the divine love. It will take the form first, of praise to God for the Jewish people, who have served him faithfully through so many difficulties and so much suffering. Secondly, of prayer for the Jewish people that they may be faithful to the Torah which God has given them. Thirdly, it will seek to serve the Jewish community in sensitive ways which are truly required i.e. in ways which help to affirm and safeguard Jewish identity.

Fourthly, it will take the form of listening to the Jewish people, and hearing their concerns and fears; of entering into their perspective and seeing with their eyes. Fifthly, in the dialogue between Jews and Christians, there will be mutual witness. Through learning from one another each will enter more deeply into their own inheritance. Each will recall the other to God, to trust him more fully and obey him more profoundly. This will be a mutual witness between equal partners.

We offer as one model of how Christian concern for the Jews remains but in a radically altered form, the work of the Sisters of Sion. The Roman Catholic Congregation of Our Lady of Sion was founded in the mid-nineteenth century with the avowed aim of the conversion of Jews. Under the impact of the ecumenical and biblical movements, the Holocaust, and for theological reasons, the aim of the congregation has completely changed. Keeping in mind the fundamental inspiration of the founders that there was a need for a congregation that would remind Christians of their Jewish roots, they moved away from the original goal to a fresh understanding of the permanent election of the Jewish people and the validity of the Jewish religion in both the past and the present. The sisters are now committed to the task of spreading among Christians an understanding of Jewish religious values and of theological issues concerning the permanent existence of the Jewish people alongside the church.

Again, as indicated in the Introduction, this section in particular was one of those that encountered fierce opposition at the 1988 Lambeth Conference. The final document, 'Jews, Christians and Muslims: The Way of Dialogue', retained this view as one option but also indicated that there were others. Sections 25, 26, and 27 of 'The Way of Sharing' read as follows:

25 Dialogue does not require people to relinquish or alter their beliefs before entering into it; on the contrary, genuine dialogue demands that each partner bring to it the fullness of themselves and the tradition in which they stand. As they grow in mutual understanding they will be able to share more and more of what they bring with the other. Inevitably, both partners to the dialogue will be affected and changed by this process, for it is a mutual sharing.

26 Within this sharing there are a variety of attitudes towards Judaism within Christianity today. At one pole, there are those Christians whose prayer is that Jews, without giving up their Jewishness, will find their fulfilment in Jesus the Messiah. Indeed some regard it as their particular vocation and responsibility to share their faith with Jews, whilst at the same time urging them to discover the spiritual riches which God has given them through the Jewish faith. Other Christians, however, believe that in fulfilling the Law and the prophets, Jesus validated the Jewish relationship with God, while opening this way up for Gentiles through his own person. For others again, the Holocaust has changed their perception, so that until Christian lives bear a truer witness, they feel a divine obligation to affirm the Jews in their worship and sense of God who is, for Christians, the Father of Jesus. In all these approaches, Christians bear witness to God as revealed in Jesus and are being called into a fresh, more fruitful relationship with Judaism. We urge that further thought and prayer, in the light of Scripture and the facts of history, be given to the nature of this relationship.

27 All these approaches, however, share a common concern to be sensitive to Judaism, to reject all proselytising, that is, aggressive and manipulative attempts to convert, and, of course, any hint of antisemitism. Further, Jews, Muslims and Christians have a common mission. They share a mission to the world that God's name may be honoured: 'Hallowed be your name'. They share a common obligation to love God with their whole being and their neighbours as themselves. 'Your Kingdom come on earth as it is in heaven'. And in the dialogue there will be mutual witness. Through learning from one another they will enter more deeply into their

own inheritance. Each will recall the other to God, to trust him more fully and obey him more profoundly. This will be mutual witness between equal partners.[2]

The resolution that commended 'Jews, Christians and Muslims: The Way of Dialogue' for study in the Anglican Communion and also recommended that the Anglican Consultative Council, through an interfaith committee, set up working parties to draw up more detailed guidelines for relationships with Judaism and Islam and other faiths as appropriate. In the event some guidelines were drawn up by a committee set up by the Churches' Commission for Interfaith Relations in response to a request from the Church of England to respond ecumenically to the Lambeth resolution.[3] These were published as *Christians and Jews: A New Way of Thinking*. The session on 'Mission and Evangelism' was shorter than the previous two documents. It read:

Jews and Christians have a mission in common. Each interprets itself as people of God, sent into the world to witness to his light and truth. Secondly, there is mission to one another, in which Christians and Jews both receive and give. Through honest sharing we enlarge and enrich our understanding of faith, rediscover neglected aspects of our own tradition and are recalled in obedience to God. In this way both communities grow as partners in the purpose of God.

There are differences of opinion amongst Christians about whether we should or should not be seeking to convert individual Jews to Christian faith. However, this difference needs to be seen against the background of the two fundamental affirmations above. Furthermore, we have to bear in mind the long history of Jewish suffering brought about by the Christian church and the Shoah. In the light of this many Christians today believe that the first task which Christ has given us is to acknowledge the hurt which Jews have

---

[2] 'Jews, Christians and Muslims: The Way of Dialogue', appendix 6 of *The Truth Shall Make You Free*, the Lambeth Conference 1988 published by the Anglican Consultative Council.

[3] In addition to myself, who chaired the working party, the others members were Rabbi Dr Norman Solomon, Sister Mary Kelly, nds, the Revd John Parry, and Rabbi Tony Bayfield. The working party produced *Christians and Jews: A New Way of Thinking: Guidelines and the Churches*. It was published by the Churches' Commission for Interfaith Relations on behalf of the Council of Churches for Britain and Ireland in 1994.

received over centuries at Christian hands, to rethink our relationship to Judaism and rebuild it on more constructive foundations. It also needs to be borne in mind that though their mission is an essential aspect of the Christian church and we cannot withhold the good news, many Jews find attempts to single them out for conversion both disturbing and threatening.

At the 1988 Lambeth Conference there was some criticism that Christians of Jewish origin had not been part of the original working party. Nor were they members of the working party that produced *Christians and Jews: A New Way of Thinking*. As a result of this concern a question was asked at the November 1996 meeting of the General Synod of the Church of England asking the Board of Mission what plans it had to express support for members of the Church of England who see themselves as both Jewish and Christian and who seek to share the good news of the messiah with their fellow Jews. As a result of this question the Interfaith Consultative Group set up a working party. The first drafts of this working party's report expressed the concerns of Jewish Christians but failed to take into account the wider and much larger context of Jewish–Christian relations generally. As a result of extensive criticism and further work and the helpful role of Michael Ipgrave, the Interfaith Relations Adviser for the Archbishops Council, a final report was published which did in fact include nearly all of the earlier report *Christian and Jews: A New Way of Thinking*. In other words, the concerns of Jewish Christians were set in the wider context of Jewish–Christian relations generally. This new report, *Sharing One Hope?*, set out to be a contribution to a continuing debate.[4] Section 4 of chapter 8 of *Sharing One Hope?*, 'Christian Mission and the Jewish People', simply sets out three positions that the authors regard as present in the Church of England today.

1. It is not appropriate for Christians to believe that they have any kind of 'Mission to Jews'.

2. It is entirely appropriate that Christians who establish relations of genuine friendship and trust with Jews should continue to see these relationships in the context of Christian mission.

---

[4] *Sharing One Hope? The Church of England and Christian-Jewish Relations: A Contribution to a Continuing Debate* (Church House Publishing, 2001). The somewhat tortuous path that eventually led to the production of this document is set out in appendix 1.

3. Christians have a responsibility to try to convince Jews about Jesus as messiah.

Each of those positions is given a dozen or so lines of explanation. No attempt is made to resolve the very different approaches: indeed the whole document, as already stated, sees itself as a contribution to a continuing debate rather than a resolution of the issues.

Before looking at the substantial issue it is just worth noting briefly some of the controversies that have erupted in relation to it. First, as already indicated, there was public concern from some quarters about the original document put to the Lambeth Conference because it rejected any idea of a mission to Jewish people.[5] Secondly, in 1992 Dr Carey became the first Archbishop of Canterbury for 150 years to decline the usual invitation from the Church's Ministry among the Jewish people to be their patron. Archbishops are ex-officio co-presidents of the Council of Christians and Jews, whose role is dialogue not mission, and Dr Carey, like Dr Runcie, was very active in that role. Dr Carey noted in his letter to CMJ that he wished to build up the trust of the Jewish community and would not be helped in this by close association with an organization 'Entirely directed towards another faith community'. Thirdly, at Christmas 1988 Jews for Jesus started to place high-profile advertisements in the newspapers. This aroused the concern of the Jewish community and again initiated a public debate about what was and was not appropriate for Christians in their relationship to Jews. Messianic Jews have continued to be active since then and another public dispute arose over high-profile advertisements in 2001. Fourthly, in 1996 the Council of Christians and Jews published 'A Code of Practice for Members'. The basis of CCJ's work is mutual trust between Jewish and Christian members. Any hint of proselytizing would destroy that trust and there was a fear that the Council might be infiltrated by people who wished to do that. The code of practice therefore said:

Insensitive comments about Christianity or Judaism, or attempts to use CCJ for missionary activity, destroy the mutual trust that is essential to our work.

---

[5] See the *Church Times* for 29 July 1998 and the *Jewish Chronicle* for 15 July 1988 and subsequent letters and reports in the press.

Aggressive proselytism is always wrong and if this or any unsuitable behaviour is reported to CCJ, appropriate action will be taken.

The code also had the phrase 'Concern will not be confined to behaviour within the CCJ'. This was a response to a particular instance when people who had engaged in unsolicited missionary activity in a Jewish community then appeared at their local CCJ branch and Jewish members were perturbed. This code again initiated a public discussion. Then, finally as already mentioned, there has been the continuing and growing concern of Jewish Christians, not necessarily those associated in any way with Messianic Judaism or indeed evangelicalism. Clearly how one responds to this interrelated set of issues depends very significantly on the prior theological questions discussed in the previous chapter.

The view presented there is that the primal covenant is between God and humanity. After the flood God promised Noah that seed time and harvest time would not fail. God would maintain life and the conditions which make life possible and through this his love for humanity is expressed. For Christians this one covenant with the whole of humanity is rooted and grounded in Jesus Christ in whom heaven and earth, God and humanity are one; united in a way never to be divided again. Nevertheless, although there is one covenant and the one God remains equally faithful to every aspect of his creation, different voices are heard in response. Jews and Christians respond with two different voices, or perhaps an analogy would be two different languages whose root is the same. Latin gave rise to both Italian and Spanish amongst other Romance languages. Spanish and Italian are now different languages but they have many aspects in common that reflect their common base. Or, to use an analogy that has often been used by the Pope, Christianity and Judaism belong to one family, with Judaism being the elder brother and Christianity the younger.

These analogies should not be taken to deny that Judaism and Christianity have a special, unique role. They do. But it should be seen not so much in terms of a covenant made with them as the covenant with humanity made more explicit. God's faithfulness and his call to us to respond with a corresponding loyalty is lived out and tested within Judaism. It was lived out and tested to the limit in Jesus Christ. But the divine promise and the divine call which evokes our response belongs to humanity as a whole.

In the previous chapter I rejected the idea that Christianity was simply Judaism for the Gentiles. Similarly, the concept of two separate covenants, one for the community and one for individuals as such, put forward by James Parkes and taken up in a more nuanced way by John Pawlikowski, is not the most helpful way of seeing the relationship between the two religions. There is a real difference and this is best seen in terms of a religion of the Torah for the one and a religion of participation in the life of God for the other. As such, the two religions live in inescapable partnership with one another, Torah reminding Christians that their religion needs to be lived out in quite specific, day-by-day practical ways in obedience to God's revealed will.

Against this background I would want to affirm the following points. First, Judaism is a living religion through which Jews relate to the one true, living God. This is the God Jesus came to believe in and trust through the Judaism he was taught in his day. This is the one he called his Father and his God, the God of Abraham, Isaac, and Jacob. Franz Rosenzweig thought seriously of becoming a Christian but felt he had to do this as a Jew not as a pagan and therefore first of all he was led back into a more thorough study of Judaism. Through this he came to the insight that 'He already was with the Father' so that John 14: 6 'No one comes to the Father except by me' did not apply to him. Jews know God as Father, the God and Father of Jesus Christ. Judaism is called into a filial relationship to this Father so that individual Jews also participate in the sonship which belongs to the community as a whole. All this is made possible through the divine Spirit which supports and leads the people of Israel. In short, Jews do not need Christianity in order to know the one true God. They can know him already through their Judaism.

Secondly, the voice or language of Judaism preserves precious insights which it is important not to lose. Today there is a great concern about losing particular species of plants or animals. We recognize that the richness and diversity of creation is valuable in itself. We feel the same about particular languages. It would be a terrible loss, if, for example, Welsh ever died out. Judaism is a language about God and what is required of us in the light of the knowledge of God, whose loss would be very great indeed. Thirdly, Jews understandably see conversion to Christianity as both a betrayal and a loss of identity. Rabbi Arye Forta has written

Shmad—Apostasy—is one of the most terrible words a Jew can hear. It expresses treachery, family breakup and national extinction. It can generate unbelievably powerful emotions; 'The missionaries are trying to do what Hitler and Stalin failed to achieve' is a not uncommon Jewish response—and understandably too. For Jews, Shmad is a subversion of their entire raison d'être on this planet.[6]

Again, as Clifford Longley has written referring to Christians who try to convert Jews to Christianity, 'They insist that Jewish identity can survive a change of religious conviction. But strong attachment to Jewish identity is one of the chief ways in which Jews have traditionally resisted attempts to convert them, which this approach seems to undermine.'[7] Or as the Chief Rabbi has put it, 'Throughout the Christian centuries the vast majority of Jews were willing to suffer persecution, expulsions and martyrdom rather than break their covenant with God.' It is because of this sense that Messianic Jews seek to retain their Jewish identity whilst at the same time confessing Jesus as the Jewish Christ. This is an issue which will be discussed shortly but the point here is that for a Jew to become a Christian is, from a Jewish perspective, the most fundamental of all betrayals.

Fourthly, in the light of the long history of the teaching of contempt, the Christian Church is called on to repent, that is to radically rethink its whole attitude to Judaism. Members of CMJ such as John Fieldsend believe that the issues of the Church's anti-Judaism and what he sees as a Christian duty to try to convert Jews today, can and should be kept separate. The Church should indeed be deeply sorry for its history but that does not preclude wanting Jews to become Christians.[8] But that is not how Jews see the matter. As Hyam Maccoby puts it:

[6] The Times (16 Jan. 1989).   [7] The Times (7 Jan, 1989).
[8] John Fieldsend, 'Antisemitism and Evangelism', in a CMJ magazine in 1994.

Should Christians Try to Convert Jews?

Mr Fieldsend also envisages a Christianity not only tolerant of Jewish observances but purged of the antisemitism that has hindered missionary efforts in the past. This is certainly a laudable aim, but I would point out that Christian antisemitism has been more than a mere unnecessary excrescence on the face of Christianity. It has arisen out of certain central features of Christianity: the compulsion to supersede the Jews as the true Israel and people of God, and, as a consequence, the representation of the Jews as the rejecters and betrayers of the Saviour. As long as Christianity retains its claim to be the unique road to salvation (a claim that Mr Fieldsend reasserts unequivocally), it will regard the Jews as uniquely wicked to have rejected that claim.[9]

I believe that Mr Fieldsend and his friends are totally sincere in their belief that repudiation of anti-Judaism and Christian mission to Jews can exist together. However, in the light of the Church's appalling record towards Jews it would seem more appropriate to show love of the Jewish people, a mission towards the Jewish people, not by trying to convert them to the Christian faith but by supporting them in the practice of their own religion. Fifthly, as emphasized by the original guidelines of Jewish–Christian relations that went to the Lambeth Conference and by *Christians and Jews: A New Way of Thinking*, Christians and Jews share a common mission. The very first petition of the Christian Lord's Prayer is 'Our Father in heaven, hallowed be your name'. This is a Jewish prayer expressing the Jewish sense of mission that God's name may be sanctified or hallowed in the world. This means so acting with justice and holiness that his reality is acknowledged and honoured. Both Jews and Christians share a sense that they are to be a witness to God's light and truth.

Most Jews feel very uncomfortable at the idea of Christians trying to convert them, in however loving or subtle a way. Nevertheless, there is some recognition that mission does belong to Christian self-definition. As Geoffrey Wigoder has put it,

If we Jews demand Christian understanding of our own self-definition, we must give considerable consideration to Christian self-definition which gives the mandate to go forth and spread the truth of Christianity. Witness is a legit-

---

[9] Hyam Maccoby article on 21 June, 1994, in response to an article the previous week by John Fieldsend.

imate enterprise as long as it fully respects the freedom of conscience of men of other faiths.[10]

Hugh Montefiore, a Christian from a Jewish background, again feels the inescapable imperative to bring Christian truth to Jews. However, he does say that 'It is better not to name the name of Christ to my fellow Jews'. Rather, mission should be done by 'manifesting the love of God through personal lifestyle' especially through the hand of genuine friendship. The reason he takes this view is quite simply that the word Christ down the centuries has been a curse to the Jewish community, not good news but very bad news indeed and this is still indelibly imprinted in the Jewish folk memory.

Reinhold Niebuhr put the whole matter rather differently when in 1926 he wrote:

If I were a self-respecting Jew I certainly would not renounce the faith of the fathers to embrace a faith which is as involved as Christianity is with racialism, nordicism and Gentile arrogance. If we want to approach the Jew at all we need a new strategy, a strategy in which repentance and love are mingled . . . what we need is an *entente cordiale* between prophetic Judaism and prophetic Christianity in which both religions would offer the best they have to each other.[11]

One person who seemed to shift his view was Donald Coggan, the former Archbishop of Canterbury, who had a very deep knowledge and love of the Jewish people. In a 1985 lecture at St Paul's Cathedral, after listing five attitudes which a Christian might bring to an encounter with a Jewish friend, he ended up by saying that for a Christian to share his or her faith is natural but this should be very much in the form of a sensitive, gentle invitation. However in 1992, in a sermon at St Paul's Cathedral to celebrate the 50th anniversary of the Council of Christians and Jews he said that Judaism and Christianity

have so much in common which is essential for the very life of the world that we should regard it as the truth of which we are common trustees and together

[10] Geoffrey Wigoder, *Jewish–Christian Relations since the Second World War* (Manchester University Press, 1988), 68.

[11] Quoted by Franklin Littell, *Reinhold Niebuhr and the Jewish People*, the 1990 Niebuhr lecture at Elmhurst College, p. 11.

we should make its light shine. We have a common message and, I would dare to say, a common mission.

In a third address on the theme, the annual Sacks lectures in 1995 at the University of Essex Donald Coggan was even more explicit.

I see two hands, grasped in a common task with Christian saying to Jew and Jew replying to Christian: 'We have passed from hatred to tolerance, from tolerance to dialogue. Now, together, we go—in obedience to a common mission—to fulfil a shared task given to us by God. We are partners. We are co-trustees. Come, let us go—and go together.'

This was a truly remarkable pilgrimage on the part of one of the most revered evangelical leaders of the last fifty years. When he was Archbishop of Canterbury, Dr George Carey, preaching the inaugural Donald Coggan lecture at the National Cathedral in Washington DC in April 2001, whilst deeply respecting his predecessor's learning and attitude, does question that final step. Dr Carey argued against what seems to have become orthodoxy in the Episcopal Church in the United States, that there are two covenants, one for Jews and one for Christians, and that Christians should not try to convert Jews. He also questions the understanding of St Paul's teaching in Romans 9 to 11 which asks Christians to regard Judaism as valid in its own right without needing any fulfilment or consummation in Christianity. In a very sensitive way that is based upon Christ on the cross sharing powerlessness he believes that Christians have a continuing duty to invite Jews to follow Christ. This is on the basis of equality, with Christians being willing to learn from Jews, and in the context of friendship when in most instances it would be the Jewish friend who would take the initiative in wanting to know something about Christianity. Nevertheless, 'I do not abandon that desire to introduce them to my faith and the way I see it.'

This lecture could have made for a major row in Great Britain because it was reported without any of the original subtleties and qualifications that the Archbishop was in the old conversion of Jews game again. However, the Chief Rabbi, in a great act of statesmanship, asked Rabbis of the United Synagogue, of which he is head, not to comment publicly on the Archbishop's lecture and they didn't. He also remarked that he understood that it was necessary for the Archbishop to say what he said and it was necessary for him to hear it. All this is an indication of how much has been achieved between the two communities, and the Chief Rabbi and the then Archbishop of Canterbury in particular, in the way of mutual respect and supportive friendship.

The views of both Hugh Montefiore and George Carey are at once deeply held and very sensitively put. I do not believe that those who share Geoffrey Wigoder's position quoted above, would take exception to them. Nevertheless, for me, the challenge is rather different and it was starkly put by Franklin Littell:

The most profound disservice of Hebrew Christian missioners is precisely this: that they continue to direct attention to the traditional crisis put by Christianity to the Jewish people, where the central issue today is the crisis put to Christianity by a crucified and resurrected Jewry.[12]

In the light of that I have to ask myself for what it is that I really want to pray in relation to my Jewish friends. Before mission there must be prayer: for mission is nothing less than sharing in the outgoing love of God.

The question is then for what should a Christian pray in relation to his or her Jewish friends? Can I pray that my Jewish friends are converted to Christianity? My honest answer is, no. I am happy if they are trying to be faithful Jews as I am trying to be a faithful Christian. They have insights as Jews whose loss would make the world a poorer place. They have spiritual riches which it is essential that Christianity keeps in contact with and is strengthened by.[13] Their Jewish identity is part of their identity as the person whose friendship I appreciate. To pray for their conversion would be to ask God to make them betray their deepest convictions and lose what is most fundamental to their identity. I can and should pray to God for them, to give thanks for the faithful witness of Jewish people down the ages despite so much suffering at the hands of Christians. I can give thanks for the good things in their

[12] Franklin Littell, *The Crucifixion of the Jews* (Mercer University Press, 1986), 92.
[13] For a powerful statement of this see Margaret Brearley, *Living Judaism for Christians* (Winter 1996, pub. by Anglican Renewal Ministries).

life and faith today. I can pray that they, like me, might be sensitive and responsive to God's will. But it would be wrong to pray for their conversion. This does not mean to say that mission, properly understood, and as measured by the five marks or strands of mission set out earlier has no place in relation to Jews. It does. Prayer for them is the first expression of this mission. The second is service, that is helping in appropriate ways for Judaism to be a living and vital force in today's world.

My own view has been reinforced by a document produced by Roman Catholic and Jewish leaders in the United States in August 2002. Building on the very positive series of Vatican documents on Jewish–Christian relations in recent years it affirms the words of John Paul II: 'In order to be a blessing for the world, Jews and Christians need first to be a blessing for each other.' The document affirms the essential task of Christian mission but says, 'This evangelising task no longer includes the wish to absorb the Jewish faith into Christianity and so end the distinctive witness of Jews to God and human history.'

Thus, while the Catholic Church regards the saving act of Christ as central to the process of human salvation for all, it also acknowledges that Jews already dwell in the saving covenant with God . . . It now recognises that Jews are also called by God to prepare the world for God's kingdom. Their witness to the kingdom, which did not originate with the Church's experience of Christ crucified and raised, must not be curtailed by seeking the conversion of the Jewish people to Christianity. The distinctive Jewish witness must be sustained.[14]

The document also contains Jewish reflections on mission. This mission has three aspects, the maintenance of the covenant, that is sustaining the Jewish people in existence with a distinctive way of life; witnessing to the world through this existence, as for example in 'the rebuilding of their nation state'; and helping to 'repair the world'. The document ends with the suggestion that there are many ways in which Jews and Christians can work together in a common mission.

The document is quite clear that what it says about Judaism is quite specific and does not relate to all religions.

[14] *Reflections on Covenant and Mission*, National Council of Synagogues and Delegates of the Bishops' Committee on Ecumenical and Inter-Religious affairs, Office of Communications, United States Conference of Catholic Bishops (Washington, 2002).

Though the Catholic Church respects all religious traditions . . . and though we believe God's infinite grace is surely available to believers of other faiths, it is only about Israel's covenant that the Church can speak with a certainty of the biblical witness.

This document does not come from the Vatican and so does not represent official Roman Catholic policy. Nevertheless, it carries the authority of Roman Catholic Bishops in the United States as a weighty contribution to the discussion and, as such, it goes further than any other Church document so far in affirming the covenant of God with Judaism as valid in its own right and decisively rejecting any targeted attempt by Christians to convert Jews.

This does not mean that Judaism and Christianity are the same. As already stated, I do not believe that Christianity is simply Judaism for Gentiles. I do believe that through Jesus something new was brought into the world. That new thing I would describe in terms of participation in the life of God revealed in him. In fact the Christian story is the most sublimely spiritually beautiful picture of the divine that I can image; which is why I am a Christian. The Christian picture of the creator of the universe making himself accessible to us in the heart and mind of a particular person, a person who entered into the darkness of utter alienation on behalf of humanity as a whole and who in his resurrection gives us a pledge that his purpose of love will finally prevail over all that is evil, including death, is an understanding of God which I, along with countless millions, find deeply moving and which more than any other brings me to my knees and gives me hope in life. This is a God who shared our life to the uttermost in order that we may be drawn into and share his life for now and eternity. This is a picture of God which the Church is called upon to put before all people, including Jews. It is the outline of this picture of God which I see already there in the Hebrew scriptures and in Judaism.

The particular strength of this understanding of God, apart from the sheer spiritual beauty, is the way it helps us to cope with the existence of so much suffering and tragedy in human existence. There is a separate chapter on Jewish and Christian responses to suffering but, for me, it is above all what Christianity says about this which enables me to have faith that life is not simply a tale of sound and fury signifying nothing. In response to this understanding of God there have been and there will be some Jews who convert to Christianity. Indeed some of the most outstanding Christians in every age have been people who have come to Christian faith from a Jewish background, some of the great saints like St Theresa of Avila and, in our own time in England, Hugh Montefiore and Ulrich Simon. In Russia there was the outstanding priest Father Alexander Men, who was probably murdered by right-wing forces just because he was Jewish. The Church rejoices that there are such people within the body of Christ. But their invaluable presence and witness does not mean to say that the Church should actively look for the conversion of Jews to Christianity and certainly not target them. I realize further that being a Jewish Christian has its own particular difficulties. Hugh Montefiore gives a subtitle to his book on *Being a Jewish Christian*: 'Its blessings and its problems'.[15]

There should be no deliberate attempt to convert Jews to Christianity; nevertheless, as already made clear, honest dialogue means sharing one's deepest convictions. It not only involves trying to see the other person in their terms and affirming common ground. It means bringing into the relationship those beliefs and practices which differ from those of the dialogue partner. In my experience of the Manor House Group, mentioned in the Introduction, there is no difficulty about this. Indeed, as trust and openness build up it becomes absolutely essential to the integrity of the relationships. In such dialogues I would expect Christians present to feel something of the appeal of Judaism and Jews to feel something of the appeal of Christianity. Indeed, I don't see how the dialogue can advance very far without that happening. When I was vicar of Fulham (1972–81) I used sometimes to have a dialogue at evensong rather than a sermon. One Advent, long before he was famous, I did a dialogue with Lionel Blue. He told me how every year as Christmas approached he 'teetered on the edge of Christianity'. He has felt the appeal of Christianity to the full but decided to remain a Jew. Indeed he calls one of his books *My Affair with Christianity*.[16] Similarly there have

[15] Hugh Montefiore, *On Being a Jewish Christian* (Hodder and Stoughton, 1998).
[16] Lionel Blue, *My Affair with Christianity* (Hodder and Stoughton, 1998).

been many Christians who have had a lifelong love affair with Judaism.[17]

Karl Barth, generally regarded as the greatest of all theologians since St Thomas Aquinas, wrote that there can only ever be a true conversion of the true Jew as a highly extraordinary event: it is as a result of the direct intervention of God himself as in the case of Paul. Otherwise Christians must look to 'the end of all things as the eschatological solution of this greatest of all puzzles'. This does not mean, thought Barth, that the Christian community has no responsibility now to discharge its ministry of witness to the Jews. But there is only one way to fulfil it. It must make the synagogue jealous. Modern versions of St Paul's chapters in Romans used the phrase 'making the synagogue emulate the church', rather than make it jealous. 'It must make dear and desirable and illuminating to it Him whom it has rejected.' But the Church has failed in this.

It has debated with him, tolerated him, persecuted him, or abandoned him to persecution without protest. What is worse, it has made baptism an entrance card into the best European society. It has seriously sought the conversion of individuals. But for the most part it has not done for the Jews the only real thing which it can do, attesting the manifested King of Israel as Saviour of the world, the imminent Kingdom, in the form of the convincing witness of its own existence. And thus it still owes everything to those to whom it is indebted for everything. This failure . . . is one of the darkest chapters in the whole history of Christianity and one of the most serious of all wounds in the body of Christ. Even the modern ecumenical movement suffers more seriously from the absence of Israel than of Rome or Moscow.[18]

Barth was writing before the modern attempt to reconstruct the relationship between Christianity and Judaism but, as he makes clear in his *Church Dogmatics* and elsewhere, the crucial issue is the credibility of the Christian Church; not any attempt to convert individual Jews but being a convincing witness to Christ in its own existence. In this it has lamentably failed: yet still to this it is called.

[17] See William D. Rubinstin and Hilary L. Rubinstin, *Philosemitism: Admiration and Support in the English-Speaking World for Jews, 1840–1939* (Macmillan, 1999).

[18] Karl Barth, *Church Dogmatics*, iv/3: 878 (English trans. 1961).

There remains the question of Messianic Jews and movements such as Jews for Jesus with their high-profile advertising in Jewish communities. When in 1989 an advertisement appeared, Elizabeth Maxwell, who has been tireless in trying to get the Christian Churches to reappraise their attitude to Judaism, wrote to Franklin Littell, who again has been tireless in the cause, to ask for his advice. He wrote back:

When I see this kind of retarded approach I just try to remember that during the Third Reich it was actually some of the old Hebrew Christian mission centres that stubbornly resisted the Nazi ideology and the churches.

He then went on to write about a particular person who had been a moving spirit after World War II in getting the German churches to change their attitude who had come out of a family that had for three generations been active in those Hebrew Christian missions. And it is certainly true that those missions had a much better record than the churches as a whole in opposing the Nazi ideology. It is also important to remember that, as already indicated, there is a fundamental dilemma for Jews who wish to become Christians, because Jewish identity is so fundamental it goes very much deeper than being Scottish or Welsh or English, for it is nationality, culture, and religion all inextricably entwined and reinforced through 1,500 years of faithful resistance to Christian hostility. However, I do not believe it is possible to be both Jewish and Christian in any true sense. The short answer is that Messianic Jews are Christians and should be warmly welcomed and affirmed as such. As Bishop Hugh Montefiore has written, 'I am primarily a Christian who happens to be Jewish, rather than a Jew who believes that Jesus was the messiah'.[19] They have their proper, cherished place within the Christian Church. It is the attempt to be both fully Jewish and fully Christian that is particularly disturbing to the Jewish community and that can lead to at least unconscious deception. Jews who come to believe that Jesus is the anointed one promised by God are Christians, full stop. That said, the churches today encourage Christians in different parts of the world to affirm their own cultural traditions and express their Christian faith in terms of their own culture rather than simply importing an English or

---

[19] *On Being a Jewish Christian*, 175.

American culture. Liturgies, hymns, prayers, and forms of church life are more and more becoming indigenous. If that is true for the Church worldwide, then it seems strange to refuse this indigenization to Jews who have become Christians. There must be some legitimate way for them to express their Christian faith through their Jewish cultural heritage, as long as this is done honestly as Christians and not as a form of hybrid Jewish-Christianity. Hyam Maccoby puts the Jewish view in these words

To practise the Torah of Sinai is to commit oneself to certain doctrines and attitudes . . . these doctrines and attitudes are incompatible with Christian notions . . . if Jews converted to Christianity were to continue to practise the Torah, this would be an empty observance, deprived of its inner drive and meaning. Such Jews would not really be remaining Jews in any meaningful sense. Christian mission to the Jews based on the idea of toleration of Jewish observances is based on a shallow and condescending attitude towards those observances as mere identity-markers.[20]

Hyam Maccoby is right to point out that a Jew, for example, taking part in a seder, the service surrounding the Passover meal, will have a different understanding of this from a Jewish Christian who might have a form of Christian seder. The two are different, and the one should not pretend in any way to be the other or a form of the other. But that should not prevent Jews who become Christians expressing their Christian faith in ways that are natural to them provided it is quite clear that this is a Christian and not a Jewish observance.

A more serious issue, from a Christian point of view, is the way that Messianic Jews wish to confine themselves to the Jewish Christian terminology of the infant Church in the New Testament. They stress the title Messiah but sit light to the developed understanding of Jesus Christ stated in the Christian creeds. The fact is that the Church has unfolded its truth, both in the New Testament itself and particularly in the early centuries. To retain early Jewish Christian categories, such as we have in some of the early speeches in the Acts of the Apostles, does not do justice to historic Christianity or the fullness of Christian truth. It also inclines Jewish Christians of this kind to set up separate

---

[20] Hyam Maccoby; above, n. 9.

congregations. To do this on a permanent basis, in isolation from the rest of the Church, is a denial of Catholic Christianity.

Most offensive of all to the Jewish community is the way that Jews for Jesus and other Messianic Jews target other Jews for conversion. A spirited defence of the legitimacy of bringing Christianity to Jews was set out by Nick Howard, the son of a former Tory Home Secretary. He had been accused of spiritual Nazism, on the assumption that this was inevitably implied when one faith is regarded as superior to another. Nick Howard argued that coming from a Jewish background he had come to see in Christianity a 'fulfilled Judaism'. For him it was Judaism plus Jesus, whom he regarded as the long-expected anointed one of God whose life had been given for the sins of the whole world. He argued that issues of truth were at stake here and that if we did not believe that issues of truth mattered, on what ground could we stand to oppose Nazism. But all attempts to share the news should be done with humility and respect.[21]

It is understandable that someone who has come to Christianity from Judaism should feel like that. But what I suspect has happened in the majority of cases of conversion from Judaism to Christianity is that the Jewish background has in practice been virtually non-existent. Others do have an observant background but find in Christianity something that they did not see in their Judaism. Again, others can have a Jewish upbringing which means something to them, perhaps quite a lot, but they go through a crisis in their life and at that time it happens to be a Christian who is of real help to them.

For me this all underlines the importance of two fundamental practical principles. First, Jewish people who are on the path of spiritual awakening should first of all be encouraged to be in touch with and explore the riches of their own tradition. This applies not just generally but if a person is looking to convert to Christianity, they should be encouraged before that to speak to a Rabbi whom they respect. When I first made this suggestion some years ago it was greeted with surprise and some horror in Christian circles. But what have we Christians to lose? Do we lack confidence in the truth in which we say we believe?

---

[21] *Daily Telegraph* (20 Feb. 1998), 26.

Religious truth is too important and precious to be part of the game of scalp hunting. Secondly, there will from time to time be Jews who are quite clear and convinced that they are being called by God to be baptized as Christian believers. Such situations will, I believe, be like that of Martin Luther: 'I can do no other'. When the call of God comes like that, then of course we have to respond, whoever we are. Jews who become Christians should be most warmly welcomed, affirmed, and supported in their faith. And there may very well be ways in which their Jewish practices can be given a Christian meaning. There may also be occasions when such Jewish Christians want to join with others from the same background in order to express their Christian faith in a way which they together find natural.[22] But this should not, I believe, lead to the permanent setting up of separate congregations.

For myself, as a Gentile Christian, I will give thanks to God for the many gifts that Jewish Christians have brought and continue to bring to the Church. But when I see a Jew I will continue to pray, 'Blessed art thou, O Lord our God, King of the universe, for your faithful people the Jews. May they be blessed and a blessing to others.'

[22] Ways in which this can be done are described by Margot Hodson in a *Feast of Seasons* (Monarch Books, 1988).

As I said in the Introduction, I had the privilege of spending a term studying in Jerusalem in 1962. The city was divided and East Jerusalem was under the control of Jordan. Since then I have visited Israel a good number of times and experienced its extraordinary diversity and vitality. Marcus Braybrooke, who has probably been more deeply involved in Jewish–Christian relations in the United Kingdom than anyone else, has written that 'Israel perhaps causes more misunderstanding between Christians and Jews than anything else'.[1] This is true: and it has been particularly acute during the terrible cycle of violence in recent years.

Some Christian theologians, notably Reinhold Niebuhr and James Parkes, early saw the need for Jews to have an independent homeland in Palestine. But for the Jewish community far more important than the work of individual theologians are the official statements of church bodies.

In 1948, the year in which the state of Israel was founded, the first assembly of the World Council of Churches met in Amsterdam. In the section dealing with Jews the emphasis was on overcoming antisemitism. The section on the emergence of Israel as a state read:

The establishment of the state 'Israel' adds a political dimension to the Christian approach to the Jews and threatens to complicate antisemitism with political fears and enmities. On the political aspects of the Palestinian problem

---

[1] Marcus Braybrooke, *Time to Meet* (SCM, 1990), 128.

and the complex conflicts of 'rights' we do not undertake to express a judgement.[2]

The second and third assemblies of the World Council of Churches in the 1950s again dealt with antisemitism but did not mention the subject of Israel. The faith and order commission of the World Council of Churches produced a longer theological study on the Church and the Jewish people in 1968. After mentioning the Holocaust as the decisive fact in bringing about a reassessment of the Christian attitude to Judaism it went on:

The second event was the creation of the state of Israel. This is of tremendous importance for the great majority of Jews; it has meant for them a new feeling of self-assurance and security. But this event has also brought suffering and injustice to the Arab people. We find it impossible to give an unanimous evaluation of its formation and of all the events connected with it, and therefore in this study do not make further mention of it.

In the Roman Catholic Church the publication of *Nostra Aetate* by Vatican II in 1965 was a decisive turning point. But there is no mention of Israel in that document, nor in the follow-up documents from the Vatican developing *Nostra Aetate* and giving excellent guidelines on various details of the relationship between the Roman Catholic Church and the Jewish people.

Jewish writers have been very critical of this ambivalent response by the Church to the creation of Israel. Why was it so slow and grudging? I am concerned with the theological factors which made for this lukewarm response. There were then and there are now a whole range of economic and political factors and no doubt these are fundamental. From one point of view there are the links which the worldwide Church has with the Christian churches in Jerusalem particularly. There is the fact that a number of Christian agencies, including Christian Aid, work in Gaza and are therefore very conscious of the conditions in which Palestinians are living and what they are

---

[2] This statement and others by official church bodies quoted here are all from Helga Croner, *Stepping Stones to Further Jewish–Christian Relations* (Stimulus Books, London and New York, 1977) and *More Stepping Stones to Further Jewish–Christian Relations* (A Stimulus Book by the Paulist Press, 1985).

suffering. There is the large Jewish community in America and their influence in the political process, the importance of Israel to America's strategic interests in the region and the numbers of settlers in the West Bank who come from America. There is the importance of oil from Arab countries and the long romance of the British with Arab culture. All these significant factors are for others to assess. My concern is a theological one and the theological factors which led to this slow response to the creation of Israel by official church bodies.

Above all there is Judaism's understanding of itself as a people, especially a people tied to a particular land. For most Christians religion is primarily something personal, to do with the individual's relationship with God. They sharply distinguish this from a person's nationality or ethnic origin. Such characteristics are important, but from a Christian point of view they are not related to that person's religion. So when Jews emphasize that to be a Jew is to be a member of a people, that religion is inseparable from people-hood and that this particular people is tied to a particular land, Christians find this difficult to grasp in religious terms. As Geoffrey Wigoder has put it, 'The relationship of covenant to land, as of the Jews to Israel, is as much outside the Christian experience as the centrality of Jesus in the mystery of the triune God is outside the Jewish experience.'[3]

Christians *are* now beginning to understand how the majority of Jews define themselves. It is one of the basic principles, and partial achievements, of interfaith dialogue that the other partner must be allowed to define themselves in their terms. The age-old tendency has been for one religion to see the other through spectacles heavily tinted with its own understanding of religion. The interfaith movement has begun to reverse this. The partners in the dialogue speak for themselves, in their own terms, sharing their own self-understanding. As a result of this Christians are beginning to grasp that a Jewish understanding of religion is not precisely the same as a Christian one. In particular they are beginning to understand that for Jews people-hood and attachment to a particular land have a crucial place in a Jewish

---

[3] Geoffrey Wigoder, *Jewish–Christian Relations since the Second World War* (Manchester University Press, 1988), 105.

religious outlook. But this major shift took time and it had not made an impact in the first two decades after World War II.

It is also worth noting that many Jews in the Diaspora had in fact come to share the Christian understanding of religion. For example, a group of American Rabbis, the so-called Pittsburgh Platform, declared in 1885:

'We consider ourselves no longer a nation, but a religious community, and therefore expect neither a return to Palestine nor a sacrificial worship under the sons of Aaron, nor the restoration of any laws concerning the Jewish state.

Closely connected with the Jewish understanding of people-hood is God's promise to be faithful in respect of the land. Time and again in the Hebrew scriptures God's promise is a promise about land. Christians have begun to reject supersessionist theology. They have increasingly wanted to affirm that God's covenant with Israel remains in place. But they have gulped somewhat when this means seeing the state of Israel as a fulfilment of God's promise. Peter Schneider, an Anglican who did much for Jewish–Christian relations, tells the apocryphal story of a Christian theologian who much enjoyed his new-found friendship with Rabbis but who was disillusioned by the Six Day War. He complained to his new friends:

We have just got over the shock of having to treat Judaism as a real religion. Indeed theologically we can now cope with that, and then immediately, you Jews go and spoil it all by insisting in this day and age in tying up your religion with a piece of real estate.

One person who did understand the Jewish case for Israel, much better than most Jews themselves understood it, was James Parkes. It has been said that his work 'represents the most sustained effort yet made by a non-Jew to defend the creation of the Jewish state'. Parkes discussed the question in *The Emergence of the Jewish Problem* (1946), *End of an Exile* (1954, reprinted with additional material in 1982), *A History of the Jewish People* (1963), and *Whose Land?* (1970). Parkes argued that the tree of Israel sprang from five roots. First, Judaism is a religion of the community. As a community the people need a place to live out the divine purpose. Secondly, the Messianic hope is for a gathering in

of the people of Israel to the land of their forefathers and this hope has
been kept alive throughout Jewish history. Thirdly, there is the Jewish
history of the Diaspora, with Jews always insecure and sometimes
persecuted. The hopes of complete emancipation for Jews and the liberal democracy of nineteenth-century Europe were shattered in the
twentieth century and this fundamental Jewish insecurity has to be
addressed. Fourthly, there is the continuing of Jewish life in Palestine
over 2,000 years. Although the numbers were never large and they
were focused in different parts of the country, often in Galilee, 'on the
whole it may be said that it was always as large as was possible in view
of conditions existing at any one time'. Fifthly, there is the integral
relationship between Palestinian Jewry and the Diaspora. There has
always been a link between the two and at certain critical periods in
Jewish history, it was only the existence of Jews in Palestine which
safeguarded Judaism.

All this is now familiar to Jews and to some Christians also. But in
the 1940s this was not true, even for Jews. As Parkes wrote, 'The
Jewish case rests on a long history little known even to many Jews and
not easy to assess in terms of a political decision'; and he went on:

The Zionists ignored not merely their strongest argument but their real case.
They were not bridging a gap of 2000 years. They were augmenting a Jewish
population which had never ceased to exist in the country, and which survived
largely because every successive Muslim ruler recognised that it had a right to
be there. The Zionist has ignored this vital relationship, probably because they
were in opposition to the religious conservatism of Eastern European
Judaism, and simply saw the existing Jews of Palestine as exponents of a religious fanaticism they disliked. But from the point of view of Arab reaction, the
real justification of Zion's presence is that the Jewish population of Palestine
has always been as large as could find the humblest means of existence in the
land of Israel.[4]

Further work, for example by Martin Gilbert, shows that after the
expulsion by the Romans in the first century a Jewish presence nevertheless continued in Jerusalem, Hebron, Safed, and Tiberias. From
637 to 1099 there were many towns with a Jewish community. From

---

[4] James Parkes, *Arabs and Jews in the Middle East* (Victor Gollancz, 1967), 21.

the thirteenth to the nineteenth century there was a majority of Jews in the western part of Galilee, with for example 10,000 in Safed in 1500. During the crusades the Jews in Palestine fought with the Arabs. In the thirteenth century a number of Rabbis came to Jerusalem and after the expulsion of Jews from Spain and elsewhere in Europe in 1492 a number came to Palestine. By 1880 there was a Jewish majority in Jerusalem. This needs to be balanced by the fact that even in 1880 there was an overwhelming majority of Arabs in Palestine as a whole. According to Martin Gilbert, 470,000 Arabs to 24,000 Jews. Nevertheless, those Jews represented a vital continuity of presence over two millennia.[5]

If the strongest argument for a Jewish state in Palestine was not deployed and was hardly known even in Jewish circles, it is not surprising that the Christian Church was tardy in recognizing the Jewish claim to the land.

James Parkes was an outstanding pioneer in putting the case for the state of Israel, which he did in more convincing terms than the Zionists themselves. Yet it is important to recognize also the grounds on which he made the case, in addition to the historical and theological factors already mentioned. Between 1919 and 1936 there were 360,000 Jewish immigrants to Palestine, with 15,000 to 25,000 a year coming in after World War II. Nevertheless a Jewish majority was not achieved until the early 1950s. So, in the light of this, what was the justification for creating a specifically Jewish state, as opposed to a secular or multi-faith one? Parkes argued that there was a special case. The examples he gave included that of an expanding town which necessitated the flooding of a valley to provide it with water or a foreign power engaged in a life or death struggle for justice putting down bases on foreign soil. Israel, he argued, had a particular history and urgent needs which gave it priority over all other claims. As the ordinary rights of those in the flooded valley may be overridden by a necessity involving the country as a whole and the rights of inhabitants in the areas where foreign bases are established are again overridden, so the ordinary rights of Arabs in Palestine could, however reluctantly,

---

[5] Martin Gilbert, *The Dent Atlas of the Arab-Israeli Conflict* (Dent, 1974), and *Jerusalem, Illustrated History Atlas* (Board of Deputies of British Jews, 1977).

Israel in Christian Thought

and of course with proper compensation, be given a lower priority than the establishment of a Jewish state. He wrote:

She was allowed to override normal rights because she had unique claims. But the permission involved a deep debt of honour to those who lost by her gains; and even those who hold, as I do, that it was right that she should receive this permission, and to recognise—as I do—that she tried hard to cushion the blow to the Arabs, make a grave mistake if they seek to support their attitude by refusing to recognise that all the normal rights were on the Arab side and the Arabs were inevitably conscious of this, and bitter at the world's refusal to acknowledge it.[6]

Again he wrote:

One day she will recognise that it is wrong to evolve far fetched arguments to deny any Arab rights in the land they had inhabited so long, or to rest her case on the legality of the Balfour declaration. She was allowed to override normal rights because she had unique claims. But the mission involved a deep debt of honour to those who lost by her gain.[7]

A great deal of bloody water has flown over broken bridges since then. Above all, from an Israeli point of view, there has been the sense of being surrounded by powerful Arab neighbours who wished to destroy it, and, more lately, suicide bombers who have targeted crowded places killing civilians, including children, indiscriminately. Understandably security has been the highest priority. Nevertheless, in Israel itself there are a good many Jews who understand the Arab sense of an injustice done, who are working for justice and reconciliation. Furthermore, there has now dawned a much more accurate historical assessment of the events surrounding the establishment of the state of Israel in 1948. Benny Morris, for example, in a detailed battle by battle, village by village, year by year analysis of what actually happened on the ground, rejects both the oversimplified assertion that the Palestinians were driven out by Jewish arms and the view that they fled because of cowardly Arab leadership and other Palestinian weaknesses, with a view to returning sooner rather than later. As he writes:

[6] James Parkes, *End of an Exile* (Micah Publications, Massachusetts, 1954, repr. 1982), 42.
[7] Ibid.

The Palestinian refugee problem was born of war, not by design, Jewish or Arab. It was largely a by-product of Arab and Jewish fears and of the protracted bitter fighting that characterised the first Israeli-Arab war; in smaller point, it was the deliberate creation of Jewish and Arab military commanders and politicians.[8]

Benny Morris's study is not of course the last word on the subject but sober, detailed studies have helped to debunk the myths and must, in the long run, enable a solution to be based upon a mutually recognized truth.

In the 1970s and 1980s church statements on Israel began to be more positive in tone. First of all there was the acknowledgement of how important the state of Israel is for Jews and therefore if a new relationship with Judaism is wanted this fact has to be recognized. This point was made in guidelines in various Roman Catholic dioceses and by the Catholic Church in the Netherlands in 1970. This point, the importance of Israel to the majority of Jewish people around the world and the necessity of acknowledging this in any genuine interfaith dialogue, was for example made by Anglican bishops at the 1988 Lambeth Conference.

Beyond the recognition of the importance of Israel for most Jews, there has been the straightforward acknowledgement of its right to exist. Sometimes this has been linked with international law and the declaration of the United Nations. Sometimes it has been linked with a need to find a secure homeland for Jews after the terrible atrocities in Europe. For example, the Evangelical Church in Germany in 1975 declared:

After all injustice inflicted upon the Jews—particularly by Germans—Christians are obligated to recognise and support the internationally valid United Nations resolution of 1948 which is intended to enable Jews to live a secure life in a state of their own.

This kind of statement has been made by a number of Roman Catholic Archdioceses, often with the qualification that recognition of the state

[8] Benny Morris, *The Birth of the Palestinian Refugee Problem, 1947–1949* (Cambridge University Press, 1987), 286.

of Israel did not imply endorsement of its political policies at any particular time.

This approach, recognizing the importance of Israel to Jewish self-understanding and acknowledging the right of the state of Israel to exist under international law, together with qualifications about the rights of Arabs has been the predominant approach of churches to the state of Israel during the last two decades. This has not been a warm enough endorsement for some Jews. For example, Rabbi Mordecai Waxman writes that there exists for many church bodies

a lurking assumption that, despite everything, Israel is actually a political rather than a theological issue . . . the niggling statement 'Israel has a right to exist' conveys no sense of religious and theological grandeur and recognition. It is the reluctant admission of foreign office bureaucrats, not churchmen reared in the Judeo-Christian tradition . . . if it is, indeed, the new posture of dialogue to understand Jews as they understand themselves, then a touch stone of a fruitful relationship may well be the ability of Christian churches to see the state of Israel with the eyes of Jews, namely, as a stage in the reaffirmation of the covenant with Abraham and his descendants. This should be the beginning of the process for which support and love must be unconditional while, at the same time, the commitment to moral goals must be unending.

Few churches have been willing to respond to this. For example, a statement of the German Lutheran Church in 1979 noted that Lutherans are supporters not of a theology of the land but of a theology of the poor with special references to the plight of the Palestinian refugees. One remarkable exception, however, was provided by the General Synod of the Netherlands Reform Church in 1970 which came to the conclusion:

If the election of the people and the promises connected with it remain valid, it follows that the tie between the people and the land also remains by the grace of God.

The Synod granted that there is no necessary connection between the biblical promise and the present state of Israel but went on to say:

As matters are at the moment, we see a free state as the only possibility which safeguards the existence of the people . . . therefore, we are convinced that anyone who accepts the union of the Jewish people and the land for reasons of faith, has also to accept that in the given circumstances the people should have a state of their own.

Other churches have not taken their cue from that statement. For example, the seventh meeting of the Anglican Consultative Council meeting in Singapore in 1987, whilst affirming the right of the state of Israel to exist within recognized and secure borders, went on to say that it

rejects the interpretation of holy scripture which affirms a special place for the present state of Israel and in the light of biblical prophecy, finds it detrimental to peace and justice, and damaging to Jews, Christians and Muslims.

Another 1987 document, that of the General Assembly of the Presbyterian Church in the United States, argues that the promise of the land is still valid but refuses to equate the land with the present state of Israel. 'The state of Israel is a geopolitical entity and is not to be validated theologically.'

Before exploring further the relationship between God's promise to his people Israel, the continuing validity of that promise, and its fulfilment in the state of Israel as we actually have it at the moment, two other justifications for Israel's right to exist can be noted. First, there are those evangelical Christians who see the state of Israel as a prelude to the end of time when Christ will return in glory and the Jewish people will be gathered from the ends of the earth in the Holy Land to acknowledge him as the true messiah. This is not a modern phenomenon. Thomas Brightman (1562–1608) prophesied the overthrow of the anti-Christ, identified with the papacy, followed by the dissolution of the Ottoman empire and the 'Calling of the Jews' who will be 'Kings of the orient'. Such a view has not been represented in official church statements and would probably not be regarded as very natural to the thinking of most Christian people today, although it has been politically influential, for example in helping to form the perspective of Lloyd George in bringing about the Balfour declaration. Christians who take this point of view are amongst the strongest supporters of the state of Israel but from a Jewish point of view, their support comes with a price. For of course they believe that the establishment of the state of Israel is simply a sign of the forthcoming end when Jews will acknowledge Jesus Christ to be the true messiah. Professor Wistrich suggests that most Jews probably take a fairly cynical view, namely that 'These guys are nuts, but we want all the votes we can get for Israel, and we can't afford to worry about the theological niceties' or, as he himself puts it more soberly, 'From the Jewish point of view, it has not always been easy to balance the advantage of such support against the disadvantage of its linkage with a programme or at least a hope for conversion.'

The second approach is based upon the importance and validity of international law. The recent Vatican document for example has said that 'The existence of the state of Israel and its options should be envisaged not in a perspective which is itself religious, but in their reference to the common principles of international law.' This is also an approach which has been taken by the Anglican Communion. Professor Wistrich welcomes this way of approaching Israel in that it disposes of what he terms unacceptable theological baggage 'at a stroke' and leaves Christians, especially Catholics, free to adopt realistic and 'normal attitudes to Israel'. I should like, however, to emphasize the theological underpinning of international law. It arose out of the work of the great theologians Francisco de Vitoria and Suarez in the seventeenth century and the Dutch theologian and jurist Hugo Grotius in the eighteenth century. International law witnesses to the possibility of universal moral standards, legally expressed. Both Jews and Christians believe that the moral law originates in the mind and purpose of God. They believe that it is apprehended in the moral consciousness of all human beings and expressed in human laws when those human laws conform to the moral law. From a theological point of view then the great body of international law which has arisen since World War II, which future historians will judge to be one of that generation's greatest achievements, will not be seen by Jews and Christians in purely secular terms. It is part of the moral underpinning, legally enacted, of human community in the purpose of God. Politically, of course, international law cuts all ways. By it the existence of the state of Israel is justified. By it, the state of Israel is called to acknowledge certain standards in relation both to its internal life and its relationship to the surrounding territories, including the Palestinian areas.

From a more directly theological point of view I would want to argue that culture is integral to our identity as human beings. By culture I mean that mixture of language, mores, rituals, history, and religion into which we are born and by which we are shaped. So as God wills to bring human beings into existence, he wills the societies and cultures without which we would not exist. For those cultures to exist it is necessary for there to be an ordered framework without which one culture could be dominated and eventually obliterated by others. This can be done in empires, if those empires safeguard the rights of minorities. But in our time we assume that cultures are defended by nation states, even though within a particular nation state there may be a range of cultures. We can then say of the Jewish people as of any other, that their culture is a precious heritage and that in the conditions of the modern world the nation state is the best means at present available for safeguarding it. Whatever the future may hold in terms of federations, under present conditions Jewish people-hood needs a defendable state.

This was the argument of Reinhold Niebuhr during World War II. He regarded it as a scandal that the Jewish people had had so little effective help from the rest of the world and that after the war they would need a state of their own. Assimilation might suit some successful Jews but Jews as a whole, especially the poor, needed a safer environment. There is 'the simple right of the Jews to survive as a people'. Niebuhr argued that there is a collective survival impulse which is as legitimate a right as an individual one. 'Justice, in history, is concerned with collective, as well as with individual, rights.' Whole peoples have an individuality no less marked than that of single persons and this should not be swept aside in the name of internationalism. He thought that America in particular after the war would have a responsibility to ensure a settlement in the Middle East in which Jews had their own homeland and the Arabs had a more unified federation. He thought that the Arabs would need to be compensated and Zionist leaders were unrealistic in insisting that their demands entailed no 'injustice' to the Arab population because Jewish immigration had brought new economic strengths to Palestine. It was absurd to expect any people to regard the restriction of their sovereignty over a traditional possession as 'just', no matter how many other benefits accrue from that abridgement. He did not believe that there could be any simple 'just' solution with competing claims. It would have to be imposed by the post-war victors but this imposition would need to do something to benefit the Palestinians.[9]

We can, however, go further than this. In Jewish thought the deliverance from Egypt does not stand alone. It is to be seen in integral relationship both to the revelation of the Torah and the coming into the land where that divine law has to be lived out. In short, the people of Israel were delivered in order to be a community living in a particular place in accordance with God's revealed purpose for them: not a dispersed, wandering people but a settled community building institutions that reflect the divine wisdom.

This vocation can be fully affirmed from a Christian point of view as well as a Jewish one, for God is faithful and remains faithful to his first love. He wills the Jewish people to exist and he wills them to exist in terms of their original vocation: to be a people settled in a particular place manifesting holiness and righteousness in every aspect of life. If Christians are serious in affirming the continuing place of the Jewish people within the providence of God; if, in other words, they reject the old replacement theology and affirm that the covenant with the people of Israel is still valid, then it follows that they must be serious about affirming the vocation of the people to be people in a place and living according to Torah.

In Israel today there are those Rabbis and lay people who stress that the purpose of the people of Israel living in a particular place is that they might live in accord with God's justice. For them justice, not adherence to the land, is primary. I have heard moving statements along these lines from Jewish Rabbis in Israel. They urged that the just claims of Palestinians, who have suffered so much, must be recognized. Their voice is not always heard. But Israel is not a static entity, it is a community which, in theological perspective, is a community in

[9] Reinhold Niebuhr, 'The Jews After the War', *The Nation* (21 Feb. 1942). A bibliography of Reinhold Niebuhr's writings on Israel and other issues is provided by Franklin H. Littell, *Reinhold Niebuhr and the Jewish People*, the 1990 Niebuhr Lecture at Elmhurst College.

152

transformation towards that ultimate community in the kingdom of God. So if the presence of Israel today is to be seen as a sign of God's continuing faithfulness to his ancient people, we must trust that faithful God for her continuing transformation towards God's future.[10]

Paul van Buren, who has reflected on all the Protestant church statements about Israel published since World War II, sets out the basis upon which a consensus might be developed. This includes concern for the Palestinian people and a right to criticize particular policies of particular Israeli governments when this is justified. However, the first principle of this minimum consensus would be that:

Because the state of Israel is in part the product of the ancient and living hope of the Jewish people and is of deep concern to almost all Jews, disregard for its safety and welfare is incompatible with concern for the Jewish people.[11]

This chapter has suggested ways in which Christian theological support for the state of Israel might go further than that but even van Buren's minimum, which he discerns in official church statements, is an important benchmark and achievement. The history and politics remain both complex and highly controversial. And the suffering of Israelis and Palestinians remains a matter of daily anguish. There are further reflections on this in the final chapter, on 'The Unfinished Agenda'.

---

[10] If this transformation is to come about, then the pain and deep sense of hurt and anguish leading to a sense of helpless anger by those who have lost out in the past or now, must be heard. See *Voices from Jerusalem: Jews and Christians reflect on the Holy Land*, ed. David Burrell and Yehezkel Landau (Stimulus, Paulist Press, New York, 1992). That future entails recognition of Palestinian suffering and proper provision for Palestinian people-hood.

[11] Paul van Buren in *The Theology of the Churches and the Jewish People*, Statement by the World Council of Churches and its Member Churches (WCC, Geneva, 1988), 173.

Jerusalem in Religious   8
Perspective

In a seminar on the future of Jerusalem held under the auspices of the Arab Research Centre in London the religious significance of Jerusalem was set aside.[1] The participants concentrated on territorial issues, the loss of Arab lands in West Jerusalem and the steady encroachment of Jewish inhabitants in East Jerusalem. Doctor Ibrahim Abu-Lughod stated, 'I have no wish to make my political position on the future of Jerusalem dependent upon its religious significance.' When Afif Safeah was asked about the role of religion he replied, 'I am totally foreign to any attempt to give this conflict religious connotations. I have always been exasperated by the use, misuse and abuse of religion in political struggle. The intrusion of religion in political debates has always exacerbated tensions.' It is easy to sympathize with those statements. Nevertheless, whatever the importance of demographic, economic, and political factors in understanding the history of Jerusalem and its significance, the theological dimension has played and will continue to play a crucial role—hopefully for good but potentially for ill. This chapter, like the previous one on Israel, concentrates only on the theological dimension. Bishop Kenneth Cragg has written, 'Over all looms the question of Jerusalem. Decision is projected into some "Final calendar" but its intractability persists—an inalienable capital of the Jewish state or an achievable

---

[1] 'Seminar on the *Future of Jerusalem*' (Arab Research Centre, London, 1994).

symbol of sheer human community possessed in the possessing of three great faiths.'[2] Jerusalem is important to all three faiths but important in different ways and it helps to understand not only why each faith values Jerusalem but why they value it in somewhat different ways and terms.

Jerusalem is a very ancient city and its name has been found on Egyptian potsherds from 4,000 years ago. It also occurs in the Tell-el-Amarna letters of about 500 years later. At some early stage it was a Jebusite stronghold but in the tenth century BCE David captured it from the Jebusites and made it the political centre of the nation. But it was more than a political centre, it was also a religious one and it rapidly became more than a place. It became a symbol for the land as a whole and the people as a whole, especially in so far as they were living both righteously and free from domination by others.

Although the first Christians were Jews, Jerusalem as a place rapidly began to lose its significance for Christians. Hopes in the Hebrew bible that had been focused on Jerusalem came, for Christians, to be focused in Jesus. Although there are Christian Zionists who believe that Jerusalem as a place still has a key role to play in the unfolding providence of God, it has been argued that this is a misreading of scripture. It is Jesus himself in whom God's promises come to fruition.[3] It was during the first part of the third century that Origen, the most learned Christian theologian of the time, developed this point of view in a more systematic way. His position came about in opposition to two very different views of Jerusalem which were being canvassed at the time. First of all there were some Christians who believed that before the end of all things Christ would return to earth and reign in an earthly kingdom centred on Jerusalem. Origen rejected this and referred to three New Testament texts which have been fundamental for the Christian understanding of Jerusalem ever since. Paul in his letter to the Galatians contrasts the earthly Jerusalem with the heavenly one. 'But the Jerusalem above is free, and she is our mother' (Galatians 4: 26). In the letter to the Hebrews we have the

---

[2] Kenneth Cragg, *Palestine: The Prize and Price of Zion* (Cassell, 1997), 68.
[3] Peter Walker, *Jesus and the Holy City: New Testament Perspectives on Jerusalem* (Eerdmans, 1996).

words 'But you have come to Mount Zion and to the city of the living God, the heavenly Jerusalem' (Hebrews 12: 22). Then there is the imagery of the book of Revelation: 'And I saw the holy city and new Jerusalem coming down out of heaven from God prepared as a bride adorned for her husband' (Revelation 21: 2).

The second group to which Origen was opposed were Jews of the Diaspora who looked to God to restore Jerusalem as a Jewish city. Ever since the razing of Jerusalem and its establishment as the Roman Aelia Capitolina by the emperor Hadrian in 130 of the Christian era Jews had been forbidden by Roman law to set foot in the city. So Jews looked for a fulfilment of the promises in the Hebrew scriptures in an earthly Jerusalem liberated from Roman rule and restored as a Jewish city into which Jews from round the world could be gathered. Origen, like the New Testament writers, believed that these promises had already been fulfilled in Jesus. He therefore interpreted the biblical prophecies about a Messianic age in which all things would be made new, in a spiritual manner. For example, Psalm 37, which refers to the meek inheriting the earth, a thought taken up by Jesus in the Beatitude 'Blessed are the meek, for they shall inherit the earth', is interpreted by Origen as referring to the new heaven and the new earth.

So in responding to these two groups, Christians who looked for an earthly rule of Christ in Jerusalem and Jews who looked for its restoration as a Jewish city, Origen put in place what has been described as a de-territorialization of Jerusalem. This was carried forward in the fourth century by the historian Eusebius and many subsequent Christian thinkers. At the same time the third century saw other developments which were to counterbalance the exclusive emphasis upon a heavenly Jerusalem. Pilgrims began to come 'for the sake of the holy places', as Jerome put it. Then in the fourth century Constantine became a Christian and Christianity became first tolerated and then the official religion of the empire. Although Constantine founded a new capital, Constantinople, a great Christian city free of all pagan influence, he also had a very keen interest in Jerusalem. He allowed Makarios, who had come to have episcopal oversight over Jerusalem, to demolish the temple of Aphrodite so that the tomb of Christ could be excavated. Later stories maintained that Constantine's mother,

Helena, had discovered the wood of the cross on which Jesus was crucified and a great church was built on the site.[4] The church covered
both the site where Jesus was crucified and the tomb where he was
laid, so it has sometimes been called the church of the Anastasis, or
resurrection, and more usually today the church of the Holy
Sepulchre.[5] Pilgrims to Jerusalem began to increase in numbers.[6] The
holy places in Jerusalem, Bethlehem, and elsewhere were held to be
signs, real evidence, that Jesus actually had lived and performed the
deeds associated with those sites in the scriptures. Christians began to
realize that seeing the holy places was a way of renewing the image of
what had happened, of making the saving events of the past present
and of allowing believers, through pilgrimage and memory, to become
spectators of the events in the ministry of Jesus. Eusebius called the
church built on the place where Christ rose from the dead 'a martyrion
of the saving resurrection', the word martyrion coming from the
Greek word to bear witness. So in John Chrysostom's words, 'The
whole world runs to see the tomb which has no body.'

Christians began to think of the church of the Anastasis as a new
temple. And as the old temple had been the centre of the universe, so
was the new one. As this was the place where Adam, the first human
being was buried, it was also the place where the second Adam had
been raised from the dead. Eusebius applied to Christian Jerusalem
the metaphor of a river flowing from the centre bringing salvation to
the whole world. He and other Christians began to think of Palestine
not as a Roman province but as a land whose character and identity
were formed by biblical and Christian history. People began to feel it
as a holy land though the term was not then in use. By the time
Justinian was emperor, about 530, there were 26 churches in
Jerusalem alone marking holy sites and catering for pilgrims. These
pilgrims took their sacred souvenirs, especially the ampullae, back to
their homelands. They also took memories of the aedicule built over
the tomb of Christ and this was reproduced, for example, on stone

---

[4] Evelyn Waugh's novel *Helena* (Penguin, 1963) is a superb evocation of this.

[5] For a history of the church see Martin Biddle, *The Tomb of Christ* (Sutton, 1999).

[6] We have a vivid account by a Spanish nun, see John Wilkinson, *Egeria's Travels* (Aris
and Phillips, Warminster, 3rd edn., 1999). Egeria visited Palestine and Egypt in 381 to 384.

crosses as far west as Ireland. What the earthly Jerusalem had come to mean to Christians can be seen in the way the aged patriarch Zachariah responded to its capture by the Persians in the year 614. He was led to captivity weeping over the city in the language of the Book of Lamentations: 'I adore you, O Zion, and I adore him who dwelled in you . . . to die and to be run through by the sword is sweeter than to be separated from you, O Zion.' John the almsgiver, patriarch of Alexander, lamented the fall of Jerusalem for a full year. As a contemporary put it, 'Wailing and groaning bitterly, he strove by his lamentations to outdo Jeremiah, who of old lamented the capture of this same city, Jerusalem.' One of the historians recording the event, Stratagos, wrote words that would have been inconceivable on the lips of Christians in earlier centuries: 'And the Jerusalem above wept over the Jerusalem below.' The Roman world had been utterly shaken by the sack of Rome by Alaric in 410 but the fall of Jerusalem in 614 had for Christians even more dismaying reverberations. Although the Byzantine emperor Heraclius recaptured Jerusalem, he held it only until 638 when it fell to the forces of Islam under Caliph Omar.

So two attitudes became firmly entrenched in Christian consciousness. The first is that our true mother is the heavenly Jerusalem, our spiritual home and destiny. Great hymns on this theme came to be written in the Middle Ages like 'Jerusalem the Golden' by St Bernard and 'O Quanta Qualia' by Abelard. At the same time there was a sense that this was the city in which Jesus had taught and ministered, been crucified and raised from the dead. So Christian pilgrims continued to go to Jerusalem during the years of the Arab conquest, making the long and difficult and often dangerous journey from all over the world. Yet there was always some ambivalence about such pilgrimages. St Jerome, although he chose to spend the better part of his life in Bethlehem, declared, 'The heavenly is open from Britain no less than from Jerusalem, for the kingdom of God is within you.'

In the year 1129 an English cleric from the Diocese of Lincoln set out on a pilgrimage to the Holy Land. On his way to Jerusalem he stopped at Clairvaux. Shortly afterwards the Bishop of Lincoln received a letter from the Abbot of Clairvaux announcing the good tidings that Philip had arrived safely and quickly at his destination and that he intended to remain there permanently. As the letter said, 'He has entered the holy city and has chosen his heritage . . . he is no longer an inquisitive onlooker but a devout inhabitant and an enrolled citizen of Jerusalem.' But this Jerusalem, he continued, 'is Clairvaux. She is the Jerusalem united to the one in heaven by wholehearted devotion, by conformative life, and by a certain spiritual affinity.'

Despite this profoundly spiritual understanding of Jerusalem, Christians continued to go on pilgrimage. The fact that they found it virtually impossible to go to Jerusalem when Turks controlled most of Asia Minor and there was an unsympathetic Islamic ruler in Jerusalem was one of the main reasons for the crusades. Jerusalem was captured in 1099 and held until it fell to Saladin in 1187. It was recaptured but then held only for a very short time, from 1229 to 1244, after which for 700 years it was in Arab, Mameluke, and Ottoman hands under Islamic influence until the British mandate and eventually the establishment of the state of Israel in 1948. As far as the earthly Jerusalem is concerned Christians desire only free and safe access to the holy sites associated with the Christian story and a supportive political environment for the local Christian churches. Christian congregations have been in Jerusalem since New Testament times and at the moment Palestinian Christians feel under very great pressure. Christians are leaving the Palestinian areas at an alarming rate, particularly in the traditionally Christian Bethlehem district.

This is the point to mention, albeit briefly, a very negative aspect of the traditional Christian understanding of Jerusalem. A belief grew up in the Church that the Jews, collectively, were responsible for the death of Jesus. The charge of deicide was held against them. For this terrible crime they were to receive a terrible punishment. So when the temple in Jerusalem was destroyed in 70 CE and later, in 130 CE the whole of Jerusalem razed to the ground and rebuilt as a pagan city, Aelia Capitolina, it was assumed by Christians that this was part of the punishment. Furthermore, the Jewish people spread around the world, as wandering Jews, were to be regarded as objects of the divine wrath. So although the Christian Church has not itself had theologically based territorial ambitions for Jerusalem, it has certainly taught that Jews have no claim to it, indeed are to be kept from it because of their responsibility for the crucifixion of God's chosen one. These appalling beliefs, which entered deeply into Christian consciousness, were decisively rejected by the authoritative Roman Catholic document *Nostra Aetate* in 1965.

Jerusalem is special, indeed sacred, for Islam for three reasons. First, it was the direction to which Muslims originally turned for their prayer: the *Quibla* was to Jerusalem not Mecca, for the Quran records the later change in direction (Sura 2: 136). Secondly, there is an enigmatic but important verse in the Quran, Sura 17: 1, which reads 'Praise be to Allah who brought his servant at night from the holy mosque to the remote mosque, the precincts of which we have blessed.' The original meaning of this passage has been much disputed and it has been doubted whether it refers to Jerusalem at all and if so whether this is a literal journey or a vision. According to the earliest traditions of Islam, however, it referred to the fact that the prophet Muhammad was miraculously transported from Mecca to Jerusalem and it was from there that he made his ascent to heaven, the *Miradj*.

According to the story, Muhammad rode a miraculous steed, Alburaq (the bright one), which is a two-winged white animal between the size of a mule and an ass. The journey occurred in the prophet's dream, which lasted a fifth of a second or, to use the language of the tradition, 'in the time it takes for a clay jar to fall over to spill the first drop'. From the furthest mosque he went to the seventh heaven, where he was met by Abraham, Isaac, Joseph, Moses, and Jesus and received their blessing to become the last prophet of God. The essence of the story is that Muhammad goes to heaven in a vision but, as Professor R. J. Zwi Werblowsky puts it, apologizing for the language of modern air travel, 'There are no direct flights from Mecca to heaven; you have to make a stopover in Jerusalem.'[7]

The third reason why Islam regards Jerusalem as its third most holy city, is the fact that it was already so prestigious from a sacred

---

[7] This chapter is indebted to R. J. Zwi Werblowsky, *Jerusalem, Holy City of Three Religions* (Jerusalem, 1976). See also Karen Armstrong, *History of Jerusalem: One City, Three Faiths* (1995). Also, Martin Gilbert, *Jerusalem, Illustrated History Atlas* (Board of Deputies of British Jews, 1977). Also Eliyahu Tal, *Whose Jerusalem?* (International Forum for United Jerusalem, 1994).

point of view for both Jews and Christians. Islam at once respected Judaism and Christianity and regarded itself as the last in the line of divine revelations. It therefore had a double motive for associating its own religion with the city. This was why prayer was originally in the direction of Jerusalem and why the definitive revelation to Muhammad, which pictured him receiving his mandate from both Jewish and Christian sacred figures, should have been thought of as taking place in Jerusalem.

After the conquest of Jerusalem by Caliph Omar in 638 Jerusalem became part of the Islamic world, part of the *Dar al-Islam*. A Muslim building programme was put in place, particularly a building to rival the great Christian church of the Anastasis. As the tenth-century geographer and historian of Jerusalem Al-Muqaddasi wrote about the mosque of Al-Aqsa and the dome of the rock, 'During the building of it they had for a rival and as a comparison the great church of the holy Sepulchre . . . and they built this to be even more magnificent than the other.' In 691 the next Caliph built the dome of the rock, which still stands today on the temple site as one of the most glorious buildings in the world, and then either he or his son built the mosque at the southern end of the temple site which came to be called Al-Aqsa (the remote mosque) and the identification with the furthest or remote mosque in the Quranic account of the journey was definitive and complete. 'Praise be to Allah who brought his servant at night from the holy mosque to the remote mosque.'

Jerusalem became for Islam, as it had been for Judaism and Christianity, a city to be joyously celebrated. To take just one example, a preacher in Damascus born in 1262 said:

The treasure of the world is Jerusalem. Who prays in Jerusalem, it is as if he prayed in the nearer heavens. . . . God directs his regard towards Jerusalem every morning, and showers upon his people his mercy and his benefits. . . . The dew which descends upon Jerusalem is a remedy from every sickness, because it is from the gardens of paradise.[8]

[8] Quoted by Walid Khalidei, *Islam, The West and Jerusalem*(Georgetown University, Washington, 1996).

Some have seen the Islamic view of Jerusalem purely in political terms but as Professor Werblowsky has written, 'The sanctity of Jerusalem in Islam is a fact. Jerusalem is *Al-Kuds* (the holy one).' Although he recognizes that the literature praising Jerusalem after the crusades is in part propaganda designed to arouse enthusiasm for a Muslim reconquest, he says nevertheless that the existence of Jerusalem 'as much as the underlying ideas belong[s] to the sphere of Muslim piety and devotion'. Furthermore, although the holiness of Jerusalem in Islam has been created out of piety rather than hard historical fact the result for all practical intents and purposes is 'as real as any other kind of "hard" fact'. Dr Zaki Badawi has written that:

The spiritual position of the city in Islamic theology has not diminished. There are many traditions passed down from the prophet concerning the spiritual value of Jerusalem. The consequence is that, in Muslim popular eschatology, it is the place where the resurrection will take place; indeed it was believed that if you died in Jerusalem, you would go to heaven. Furthermore, the dome of the rock itself symbolises in concrete form the Muslim concept of Islam as the ultimate and complete revelation of Allah, in that it is located in the city which is at the heart of Christian doctrine and close to the site of the temple of Judaic tradition. It is for these reasons that simple access to the Muslim holy sites in the city is insufficient, for it militates against the very core of Islam itself. All places of worship in Islam are 'The house of God' and cannot be owned by individuals or communities, who have the power to bar others from them. The house of God is the place where *everybody* should have right of access and feel at peace. If you are made to feel a stranger, if you are made to feel excluded, then it is not the house of God; not the God that spoke to Abraham, Moses, Jesus and Muhammad. Here lies the truth. It is a Muslim's duty, therefore to preserve such access to the city which is the third most significant and holy site in Islam.[9]

The importance of Jerusalem for Judaism hardly needs to be spelt out. As a symbol it has entered every aspect of Jewish life and consciousness. It is there in the wedding service when one of the benedictions reads, 'May she who was barren be exceedingly glad and exult: when her children are gathered within her in joy. Blessed are

---

[9] Zaki Badawi, 'Jerusalem and Islam', in Ghada Karmi (ed.), *Jerusalem Today* (Ithaka Press, 1996), 141.

thou, O God, who makest Zion joyful through her children.' One of the benedictions recited every Sabbath after the reading of the prophetic lesson says, 'Have pity on Zion which is the home of our life . . . blessed art thou, O Lord, who makes Zion rejoice in her children.' It is a theme of which endless examples could be given. The role of Zion or Jerusalem is markedly present in the daily liturgy, in the grace after every meal, and in the poetry and writings of Judaism in every age. But it has been more than a symbol. Every year at the seder Jews say, 'Next year in Jerusalem', expressing the hope that one day Jews from round the world will be gathered in their transformed holy city.

Jerusalem became an important symbol for Christianity but in Judaism there is a crucial difference. For Judaism the actual geographical place has always remained important, not just as a symbol of a world governed by peace and justice but as the hope of an ingathering on this earth of the people to their promised land. One Rabbinic saying goes, 'You also find that there is Jerusalem above, corresponding to the Jerusalem below. For sheer love of the earthly Jerusalem, God made himself one above.' So whilst for Christianity Jerusalem has become an important symbol, for Judaism the symbolic aspect is integrally bound up with the actual city. As Professor Zwi Werblowsky puts it, 'Jerusalem and Zion are geographical terms beyond mere geography, but not without geography.' Christians have holy sites in Jerusalem, sacred places for pilgrimage. But in Judaism there are no shrines and no special sites. Its religion is tied not to sites but to the land itself, not to what happened in Jerusalem but to Jerusalem.

I do in fact believe that a political agreement on Jerusalem has long been possible and it was not failure over this that resulted in the collapse of the Oslo accords.[10] What contribution might a religious understanding of Jerusalem make then to a political agreement? I believe that an attempt to at least try to understand how the other partners in a discussion view the matter, is crucial to any process of negotiation. This means sharing something of how the others, whether they are Jews, Christians, or Muslims, view Jerusalem and feeling

---

[10] See for example the proposition put forward by Bernhard Wasserstein, *Jerusalem: Past, Present and Future* (Institute of Jewish Affairs, 1995).

something of their pain at the lack of realization of their vision. Rabbi David Goldberg quotes a well-known Hasidic story about two friends walking along and one asks the other, 'Do you love me?' 'Of course I love you,' his friend replies, 'Why do you ask?' The first one answers, 'If you love me, can you feel my pain?' Goldberg goes on to write, 'There are many Jews living in Israel or the Diaspora who would hope that they can feel, and sympathize with something of the pain experienced by Palestinians in Jerusalem and the West Bank.'[11]

Understanding the other's point of view and feeling something of their pain is not of course a guarantee that progress can be made towards a settlement. As one Italian prince said to the other, 'We understand one another perfectly. We both want Italy.' But if it is not a guarantee, it is at least an essential prerequisite for any move towards reconciliation, not just at a political level but from a human point of view, which in the long term is going to be no less important.

What strikes every visitor to Jerusalem is the terrible contrast between Jerusalem as an ideal, a symbol of peace and righteousness, and the hate-filled, violent reality. Every day in the liturgy Christians, like Jews, say Psalms and read from the Bible, the sublime things said about 'Jerusalem'. Every time I hear that word in the liturgy I cannot help contrasting the ideals with which it is associated and the reality that we read and hear about daily through the media. It seems a divine irony, except that is much too light a way of putting it, for it is a divine tragedy, that the city which is meant to symbolize so much in the way of human aspirations should in reality provide such a stark contrast to the ideals espoused. But, without in any way romanticizing or valorizing that suffering, perhaps we have a clue here to Jerusalem's ultimate purpose. Yehezkel Landau has written:

The Palestinians, for their part, have not undergone a genocide, but the loss of Palestine to the Jews, compounded by their being manipulated and occasionally massacred by almost every other group in the Middle East . . . has left them traumatised, resentful and as mistrustful of others' intentions as we Jews are. Now these 'Crucified' peoples—the Armenians, the Israeli Jews, and the Palestinian Muslims and Christians—share Jerusalem, as they mourn their

---

[11] David Goldberg, 'Jerusalem and Judaism', *Jerusalem Today*.

martyrs and try to stay faithful to their respective faith traditions. In addition to the deep wounds suffered in the flesh, the spiritual suffering of exile, of being refugees in strange lands, is another common denominator linking the three nations. Could these similarities of fate be tied in any way to the fact that all three communities share identity elements linking particularity of people-hood, faithfulness to religious tradition, and attachment to a land each calls holy? Could these common denominators, and the juxtaposition now in Jerusalem, be of service to a bewildered humanity struggling to find a healthy balance between cultural particularities and universality? And most essentially, could this challenge be part of Jerusalem's Messianic vocation, calling on Jews, Christians and Muslims to work together as partners in the task of consecration so that our crippling traumas may be healed and we, in turn, may be truly liberated?[12]

Kenneth Cragg too looks to the Messianic ideal, as interpreted by Christianity in terms of the divine sovereignty which wears a crown of thorns. If for Christians the crucified one is 'the place of the name', then, he suggests, this is the clue to comprehending the final measure of Jerusalem.

To interpret Jerusalem in these terms must mean a lively participation in the Jewish rationale for Zionism, arising as this does from the anguish of Jewish experience at the hands of the European world. If we are drawing the final significance of Jerusalem from a perception of divine suffering, then 'Suffering' must be a clue concerning *all* parties in contemporary history. The suffering of the Palestinian identity, its economy, its people and its territory is not in doubt.[13]

He goes on to suggest that even though Israel is now empowered it still 'suffers', being heavy with the ambiguous issue of its great ideals which at the moment are so far from realization in the political realm.

Jerusalem, as an ideal, is a joyous city, a special place to be for both Israelis and Palestinians, for Jews, Muslims, and Christians. It is now a suffering city. If, as was suggested in an earlier chapter, God shares in and helps to bear our human anguish, then in a very special way he is present in Jerusalem. But he is present in order that some good

---

[12] Yehezkel Landau, 'Sharing Jerusalem: The Spiritual and Political Challenges', in *Jerusalem, Prophecy of Peace* (SIDIC 29/2–3; 1996, English edn.).

[13] Kenneth Cragg, 'The Place of the Name', *Jerusalem Today*.

might come out of the present travail and that good must come by human hands through human actions overcoming the suspicion and hatred of the past and drawing on all the best resources of our respective religions to find an agreed way forward. Religion can exacerbate conflict and too often has done just that. But it can also help to bring about greater understanding and can motivate people to continue to work for peace. Over the west door of a church in the English village of Staunton Harold is the following inscription:

> In the year 1653
> when all thinges Sacred were throughout ye nation
> either demolisht or profaned
> Sir Robert Shirley, Barronet,
> Founded this church;
> Whose singular praise it is,
> to have done the best things in ye worst times,
> and
> hoped them in the most callamitous.
> The righteous shall be had in everlasting remembrance.

It should be the particular contribution of true religion to do the best things in the worst times.

I will rejoice in Jerusalem and be glad in my people; no more shall be heard the sound of weeping and the cry of distress.   (Isaiah 65: 19)

When that verse refers to 'my people' to whom does it refer today? It must, I believe, embrace all the inhabitants of Jerusalem and the adherents of all the religions there.

Jewish Attitudes Towards Christianity

9

For most of its history Judaism has, understandably, had a very negative attitude towards Christianity. Jesus was regarded as an apostate, a false messiah who had led people astray. After centuries of persecution Jews had good reason to dislike Christianity.

Until recently Christianity tended to be regarded as more than unclean: It was felt to be tainted with evil, and not just because of its hostility to the Jews. And this may explain why Jewish parents are much less distressed if their children drop the practice of their religion and profess themselves agnostic or atheist, than if they adopt Christianity.[1]

Within this overall bleak picture, however, there were some outstanding exceptions, Jewish thinkers who sought a more positive evaluation of Christianity. One such was Judah Halevi (1075–1141), a Spanish Hebrew poet, philosopher, and physician. He wrote of the preparatory role played by both Christianity and Islam for the coming Messiah:

The nations merely serve to introduce and pave the way for the expected messiah, who is the fruition, and they will all become his fruit. Then they will revere the origin which they formerly despised.

Both Christianity and Islam grudgingly admitted Judaism to be their source. However, Halevi argued that it is Judaism which is the

---

[1] Clifford Longley, *The Times* (7 Jan. 1989).

original most authentic monotheism. It is the only religion that has remained pure and unadulterated by pagan additions and distortions. Christianity and Islam put forward the supersessionist claims of their own religion. Halevi and Maimonides (1135–1204), philosopher, physician, and one of the greatest legal authorities of all time, reversed the argument and argued that it was the source of these religions that had remained true.

Maimonides also argued that Christianity and Islam were preparing the way for the messiah.

How is this so? The whole world is already filled with the words of (their) messiah and the words of the commandments, and these words are spread to the furthest islands and among many obstinate peoples, and they discuss these words and the commandments of the Torah. They say, 'These commandments were true but are already invalid today, and are not meant to be perpetual' . . . For when the true messiah arises and will triumphantly be uplifted and exalted, all of them will immediately return and comprehend that their ancestors misled them.[2]

Maimonides saw the messiah as a political ruler who would be able, without supernatural intervention, to bring about universal monotheism by putting the Torah into practice and having full authority. In this way the world would be united. The Messianic failure of Christianity and Islam indicates that their versions of monotheism cannot bring about unified and harmonious world order. So although Maimonides and Halevi argued for the truth of Judaism against Christianity and Islam, they have a place for both these religions within the providence of God.

For the last 2,000 years it has hardly been possible for most Jews to have a public view about Christianity. As Geoffrey Wigoder has written, 'Silence was the safest course. Even when interest in Christianity was evinced, it was dangerous to speak of the faith of the persecutor.'[3] Against that background the positive attitude by some Jews towards Christianity is even more remarkable.

---

[2] The quotations from Halevi and Maimonides are cited in David Novak, *Jewish–Christian Dialogue: A Jewish Justification* (Oxford University Press, 1989), 62 and 63.

[3] Geoffrey Wigoder, *Jewish–Christian Relations since the Second World War* (Manchester University Press, 1988), 48.

Since World War II it is again understandable that Jews, until recently, have found it difficult to have a positive view of the Christian faith. The emphasis has been upon the complicity of Christians in Nazi Germany and the way anti-Judaism sowed seeds which sprang up as the poisonous weed of antisemitism. However, before World War II there were a number of remarkable Jewish thinkers who, in their different ways, came to a positive understanding of Christianity—and indeed some of these remained influential after the war. It is this group of Jewish scholars, Leo Baeck, Martin Buber, Franz Rosenzweig, Will Herberg, and Abraham Heschel, that I want to consider.

Leo Baeck (1873–1956) was born in Prussia, where his father was a Rabbi. He began his rabbinical studies at 18, studying in Berlin and elsewhere. He believed that Judaism, properly understood, was concerned with the whole of humanity. As he wrote, 'One can be a Jew only if one sees the totality, only if one thinks in a universal manner. There is the person whose horizons remain confined to certain bounds, groups, parties, interests; such a person is perhaps on the way to that which is Jewish, but is not yet completely a Jew.'[4]

He thought that what mattered about Christianity are the Jewish elements within it and their persistence. The converse of this, as Baeck believed it, was that Christianity had included certain non-Jewish elements and as a result it failed to be truly universal. Baeck was highly critical of the influential scholar Harnack for arguing in his book *What is Christianity?* that Jesus was not properly versed in Judaism. He may not have been an expert on Halakhah, Jewish law as derived from the Bible and Rabbinic literature, but his teaching is imbued with the spirit of Haggadah, the elaboration of Jewish teaching often in story form. Harnack seemed to claim that the essence of Jesus' teaching was non-Jewish. On the contrary, Baeck claimed that the kernel of Jesus' teaching lies in its fidelity to the essence of Judaism and only there. As he wrote, 'In all of his traits, Jesus is through and through *a genuinely*

---

[4] Quoted in Fritz Rothschild (ed.), *Jewish Perspectives on Christianity* (Continuum, New York, 1996), 23.

Jewish character. Such a man as he could grow up on the soil of Judaism, only there and nowhere else.'[5]

Some of Baeck's profoundest thoughts come in his essay on *Mystery and Commandment*. He believed that both mystery and commandment were necessary and that in Judaism they are properly united: 'Every mystery means and suggests also a commandment; and every commandment means and suggests also a mystery.'[6] Properly understood, there is no opposition between mysticism and ethics: 'All absorption in the profundity of God is always an absorption in the will of God and his commandment.'[7] On the other hand, even when we are coping with the difficulties of life we are related to the mystery of God.

It was on this basis that Baeck was critical of Paul, whom he accused of being an exponent of romantic religion. He saw this as placing an undue emphasis on feeling, on being lost in the divine, of being passive, in danger of creating an imaginary world that avoided reality and wished only to sink in bliss. Paul, in Baeck's view, was unduly influenced by the mystery religions of the ancient Roman world with their emphasis on dying and rising again and this led him into a similarly romantic understanding of religion. The result is that 'what is called The Victory of Christianity, was in reality this victory of romanticism'.[8] It was this that took hold of the Roman Empire. It is true that the Jewish elements in Paul continue to tug and struggle within him but in the end we can only call him a romantic because of his emphasis on faith alone, an emphasis that continued in Lutheranism, though less so in Calvinism and Roman Catholicism. One of the results is that Christianity has failed to conform to Baeck's criterion of universalism, it became a religion only for the redeemed and at its worst was indifferent to the wrongs of the world.

It is not my purpose now to defend Christianity against such criticisms, rather to expand the positive view of Christianity that is also present. Nevertheless, it does have to be pointed out that few today would accept the description of Paul as a romantic. It is true that he

---

[5] *Jewish Perspectives on Christianity*, 26.

[6] Leo Baeck, 'Mystery and Commandment', in *Jewish Perspectives on Christianity*, 47.

[7] Ibid. 49.

[8] Leo Baeck, 'Romantic Religion', in *Jewish Perspectives on Christianity*, 62.

had some extraordinary mystical experiences and saw himself as having died and risen again with Christ, but his letters contain as much ethics as they do theology or spirituality. They are full of exhortation and injunctions.

Nevertheless, the positive point in Baeck's understanding of Christianity is that the Jewish elements within it were never finally crushed or eliminated. It is these that give it its validity and universal horizon. As he wrote,

There is such a thing as a history of Judaism within the church. Judaism has an indestructible life by reason of its ideas; it can be fought against and can be forced to give ground yet it always becomes reanimated. 'Et inclinata resurget' even when it is bowed down, it only rises again to still loftier heights.[9]

Martin Buber (1878–1965) was brought up by his grandfather, a midrashic expert, in the Austrian sector of Galicia. As a consequence Buber always thought of himself as a Polish rather than a German Jew. He studied at many universities and was influenced by Zionism, which he saw primarily in terms of a cultural and religious renewal. But his main religious renewal came through his contact with Hasidim. Central to Buber was the dialogical principle. For example, he wrote:

The great deed of Israel is not to have taught the real God . . . but to have shown the addressability of this God as a reality, the ability to address him as a thou.[10]

He published his famous work *I and Thou* in 1923 but in 1933 was ousted from his post by the Nazis and eventually went to Palestine in 1938. He started to translate the Bible into German in 1925 with Franz Rosenzweig, a task which was eventually finished in 1961. His contribution was not simply to Judaism but more generally to European thought and he was highly respected by and influential on Christians. When I first went up to Cambridge in 1958 a Canadian research student was doing his doctorate on Buber. He told me that he had read *I and Thou* 500 times.

---

[9] Leo Baeck, 'Judaism in the Church', in *Jewish Perspectives on Christianity*, 108.
[10] Martin Buber, *Jewish Perspectives on Christianity*, 112.

Buber stressed Haggadah rather than Halakhah and his concern was history and the prophets rather than law. He saw Jesus as a great reformer who taught a return to 'What the prophets taught: the absoluteness of the deed'.[11] He believed that Paul had distorted this message with his undue emphasis on faith. Like Baeck he thought that what really counted in Christianity was its Jewish elements. As he put it, 'Whatever is creative in Christianity is not Christianity, but Judaism.'[12] He believed that Jews should recognize this Jewish element in Christianity and take possession of it but there should be no rapprochement with the rest, the non-Jewish elements.

Dialogue for him was crucial not only between humanity and God but between human beings on the basis of equality.

One person's truth is not the other person's untruth . . . only partnership . . . no head start with a view to eternity . . . the charisma of brotherliness.[13]

Buber speaks of the soul of Judaism, not Judaism as such because he was personally nonconformist. What mattered to him was faith, which is a fundamental trust in God. He believed that God can be known by anyone at any time as a faithful father.

God speaks to every man through the life which he gives him again and again. Therefore man can only answer God with the whole of his life—with the way in which he lives this given life.[14]

But although God's redeeming power is at work everywhere there is no redemption now.

The Jew, as part of the world, experiences perhaps more intensely than any other part the world's lack of redemption. He feels this lack of redemption against his skin, he tastes it on his tongue, the burden of the unredeemed world lies on him.[15]

Ultimately there will be redemption, redemption for all: 'There can be no eternity in which everything will not be accepted into God's atone-

[11] Martin Buber, *Jewish Perspectives on Christianity*, 116.   [12] Ibid. 116.
[13] Ekkehard Stegmann, 'Summing up Buber's Emphasis on Dialogue', *Jewish Perspectives on Christianity*, 117.
[14] Martin Buber, 'The Two Foci of the Jewish Soul', in *Jewish Perspectives on Christianity*, 126.
[15] Ibid. 127.

ment.' He quotes the Rabbi of Koynitz: 'If you do not yet wish to redeem Israel, at any rate redeem the Goyim'.[16]

As the book of Jonah teaches, anyone who turns to God will be saved. Israel has a special vocation, a response demanded by the community, the people as a whole, on the basis of Isaiah 49: 2: 'He made me a polished arrow, in his quiver he hid me away'. As Buber wrote,

A suffering for God's sake, the concealed history of the arrows which God does not dispatch, which do his work in the darkness of the quiver: it is for this that we, as Israel, endure.[17]

Israel is the servant of God, a servanthood which is to embrace the whole of human existence, not just a so-called spiritual realm.

In a moving passage Buber wrote that he lived near the city of Worms, where his forebears came from. When he goes to the city he goes first to the cathedral 'gazing at it in perfect joy'. Then he goes to the Jewish cemetery which is full of cracked and crooked stones without shape or direction. Here there are only stones with the ashes beneath them. But he feels that this is where he belongs.

I have stood there; I have been united with the ashes, and through them with the patriarchs. That is a remembrance of the divine–human encounter which is granted to all Jews. The perfection of the Christian God cannot divert me from this; nothing can divert me from the God-time of Israel.

I have stood there and I have experienced everything myself. I have experienced all the death that was before me; all the ashes, all the desolation, and all the noiseless wailings become mine but the covenant has not been withdrawn from me. I lie on the ground, prostrate like these stones. But it has not been withdrawn for me. . . . The cathedral is as it is, the cemetery is as it is. But nothing has been withdrawn from us.[18]

Martin Buber ended this essay with two quotations. The first from the Talmud:

If in this day and age a convert comes in order to be received into Judaism let him be told: 'What have you seen in us, that you wish to be converted? Do you know that the people of Israel are at this time tortured, battered, buffeted,

[16] Ibid. 128.
[17] Martin Buber, 'Church, State, Nation, Jewry', in *Jewish Perspectives on Christianity*, 138.
[18] Ibid. 141.

driven about, that suffering has overtaken them?' If he says: 'I know, and I am
not worthy', then let him at once be received.[19]

The other quotation is from the Midrash:

The Holy one, blessed be he, declares no creature unworthy, rather he receives
everyone. The gates are opened at every hour, and whoever seeks to enter, will
enter.[20]

The gates are open to all the righteous who turn to God, but Judaism
has a special vocation. I mentioned earlier that for Buber, faith understood as confident trust in God is fundamental—the Hebrew *emunah*.
Buber was critical of Paul, whose faith he took to be *pistis*, a much
more Greek concept, but it is doubtful whether that interpretation
would stand up today. For Paul, faith is the faith of Abraham and
pistis, though a Greek word, is always imbued with a strong sense of
the Hebrew *emunah*.

Franz Rosenzweig (1886–1929) had four years at the front in World
War I, first in the Red Cross and then as a combatant. He wrote his
famous book *The Star of Redemption* in 1921. Rosenzweig seriously
considered becoming a Christian. He had two talented cousins who
were Christians who influenced him in that direction. But as mentioned earlier he came to think that he could only become a Christian
as a Jew, not a pagan, and this led him back into Judaism. Through
Judaism he came to the insight that 'He already was with the Father',
so that the words of Jesus in John 14: 6 'No one comes to the Father
except by me' did not apply to him.

Rosenzweig's thought is not easy to understand because he struc-
tured truth in polar terms. Creation was wrought in pairs, in opposites.
To us humans truth never appears as one. This oneness only exists in
God. Both Christianity and Judaism are committed to the truth but
only before the one, God himself, is truth one. This means that both
Torah and Jesus Christ can be affirmed. The decision between them
cannot be decided by us human beings, because we are creatures; 'The

[19] Martin Buber, 'Church, State, Nation, Jewry', in *Jewish Perspectives on Christianity*, 142.
[20] Ibid. 142.

proof lies with God himself, only before him is truth ONE'.[21] Rosenzweig read the Church Fathers in the trenches and he knew Christianity very well, though the theology he reflected on may have moved on since then.

Both Jews and Christians have 'an identical final hope' and in this world they are destined to suffer in an equal degree. Both are responsible for history and that responsibility inflicts suffering on them, albeit n different ways. Judaism is separated from the world by election and this leads to her suffering. Christianity is called to be a missionary religion and this will bring its own suffering. Nevertheless, 'before God, both Jew and Christian are labourers of the task'.[22]

The title of Rosenzweig's book *The Star of Redemption* provides an image which includes both Christianity and Judaism. The burning heart of the star is Judaism: the rays that go out to the world are Christianity. The world remains unredeemed so Jews say to Christians:

We are to you the ever mindful memory of your incompleteness for you who live in a Church triumphant need a mute servant who cries out every time that you have partaken of God's bread and wine, *despota, memnesa, ton eschaton* 'Master, remember the last things'.[23]

In those last things both Christianity and Judaism leave behind their special vocations:

The people of Israel, chosen by its father, fixes its glance on that ultimate, most distant point, beyond world and history where its father, the father himself, will be the one and the only—will be 'all in all!' At that point, when Christ will cease to be the Lord, Israel will cease to be chosen; on that day God will lose the name by which only Israel calls on him; God will then no longer be 'their' God. Until that day, however, Israel will live to anticipate it in belief and deed to stand tall as a living harbinger of that day, a nation of priests, following the law which requires that one make the name of God holy by being holy oneself.[24]

---

[21] Franz Rosenzweig, *Jewish Perspectives on Christianity*, 163.   [22] Ibid. 167.

[23] Franz Rosenzweig, 'The Star of Redemption', *Jewish Perspectives on Christianity*, 182.

[24] Ibid. 170.

Will Herberg (1901–77) was once a Marxist and a communist. But when he was working for the International Ladies Garment Workers Union he became critical of the use of power by the communists. Like a number of other ex-Marxists at that time, he responded to the thought of Reinhold Niebuhr. He was drawn to the way Niebuhr spoke like a prophet and urged that all human powers are ultimately subject to the judgement of God. He was very attracted to Christianity but Niebuhr said that he should become a Jew first in a full theological sense. This he did and he remained a Jew. Much influenced by Franz Rosenzweig he took a double covenant view of the relationship between Judaism and Christianity. He urged Christians to hold fast to Christian orthodoxy and not be distracted by either a purely social gospel or an attenuated liberalism. He believed that biblical theology was not simply a passing phase. For both Judaism and Christianity faith is 'faith enacted in history'. We are co-workers with God with the aim of redeeming humanity.

Herberg stressed the many beliefs and features that Judaism and Christianity have in common and he rejected many of the traditional polarities as well as some modern ones. For example, he rejected Buber's distinction between Hebrew *emunah* and Greek *pistis*. He argued that the Hebrew scriptures are full of grace and the New Testament also contains law. The concept of covenant is basic to both but through Jesus that covenant goes out from Israel to humanity as a whole: 'Through Christianity God's covenant with Israel was opened to all mankind.' Christ 'is quite literally, an incarnate or one man Israel, the remnant man', 'through union in faith with him the Gentile believer becomes part of Israel'.[25]

For both Jews and Christians, there is the vocation of sanctifying the name, *Kiddush Ha-Shem*. But Jews do this by staying with God and Christians by going out to the world. Jews by their distinctive, separate existence are witness to the divine reality. The very anomalous nature of this existence points beyond itself. Christians witness in a different way, by going out.

---

[25] Will Herberg, 'Judaism and Christianity: Their Unity and Difference', in *Jewish Perspectives on Christianity*, 244.

As I said, Herberg was concerned to disabuse people of the usual stereotypical differences between Judaism and Christianity. For example, whereas people in the past have contrasted alleged Jewish works with alleged Christian grace he emphasized the element of grace in Jewish writings.

'Our father Abraham inherited this world and the world to come solely by virtue of his faith' is one quotation from the Mekilta. Every morning a Jewish person prays 'Our Father, Our King, be gracious unto us, for we have no works, save us according to thy grace.'[26]

At the same time, Israel's vocation is to stay with God through obedience to the Halakhah, through this discipline of life. Christianity has a charism or gift of the Spirit to go out to others. Israel can go out to others and Israel can bring the world to God only through Christianity. Christianity in fact is Israel's apostle to the Gentiles.

Judaism's great service to Christianity is to recall it to its origins. For it is always in danger of accommodating to the spirit of the age.

When it comes to Jesus, Herberg considered him not only a great moral teacher and prophet but, in accord with his overall understanding of Christianity, as he put it, 'Through Christ God's covenant with Israel is—in the fullness of time—open to all mankind.'[27]

Abraham Heschel (1907–72) was regarded by the great Jewish scholar Neusner as 'the greatest Judaic theologian of this century'. He spoke powerfully and uniquely to both Jews and Christians.

He was born in Warsaw into a learned and pious family. He pursued academic life in Germany but was deported to Poland in 1938. He left for the United States six weeks before the Nazi invasion. In America he was not only a prolific writer but very active on behalf of the civil rights movement, against the Vietnam war, in support of Soviet Jewry, and was very influential at Vatican II.

He was clear that Jews must keep the Torah but that the diversity of religions was the will of God: 'The Jewish attitude enables us to acknowledge the presence of a divine plan in the role of Christianity

[26] Ibid. 250.
[27] Will Herberg, 'A Jew Looks at Jesus', in *Jewish Perspectives on Christianity*, 259.

within the history of redemption.'[28] However, Christians needed to recover a Messianic sense, that is a belief that God's kingdom could come in this world. Then the Church might 'consider itself an extension of Judaism'.

Christianity was based upon a new covenant but this did not mean that the first covenant was superseded or surpassed. It meant that the covenant was renewed as an anticipation, not a fulfilment, of the final realization of the covenant pointed to by Jeremiah and Ezekiel (Jeremiah 31: 31 and Ezekiel 16: 59).

We have a sense of the profoundly Jewish and profoundly spiritual nature of Heschel's thought in his statement that 'For Judaism, religion is not a feeling for something that is, but an answer to him who is asking us to live in a certain way.'[29]

Like Herberg, Heschel was both a great admirer of, and influenced by, Reinhold Niebuhr. Niebuhr had a brutally realistic view of human existence and the way that evil permeates everything. Heschel argued that this insight is also contained within Judaism. The problem is not simply evil but the fact that evil is mixed with the good; good and evil are so often confused, so that evil can get into religion and all human virtues are likely to be ambiguous. He quotes a Hasidic rabbi who was asked by his disciples whom they should choose as their master after his death. He said, 'If someone should give you the way to eradicate "alien thoughts" know he is not your master.' In other words, we have to have an utterly realistic understanding of human nature and this includes knowing that alien thoughts remain part of all of us until the end of time. Yet Heschel shows his quintessential Jewishness in insisting upon the reality of the deed: 'Judaism insists on the deed and hopes for the intention'.[30] He argues that deceitful though the heart is, the ego can be redeemed through absorption in the power of the just task, in the same way that a musician can be caught up by the music. It may be true that possibilities of evil grow with possibilities of good but there are good moments in history, 'Unalloyed good moments are

[28] Abraham Heschel, *Jewish Perspectives on Christianity*, 274.

[29] Abraham Heschel, 'More than Inwardness', *Jewish Perspectives on Christianity*, 278.

[30] Abraham Heschel, 'A Hebrew Evaluation of Reinhold Niebuhr', *Jewish Perspectives on Christianity*, 295.

possible.'[31] Mitzvah can be done and the worth of good deeds remains for eternity.

History is indeed a nightmare but 'It is an act of evil to accept the state of evil as either inevitable or final.' There is redemption. There is a waiting for redemption. But deeds are acts in the long drama 'And every deed counts'.[32]

Heschel protested against both the de-Judaizing of Protestantism and the de-sanctification of the Bible in the modern world. By this he meant the way many Protestants considered Jesus or the New Testament apart from the Hebrew scriptures and often treated the Bible simply as a historical book rather than a divine revelation.

Heschel was not only theologically profound but spiritually sustaining. Asking the question about the purpose of interreligious co-operation, he answered:

It is neither to flatter nor to refute one another, but to help one another; to share insight and learning . . . and what is even more important to search in the wilderness for well-springs of devotion, for treasures of stillness, for the power of love and care for man. What is urgently needed are ways of helping one another in the terrible predicament of here and now by the courage to believe that the word of the Lord endures forever as well as here and now; to cooperate in trying to bring about a resurrection of sensitivity, a revival of conscience; to keep alive the divine sparks in our souls, to nurture openness to the spirit of the Psalms, reverence for the words of the prophets, and faithfulness to the Living God.[33]

The scholars just discussed, Leo Baeck, Martin Buber, Franz Rosenzweig, William Herberg, and Abraham Heschel, were a remarkable group with fresh, positive things to say about Christianity. Yet, for other understandable reasons, the dark cloud of the Holocaust and the challenge to Christianity to reappraise its whole understanding of Judaism, their voice and their concerns have been in abeyance for the last fifty years. Jacob Neusner looks back to that group of Jewish scholars with admiration and argues that, since then, Jewish–Christian dialogue has not really begun. Neither religion has really faced the

---

[31] Ibid. 297. [32] Ibid. 300.

[33] Abraham Heschel, 'No Religion is an Island', *Jewish Perspectives on Christianity*, 324.

difference presented by the other, in the case of Christianity its doctrine of the incarnation of God in Jesus Christ. Neusner argues that real dialogue involves trying to understand the most difficult beliefs of the other religion, rather than simply dismissing them out of hand as inconceivable, as traditionally Judaism has done with the Christian doctrine of the incarnation of God. Neusner argues that we have to make an imaginative attempt, drawing on the resources of our own religion, to enter into the understanding of the other. He believes that this can and must be done, using Jewish rabbinical thought, to understand the Christian concept of incarnation. As he writes:

At issue here . . . is not what Christianity says about Jesus Christ or what Judaism responds. It is, can we find in the resources of Judaism a way of understanding what Christians might mean when they speak of Jesus Christ God incarnate?[34]

He then builds on the thought of Abraham Heschel, who said that what defined God was his pathos, 'the divine pathos, the fact of God's participation in the predicament of man, is the elemental fact'; this means that human actions not only affect other human beings but affect God himself: 'he is a consort, partner, factor in the life of God'. Neusner then looks at various rabbinic discussions and argues from these that the Rabbis thought of God in very human terms. God has traits which are reflected in Israel and Israel has traits which have their counterpart in God. In particular God is sometimes portrayed as like a sage:

A story built on the premise of the incarnation of God, fully exposing God's traits of personality and portraying God like a sage, engaged in argument with a man as the master engages an argument with a disciple, serves a stunning purpose, which contradicts its academic form. It is to show that God, while like a sage, is more than a sage—much more.[35]

God is in the end ineffable but

When I tell my stories, in which I learn how the Torah reveals God, both the stories of the prophets and what God said to them, and the stories of our sages of blessed memory and how they knew God in incarnate form, I can under-

---

[34] Jacob Neusner, *Telling Tales* (Westminster/John Knox Press, 1993), 124.
[35] *Telling Tales*, 137.

stand how someone else may tell stories about God in us, and about how we can become like God. And I then listen with sympathy to the Christian story of Jesus Christ God incarnate? Without doubt: I can listen with sympathy, because the Torah teaches me how.[36]

Neusner is not of course suggesting that this necessarily leads to Jesus Christ. Nor is he suggesting that Christians would be content only with this way of understanding the incarnation. But he is showing how, using Jewish traditional sources, it is possible to understand what traditional Judaism has regarded as totally alien and theologically inconceivable.

Now, suddenly, a new group of Jewish scholars has decided to reflect seriously on Christianity again, its relationship with Judaism and its role within the providence of God. *Dabru Emet*, word of truth, subtitled as a Jewish statement on Christians and Christianity, was signed by 179 Rabbis and scholars from different Jewish traditions, predominantly from the USA, Canada, and the United Kingdom and published in 2000. It begins by recognizing that Christianity's attitude to Judaism has changed dramatically since World War II and 'We believe these changes merit a thoughtful Jewish response.' The paper sets out eight fundamental propositions.

Jews and Christians worship the same God

Jews and Christians seek authority from the same book—the Bible (what Jews call 'Tanakh' and Christians called the 'Old Testament')

Christians can respect the claim of the Jewish people upon the land of Israel

Jews and Christians accept the moral principles of the Torah

Nazism was not a Christian phenomenon

The humanly irreconcilable difference between Jews and Christians will not be settled until God redeems the entire world as promised in scripture

A new relationship between Jews and Christians will not weaken Jewish practice

Jews and Christians must work together for justice and peace

[36] Ibid.

Each of those principles is followed by a few lines of explanation. What is no less remarkable than this brief statement is a book *Christianity in Jewish Terms*,[37] mainly by Jewish scholars, which sets out to give substance to those eight principles, which are quoted at the beginning.

One of the problems about any kind of dialogue is that it can be dominated by the agenda of the other. Christians, for example, would always want to have Jesus on the agenda but it is not natural for Jews to think about him at all. Jews would want to have Israel on the agenda but Christians have difficulty in seeing attachment to a particular land as part of a religious outlook. One of the strengths of *Christianity in Jewish Terms* is that the sections reflect equally the concerns of both Jews and Christians. They are:

The Shoah and the legacy of antisemitism
God
Scripture
Commandment
Israel
Worship
Suffering
Embodiment
Redemption
Sin and repentance
Image of God.

From a Christian point of view this table of contents includes such fundamental Christian beliefs as incarnation and God as Holy Trinity as well as the cross of Christ. The plan followed by the book is that in each section there is a first essay by a Jewish scholar teaching about a particular area of Jewish theological tradition and offering a way for Jews to understand a corresponding set of Christian beliefs. In the second essay another Jewish thinker describes from her own perspective another way to understand both Jewish and Christian beliefs. In the third essay a Christian scholar responds to the first essay and answers

[37] Tikva Frymer-Kensky, David Novak, Peter Ochs, David Sandmel, and Michael Signer (eds.), *Christianity in Jewish Terms* (Westview Press, 2000).

the questions 'Do I recognize my Christianity in what has been written? What is the significance of Judaism for my understanding of
Christianity?' In short, starting from Jewish premises, an attempt has
been made to see how far these can be made congruous with or at least
seem to have some affinity with central Christian beliefs. The scholars
are also quite clear that issues of truth are at stake, that relativism
needs to be avoided.

Relativism is especially dangerous to the dialogue because it denies that some
things are true all the time everywhere for everyone. But Judaism and
Christianity make such claims. Indeed, these claims, like 'God elects Israel' or
'God is incarnate in Jesus' are what Judaism and Christianity are all about. In
fact Judaism requires Jews to die as martyrs rather than exchange Judaism for
anything else, even something as similar to Judaism as Christianity.
Christianity makes a similar claim on Christians.[38]

In a previous chapter, 'The Covenant with Humanity' I argued that
central Christian beliefs like the trinity and incarnation, which traditionally have seemed to set up an abyss between Christianity and
Judaism, do in fact have resonances within Judaism itself. That this is
not simply wishful thinking is borne out by the chapters in *Christianity
in Jewish Terms*. Some of the insights there are referred to elsewhere,
for example, in the chapter on suffering. Here we simply focus on two,
the trinity and incarnation. Peter Ochs in his section on incarnation
and trinity writes that 'At this third epoch of Judaism, however, Jews
are called to do more than throw up our hands in the face of Christian
doctrines; we must, instead, find a way to reason Jewishly about
them.' This he does, for example by comparing the Jewish concept of
God's being the author of the divine speech with Christian theology's
understanding of the Father begetting his divine son. He finds the suffering servant passage of Isaiah helpful when it is taken to refer both to
Israel and to the one Jew, Jesus. Here suffering is not just experiencing
pain but receiving God's presence.

Jews can find a bridge to discussion in the biblical analogy of Israel's own suffering for humanity and in the theological reflection that Israel knows God the
infinite only by 'Suffering' (that is, receiving) God's presence.

[38] Ibid. 4.

He links this up with the idea of the infinite suffering finitude in some way.

We who speak of the difference between our finitude and God's infinity must, if we reason consistently, also talk about our 'Suffering' (sharing in) a relation to God and God's suffering a relation to us, however mysterious this notion may remain to us.

He also finds a bridge to Trinitarian usage about the Holy Spirit through Jewish references to being touched by the divine wisdom and mystical experience.[39]

David Ellenson, another Jewish scholar, finds hope in the Jewish tradition of thinking about the Trinity, because a number of scholars who said that although Trinitarianism constituted idolatry for Jews it did not do so for Christians. He quotes an eighteenth-century Rabbi, Yehuda Ashkenazi:

In our era . . . when the gentiles in whose midst we dwell . . . [speak of God], their intention is directed towards the one who made heaven and earth, albeit that they associate another personality with God. However, this does not constitute a violation of Leviticus 19, 14, 'You shall not place a stumbling block before the blind' for non-Jews are not warned against such association.[40]

He also quotes Rabbi Jacob Emden (1697–1776), who said about Jesus:

The Nazarene brought about a double kindness in the world. On the one hand, he strengthened the Torah of Moses majestically . . . on the other hand he did much good for the gentiles . . . by doing away with idolatry and removing the images from their midst. He obligated them with the seven commandments so that they should not be as the beasts of the field.[41]

The section on embodiment is rather fuller and perhaps from a Christian point of view more satisfactory. Elliot Wolfson begins by saying that imaginative attempts to conceive God in embodied terms is not the same as idolatry. The forbidding of images does not mean forbidding imaginative attempts to grasp God in human terms. This means that the doctrine of incarnation in general is not antithetical to

---

[39] Peter Ochs, 'God of Jews and Christians', *Christianity in Jewish Terms*, 65–7.
[40] *Christianity in Jewish Terms*, 74.   [41] Ibid. 74.

Judaism. On the contrary, the idea of incarnation unique to Christianity should be viewed as a 'particular framing' of the conception of incarnation that was 'idiomatic to a variety of Judaic authors who represented God as a person. . . . Incarnation of the divine body in Judaism relates to theophanic images that are localised in the imagination.'[42] An example given of this kind of theophanic image is the story of Jacob's struggle with the mysterious 'man' who is explicitly identified as *Elohim*. Another example of the incarnational orientation occurs in the verses in the book of Deuteronomy where the divine name is described as dwelling in the sanctuary. The glory of God thus inhabits the earthly temple through the agency of the name. Again, there are very many passages where there seems to be a deliberate confusion between the angel of God and divinity itself. In some Jewish sources this identification is made more explicit. 'In every place that the angel is seen, the *Shechinah* is seen, as it says "An angel of the Lord appeared to him in a blazing fire out of bush" and immediately "God called out to him (out of the bush)".'[43] Further examples are the way in which every word that comes from the mouth of God at the same time creates an angel.

Another line of thinking explores the idea of God being present in the Torah, especially in the body of scholars studying the Torah. Quotations are given from Jewish sources which indicate that the Torah is the means by which one lives in the immediate presence of God. Again, prayer opens the believer to the indwelling of the divine presence. Randi Rashkover also concentrates on the Torah as the embodiment of the word of God: 'The Jews are not only to follow God's laws but also to embody them.'[44] This is done in quite tangible ways such as binding the commandments as a sign upon the arm and between the eyes. Circumcision is also a very specific way in which the law is inscribed on the human body. 'Embodying God's Torah, the Jews become a corporeal sign of God's presence. Bearing the mark of

---

[42] Elliot Wolfson, 'Judaism and Incarnation: The Imaginal Body of God', *Christianity in Jewish Terms*, 240–1.

[43] Ibid. 245.

[44] Randi Rashkover, 'The Christian Doctrine of the Incarnation', *Christianity in Jewish Terms*, 255.

God's word, the people of Israel become a sign or a testimony to God's reality here on earth.'[45] Like Elliot Wolfson she refers to the text about the community of scholars embodying the Torah by interpreting and inscribing it in their minds. In one remarkable story God seems to have delegated his decision-making to such a body. More specifically, 'If ten men sit together and occupy themselves with the words of the Torah, the *Shechinah* is in their midst.'

There is of course great scope for discussion of these themes, as to how far they really do encompass the Christian concept of incarnation and how far they do not. My point here is to reiterate what was said earlier that the historic total rejection by Judaism of certain central Christian doctrines need not continue today. There are resonances and congruities so that such Christian doctrines can at least be discussed in Jewish terms and not regarded as totally alien. The scholars who have contributed to *Christianity in Jewish Terms* have made a remarkable contribution to Jewish–Christian dialogue which, in fact, goes significantly beyond the constructive contribution of the previous group of Jewish thinkers discussed earlier.

The minister of the orthodox synagogue in Hampstead, the Revd A. A. Green, introduced the study of the New Testament to the senior level of his religion school in 1921. It received the initial backing of the then Chief Rabbi, Hertz, although there was a furore in the Jewish community when it became public knowledge and was quickly dropped. Rabbi Jonathan Romain wrote in 1990: 'Nowadays such an initiative would be unthinkable . . . It seems we have a long way to go to catch up on an earlier spirit of liberalism.'[46] But perhaps even in ten years something has changed. Rabbi Dr Sidney Brichto has written:

We Jews remain as negative as ever about the Christian faith. We are always alert to any Christian claim of superiority to our own faith, but without giving up our own claim to chosenness. We totally ignore the contribution of Christianity to human culture. We will not read the New Testament nor take any interest in understanding why it succeeded in conquering the Western world where we failed. . . . Since translating the letters of Paul, I have begun to

[45] Randi Rashkover, 'The Christian Doctrine of the Incarnation', *Christianity in Jewish Terms*, 256.

[46] Private letter to the author, 22 Mar. 1990.

realise how great a deprivation it is for Jews not to understand the foundations of our sister faith.

Dr Brichto then goes on to make some very perceptive comments about the difference between Paul's religion and Judaism, ending with the words:

Reading the sacred literature of Christianity will not threaten our faith but make it stronger. Also, it is only through the understanding of each other's faith that ignorant prejudice between Christian and Jew and Jew and Christian will end.[47]

---

[47] Rabbi Dr Sidney Brichto, *Jewish Chronicle* (22 June 2001).

The Jewish Jesus and the Christian Christ

10

The nineteenth-century quest to discover the historical Jesus gave way for a couple of decades to a radical scepticism about the possibility of doing this. This in turn was followed by a new search for the Jesus of history. Using the most stringent criteria and offering only tentative conclusions, there are nevertheless some propositions about Jesus that command a consensus amongst serious scholars. One of the points of agreement is that Jesus must be set and seen firmly within the context of the Judaism of his time. Geza Vermes, to whom more than anyone else this emphasis is due, has written:

The Jewishness of Jesus is now axiomatic whereas in 1973 the title of my book *Jesus the Jew* was still capable of sending shock waves across many a sector of the traditional Christian world. The legitimacy of the 'Jewish approach' to the study of the historical Jesus is universally acknowledged, even by those New Testament scholars who can only pay lip service to it.[1]

Another scholar, E. P. Sanders, who has been very influential both in locating Jesus in the Judaism of his time and using the most stringent methods of historical criticism to recover something about the historical Jesus has written:

Historical reconstruction is never absolutely certain, and in the case of Jesus it is sometimes highly uncertain. Despite this, we have a good idea of the main

[1] Geza Vermes, *The Changing Faces of Jesus* (Penguin, 2000), 268.

The Jewish Jesus and Christian Christ

lines of his ministry and his message. We know who he was, what he did, what he taught and why he died.[2]

It is not the intention here to spell out that historical portrait. It is only necessary to assert that Jesus was a Jew, born and brought up in a Jewish culture which shaped his whole understanding of life and his approach to God. The God he was taught to believe in was the God of Abraham, Isaac, and Jacob, a God whom Judaism encouraged him to address as Father. He knew that the Father's will had been disclosed to his chosen people in the Torah by which he sought to live. He shared not only Judaism's faith but Judaism's hope that God would redeem his people Israel. He did all this, if we follow Vermes, mainly in Galilee and he stood in a Galilean tradition of charismatic teachers, healers, and exorcists.

At the heart of the message of Jesus was his teaching about the kingship of God and his rule in human affairs, the kingdom of God. It is tempting to think of this kingly rule of God as a timeless truth and that Jesus simply invited people to turn away from what they knew to be wrong and put themselves under that rule as revealed in the Torah. Some of the sayings of Jesus certainly fit that understanding. However, most do not. It seems clear that the teaching of Jesus about the Kingdom of God has to be seen in relation to the hope running all through the Hebrew scriptures and strongly expressed in the inter-testamental literature, that one day God would decisively intervene in human history to rescue his people, reorder human affairs, and establish his kingly rule over the earth. There is an urgency about the teaching of Jesus that it is impossible to ignore. He summoned people to radically rethink their lives in the light of the near presence of this kingly rule of God in human affairs. He made it clear that there was a crisis, a moment of decision, because the long expected reign of God was even now breaking into human history and would shortly come to its climax.

Together with this there are a number of features of the ministry of Jesus that do not fit easily with the picture of an ordinary freelance Rabbi. There is, for example, the authority with which he taught. He

[2] E. P. Sanders, *The Historical Figure of Jesus* (Penguin, 1993), 280.

directs people to the teaching of the Torah and then says, 'But I say unto you'. The gospels report that people were astounded at the authority with which he taught. Then there is the way in which he forgave sins. Often this forgiving of sins was linked to a healing miracle. The healing was a sign that the person's sins had been forgiven. But forgiving sins was a prerogative of God.

There is also his message that the pattern of God's love was identical with the pattern of his own ministry. He went out of his way to mix with and eat with those who failed by the standards of the law, those who from a religious and hence social point of view, were marginalized, tax gatherers and prostitutes. At the same time he taught that this kind of going out and inclusive gathering in is what God does. God is like a woman who loses a coin and scrabbles all over the floor for it, or like a shepherd who searches the hills for the one lost sheep. Then there is the intimacy of his relationship with the one he called Abba, Father. Finally, there is the way that he saw his own destiny bound up with the coming of 'the Son of Man'. I do not myself think that Jesus claimed to be the messiah. He left that issue open. But he did use the enigmatic title Son of Man. He associated it with a vocation to suffering but still affirmed its traditional associations of vindication and glory.

Jesus was crucified and that, from one point of view, was the end of the matter. Jesus the faithful Jew who called people to a radical rethink of their lives and to live under the kingly rule of God's coming kingdom as they followed him in the way of love, died and everything he stood for might have died with him. But it didn't.

Within three decades the followers of Jesus were attributing to him the most extraordinary status. Sometime between the years 61 to 63 in the Christian era Paul wrote from prison to the church in Colossae to say about Jesus:

He is the image of the invisible God; his is the primacy over all created things. In him everything in heaven and on earth was created, not only things visible but also the invisible orders of thrones, sovereignties, authorities, and powers: the whole universe has been created through him and for him. And he exists before everything, and all things are held together in him.   (Colossians 1: 15–17)

Some scholars, such as Geza Vermes, believe that the letter to the Colossians is not by Paul and should be dated a couple of decades later. Personally I believe that Colossians, unlike Ephesians, was written by Paul and is earlier, but whatever the dating, the affirmation of Jesus in these terms within decades of his death is mind-boggling. In his letter to the Philippians Paul wrote:

Let your bearing towards one another arise out of your life in Christ Jesus. For the divine nature was his from the first; yet he did not think to snatch at equality with God, but made himself nothing, assuming the nature of a slave. (Philippians 2: 5–7)

Geza Vermes believes that this is part of a hymn, interpolated into a genuine letter of Paul somewhat later. I think it is probably a hymn but one which antedates Paul's letter and which he himself included. But again the issue of dating is not crucial for the point, that these extraordinary statements were being made within a lifetime of the death of Jesus. By the turn of the century this view was being stated by other writers in other terms. The letter to the Hebrews begins:

When in former times God spoke to our forefathers, he spoke in fragmentary and varied fashion through the prophets. But in this the final age he has spoken to us in the son whom he has made heir to the whole universe, and through whom he created all orders of existence: the son who is the effulgence of God's splendour and the stamp of God's very being, and sustains the universe by his word of power.   (Hebrews 1: 1–3)

Then in the prologue to John's gospel the divine word or logos who is made flesh, in whom the writer saw the divine glory, 'such glory as befits the Father's only son, full of grace and truth', is also the logos who 'dwelt with God, and what God was, the word was' (John 1: 1 and 14). What brought about this change of perception of Jesus from faithful Jew to divine son? The terminology was already present in Jewish thought. In the wisdom literature, for example, divine wisdom is personified so that she is at once part of God and separate from God. Similarly, it did not take very much reflection on the idea of the word of God, the word of God which created the universe in the first place and which spoke through the prophets, to see how a word can be at once part of the divine mind and uttered by the divine mind and have as it were a life of its own. But that which motivated Christians to start hunting in this literature to say what they wanted to say was of course what they believed about the resurrection of Jesus from the dead. It is part of the earliest Christian preaching that on the third day God raised him. It is best, I think, to think of this raising as a raising to the 'Right hand on high', to put it in picture terms. Jesus was exalted to heaven, to be with God. The appearances to the disciples are, as it were, appearances from heaven. This is not of course the Lucan scheme, which thinks in terms of Jesus being raised from the dead, appearing for forty days and then ascending to heaven. However, it is one which is much closer to the Johannine view. In my little book *Christ is Risen*[3] I argued that the tomb was indeed found empty, and that Jesus had been transfigured, in a unique miracle comparable only to the creation of the universe *ex nihilo* in the first place and the dematerialization of the physical universe at the end of all things. It also suggested that the appearances to the disciples should be seen as 'objective visions', in which the risen Christ appears to some of his followers in terms of their own needs and vocation, though the stories of these appearances are written up from specific theological points of view. At the same time, every word in the gospels also reflects faith in the risen Jesus. They are written up in that light, which is one of the reasons why it is so difficult to get behind them to identify the Jesus of history.

Resurrection was a Jewish, and more particularly, a Pharisaic idea. It was a commonplace that in the end God would raise the dead, and in particular he would vindicate martyrs and his chosen people. So St Paul sees the raising of Jesus as the beginning of the end, an end which in his earliest letters he clearly expected quite soon. Jesus would return in glory and the dead would be raised.

For people at that time, as for us in the West now, time is linear: it has a beginning, a middle, and an end. This means that the meaning of the history, and the meaning of any particular event that occurs, can only truly be assessed at the end, when the goal has been reached, and history can be seen as a whole. History as we know it is a continuing interaction of the present with the past, with the past continually being

---

[3] Richard Harries, *Christ is Risen* (Mowbray, 1987).

reinterpreted. The final reinterpretation will come at the end. For the first Christians the resurrection of Jesus was a revealing of the end, an event in which the essential meaning of the whole could be discerned.[4] This meaning was, quite simply, the glory of God in man. What they saw was the glory of God in a particular man, Jesus Christ. But through this particular man the glory of God is to suffuse and transfigure all humanity.

This view depends upon and makes sense of those features of the ministry of Jesus, already outlined above, which do not fit easily into the pattern of a freelance teacher and healer. Those features included the authority with which Jesus taught, his willingness to forgive sins, his closeness to the Father and enactment of the pattern of his Father's ministry to the excluded, and his sense that in his teaching and above all in his physical healings and exorcisms the Kingdom of God was actually breaking into human affairs. In the light of this, Jesus trusted that at the coming of the Son of Man, with whom his mission and indeed identity were integrally bound up, he and those who put their trust in him would be vindicated. At the crucifixion all those features seemed to be negated. Jesus was clearly wrong, mistaken, tragically and foolishly mistaken. But if God had raised him from the dead, had taken him to himself and shown his followers that he now lived with a universal contemporaneity, then what Jesus stood for and his own person were both vindicated and fully disclosed. In the resurrection those features of the ministry of Jesus were retroactively validated. More than this they revealed that Jesus really was at one with his heavenly Father. He was not after all tragically and foolishly mistaken. On the contrary, the Father's work was going on in and through him and in him the Father's glory is revealed. There is a hiddenness about this glory both in the ministry of Jesus and in the resurrection, which was not such as to stun the whole world into submission. But there were those who came to see in Jesus and his self-giving into and through death, the glory of the Father. This is of course the great theological motif running through the fourth gospel. But the same theme is there in St Paul, who wrote:

---

[4] For a detailed working out of this see Wolfhart Pannenberg, *Jesus God and Man* (SCM, 1968).

For the same God who said, 'Out of darkness let light shine', has caused his light to shine within us, to give the light of revelation—the revelation of the glory of God in the face of Jesus Christ.   (2 Corinthians 4: 6)

It is this which the gospel writers reflect in their story of Jesus being transfigured before Peter, James, and John for, as later theologians put it, they saw in him the uncreated light of God.

The resurrection, as the telos or goal of history, reveals God in the life and death of Jesus Christ, discloses his unbreakable union with his heavenly Father and shows forth the divine glory. But all this is not just for his sake, but for his sisters and brothers and in principle the whole of humanity.

We tend to contrast patterns of action with states of being. As far as patterns of action are concerned, it is the desire of every sincere Jew and Christian to live at one with the revealed will of God. We believe that in saints something of this has been achieved, in however fragmentary or opaque a form. The Christian claim, however, has always been that it is not just the pattern of Jesus' life and death that is one with his heavenly Father but that his essential being is one. But perhaps there is a point where action and being coincide. A person acts with such consistent bravery that we call him a brave person. He is brave through and through. A person always tells the truth, so that we say he is essentially truthful. The life of Jesus is shown by the resurrection to have been an unbroken union with his heavenly Father. So Christians have wanted to say he is one with his heavenly Father.

Although Jesus acted with authority, in some sense with the authority of God, he did not I have suggested, claim to be the messiah and he deliberately left open who he was and the way in which God might vindicate him. His destiny was integrally bound up with the coming of the Son of Man but beyond that he put himself utterly into the hands of his heavenly Father. He lived a life of total dependence on and complete responsiveness to that Father. It is in this way that he becomes transparent to God. As human beings we tend to try to draw attention to ourselves. The ego keeps getting in the way. But sometimes we are able to give ourselves totally to something or someone else. An artist like Constable struggles with the truth of the landscape before him trying, as he put it, to avoid bravura, which he defined as 'going beyond the truth'. In giving himself to the truth of the landscape with such artistic integrity, his work becomes transparent to that which he seeks to convey. So saints, in their different ways, are also partially transparent to God. Their ego does not get in the way, they are, so far as they can be, totally given over to God's purpose, moment by moment dependent upon him and his grace, and in so doing the divine radiance shines in and through them. Yet, Christians claim, Jesus is not just one among the saints. He is the fount from which their sainthood flows. Here we come up against a fundamental difficulty. In order to talk about the relationship of Jesus to his heavenly Father, it is necessary to use human analogies. That is inevitable in all religious discourse. But Christians have always wanted to claim that the union of Jesus the son of God with his heavenly Father is of a unique kind. If it is indeed unique, then it means that in the end all analogies break down. This is why, in the end, all Christologies go out into mystery and why some theologians say that all christological propositions must be doxological, opening out into praise and glory. They are not propositions on the basis of which further deductions can be made. Most obviously we call Jesus Son of God, taking the language which is common to all human beings, for we are all daughters and sons of God. But in the case of Jesus, so the Church has wanted to maintain, that sonship is of a unique order. It is a sonship in and through which we find our proper sonship.

One of the most unsatisfactory features of a literal reading of the Bible is that people think that Jesus went around claiming that he was God, or at least claiming that he was the messiah. They get this impression above all from a reading of St John's Gospel. This is, in my judgement, the most profound of all the gospels, but it is much more in the nature of a theological meditation upon the life and death of Jesus in the light of the resurrection and the coming of the Holy Spirit. It explores, as no other New Testament writing does, the meaning of Jesus, including his meaning in the life of the Church. But although there are historical nuggets buried within it, it is not an accurate record of his human ministry. In fact, it is Jesus' nothingness, as it were, his emptying out of himself, his total abandonment to his heavenly Father, which is the essential precondition of disclosing that Father.

As Hans Urs Von Balthazar has explored, it is the combination of authority and poverty in all its senses in the ministry of Jesus, combined with his self-abandonment to his heavenly Father for the meaning of his mission and person, that in fact enables his mission and person to be revelatory.[5] He goes to the limit of identification with sinful humanity, even descending into hell, handing over his life and its meaning to God. In the resurrection that life is revealed to be at one with God, not simply in the human ministry of Jesus, but in essential being.

Marcus Braybrooke has done as much as anyone to bring about greater understanding between Jews and Christians. In his most recent book *Christian–Jewish Dialogue* he suggests that the relationship is at the moment on a plateau and we need to take some next steps.[6] One of the steps he would like to take is to stop thinking of the resurrection as an objective event. 'For me faith in the risen Christ is commitment in his strength to seek to follow his self-giving way of life.' The other is to rewind the clock of Christian doctrine and start again with Jesus the man, in whom Christians encounter God. He does not wish to understand the doctrines of the incarnation and the trinity in a traditional sense because, he believes, they divide Christians from Jews and Muslims. A number of Jewish thinkers welcome such changes of direction in Christian theology as do Muslim thinkers, because it does indeed seem to dissolve the most fundamental differences between Christianity and the other two religions.

The traditional Christian understanding of Jesus as uniquely the Son of God, the one in whom God is incarnate, whom he raised from the dead, is indeed very difficult to believe. It was difficult in the ancient world and it is no less difficult today. Even before the question of believing such doctrines is considered, however, there is the sheer difficulty of actually grasping what they might mean. Their very meaning is elusive. So I have every sympathy with those of whatever religion or none, who simply cannot go along with the central Christian claims. Furthermore, as the very purpose of this book indi-

---

[5] Hans Urs Von Balthazar, *The Glory of the Lord*, vol. vii (T. and T. Clark, 1989).
[6] Marcus Braybrooke, *Christian–Jewish Dialogue: The Next Steps* (SCM, 2000).

cates, I wish to do all I can to bring the different religions of the world closer together, particularly Judaism and Christianity. However, the road that Marcus Braybrooke has gone down and which Geza Vermes, Hyam Maccoby, and other Jewish scholars want Christians to go down, is not a road I am taking. There are three main reasons for this. First, my reading of the New Testament is that Jesus did present a challenge to the Judaism of his time. That challenge was couched in essentially Jewish terms, the imminent rule of God in human affairs, but he presented people with a point of decision, a crisis. It is very tempting to subsume Jesus under the category of a teacher of eternal truths but though such a description is in part true, it cannot do justice to the urgency and impact of his historical ministry.

Secondly, the very identity of Christianity is bound up with claims about Jesus. It was the nature of these claims and how they were to be reconciled that preoccupied the Church for five centuries or more. This is not to set up what Braybrooke laments as a new credal fundamentalism replacing biblical fundamentalism. All the articles of the creed have to be interpreted afresh for our time, and sometimes the interpretation is indeed radically different from what the Fathers of the council of Chalcedon or Nicaea might have meant. But it is difficult to see how one could do away with belief in Jesus as a unique disclosure of the heart and mind of God in human terms, without doing away with Christian identity altogether.

Thirdly, from a more personal point of view, I find the Christian story of God supremely spiritually beautiful. I don't of course mean in a pretty pretty sense. The Greek word *kalos*, which was so central for the Church in its formative centuries, meant both goodness and beauty. I actually came to a belief in the incarnation not through reading the Bible but through reading a non-Christian book, *The Perennial Philosophy* by Aldous Huxley. Sitting in my room in a German barrack block in the 1950s I read how, in Huxley's view, at the heart of every religion is a common theme, the idea of giving oneself away in order to find oneself. It dawned on my mind, that if this is how every religion conceives reality, then what could be more congruous with this than the idea of a creator who totally gives himself away, who makes himself nothing in his incarnation in Jesus. Since then there has been the influential book by W. H. Vanstone, *Love's Endeavour, Love's Expense*, which argues that the utter self-giving of God which we see in Jesus is also a characteristic of creation. God doesn't as it were simply toss the creation off, holding reserves of himself back. The very act of creation involves putting his whole self into it even to the point of being drained utterly. So in both creation and incarnation God gives himself away; so focuses on the other, that he himself is hidden. Yet in this very hiddenness it is possible to see the glory of the divine. The Jewish story of God is also very beautiful, the God who is eternally faithful to his people and who shapes their life through Torah and who is with them in all their travail. There are different kinds of beauty but I cannot imagine anything more sublime than the Christian understanding of God despite all the cruelties carried out in the name of that God. Earlier in the book I argued that Christianity is not simply Judaism for the Gentiles. It is indeed through Jesus that Gentiles are brought to believe in the God of Abraham, Isaac, Jacob, and Moses. But Christianity is not primarily a religion of Torah but of participation in the life of God as that life has been made known to us in Jesus. There is a good example in the first letter of John. The writer says that his theme is the word of life that has been made visible:

What we have seen and heard we declare to you, so that you and we together may share in a common life, that life which we share with the Father and his son Jesus Christ.   (1 John 1: 3)

That passage twice uses the Greek word *koinonia*, once to refer to the life which Christians share with one another within the Church, and the other time to refer to that life which is drawn from God himself. To be drawn into the Christian fellowship is at the same time to be drawn into the life of the Godhead.

It is fundamental to any true dialogue, that the partners bring into it their most deeply cherished convictions. It is important that Jews bring what is distinctive about Judaism. It is no less important that Christians bring what is distinctive about Christianity. In my experience this brings mutual enrichment. But this does mean facing real differences which we cannot expect to overcome in this life. As the novelist and theological writer Charles Williams put it some years ago, for many people religion is simply a matter of behaving as decently as possible under the stresses of the world:

But for the orthodox on both sides it is very much more. There is a burden on each. The Jew is confronted with (as it seems to him) the preposterous blasphemy, the most awful of blasphemies; . . . The Christian is confronted by the rejection of the faith by that from which the faith sprang.[7]

It is important, however, at this point to reiterate what has been argued for earlier in this book. First, through Judaism people can truly know the true God. Secondly, although the resurrection of Jesus validates his mission and message and discloses his unbreakable unity with the heavenly Father it is also, as I suggested earlier, a validation of Judaism. For Jesus put all his trust in the faithfulness of God, the God of his forebears. He did this as God's son focusing in himself the vocation of the people of Israel to be God's son. So in the resurrection Israel's sonship and God's faithfulness to his people is confirmed.

Thirdly, again as I argued in earlier chapters, although traditionally the Christian doctrines of the trinity and the incarnation have seemed utterly alien to Judaism, which has stressed the transcendence of God, nevertheless there are counterparts to these doctrines within Judaism itself. As some modern Jewish writers have shown, both the doctrine of the trinity and the doctrine of the incarnation can at least begin to be understood in Jewish terms.

As Christians we are like the prodigal son in the parable. We have returned to our heavenly Father. Without in any way implying that Judaism shares the begrudging attitude of the elder brother, nevertheless, I believe that the words of the father are fully applicable to it. 'My son, you are with me always, and all that I have is yours' (Luke 15: 31).

Traditionally Christians have wanted to say that those who do not put their faith in Jesus Christ will be damned eternally. This is, as Hugh Montefiore has written, a monstrous belief. I believe that we will be judged by our response to the light we have and the actions we

---

[7] Charles Williams, *The Image of the City*, selected by Anne Ridler (Oxford University Press, 1958), 162.

take in response to that light. Here, I think, there should be no dispute between Jews and Christians. Jesus is reported as saying 'Not everyone who calls me "Lord" will enter the kingdom of heaven, but only those who do the will of my heavenly Father' (Matthew 7: 21). Then he told a parable about two sons. The first said he would go and work in the vineyard but never went. The second told his father that he wouldn't go but did in fact do so. It is the second one who is commended. What matters is what we do, not what we say we will do. Then there is the famous parable in Matthew 25 in which those who have done good discover that they have in fact done it to Jesus Christ. Conversely, those who have failed to meet the need of others have failed to meet the needs of Jesus. This is of course to put it in Christian terms. From the standpoint of Judaism, Christians will be judged by the extent to which they have responded to the moral law which is discernible by all human beings, the so-called Noachide covenant. Thank goodness that the good in other religions is now recognized in official church documents. *The Mystery of Salvation*, a report by the doctrine commission in the Church of England, referring to the fruits of the spirit in Galatians 5, love, joy, peace, patience, kindness, goodness, trustfulness, gentleness, and self-control says:

Our judging that the spirit may be found outside the church is not an arbitrary one nor does it mean that the work of the spirit can be identified everywhere. Those of other faiths and indeed of none who display such fruit are we believe amongst those who have responded to the spirit of God; there is evidence that God is savingly at work in them, and he will bring his worth to fulfilment.[8]

It would be both absurd and cruel to limit the work of the spirit of God to those who profess the name of Jesus Christ. That spirit is at work throughout the length and breadth of creation, stirring in the heart of every human being. As a Christian I know the self-giving of God in Jesus. 'The drawing of this love and the voice of this calling', to use words of the fourteenth-century mystical writer of *The Cloud of Unknowing* taken up by T. S. Eliot in *Four Quartets*, will, I believe, continue to draw me into the Divine Mystery but I am quite sure that my

---

[8] *The Mystery of Salvation* (Church House Publishing, 1995), 173.

response to this calling has been less wholehearted than the response of millions of Jews down the ages to God's disclosure of his purpose and will in the Torah. It is the same God of grace to whom we look and in whom we trust.

Shared Hope and a Common Task   11

Jews and Christians both believe that behind this world, at once beautiful and anguished, there is a wise and loving power who has brought it into being. We are creatures who, moment by moment, are held in existence by the ground of all being, who has only goodwill towards us. We have this faith in common. We also share a hope that the good God who has brought a good world into existence will not allow his purpose to fail. Of course there is risk in creation, for it means letting what is created go its own way. There is a special risk in creating free beings who can rebel against their own best interests. But if God were ultimately to fail in his purpose we would have to ask whether he was justified in creating a world of such suffering in the first place or we would doubt whether we were justified in putting our faith in one who could not bring his creation to completion. So faith is inextricably linked to a hope that God's purpose in creation cannot ultimately be thwarted.

The form that this hope has taken has varied enormously both within Judaism and Christianity. In the New Testament it is recorded that Jesus said to the penitent thief on the cross, 'Today you will be with me in paradise' (Luke 23: 43). The word paradise is ultimately derived from the Persian word for garden. The statement of Jesus implies that the penitent thief, presumably his soul, will go immediately to a beautiful heaven. On the other hand, Jesus stood four square with the Pharisees in championing the idea of the resurrection of the dead, against the Sadducees who did not share this belief. When the Sadducees asked him a question about the resurrection, which they denied, Jesus said to them, 'You know neither the scriptures nor the power of God' (Mark 12: 24). At the same time, central to the teaching of Jesus was his proclamation of the long-expected rule of God in human affairs with all that that meant for the restoration of Israel and God's writ running across the world. In fact the concept of an afterlife, whether in the form of an immortal soul that lives on or the resurrection of the dead, seems to have come into Judaism rather late, both ideas perhaps from Persia. Much more central to the whole biblical story is the idea of God decisively acting in order to establish his reign of justice and peace on earth.

After the biblical period both Judaism and Christianity came into contact with other concepts, which they tried to combine in one form or another. They were both influenced in the early centuries by Platonic and Neoplatonic ideas with their emphasis on an immortal soul. So it is that when the Jewish martyrs at Masada met their deaths, they did so, according to Josephus, with a firm belief that their souls would go straight to God. On the other hand Rabbinic Judaism in its formative period very much stressed the concept of the resurrection of the dead, even though they might have been expected to react against a similar emphasis on this in Christianity because of the resurrection of Jesus Christ. Both Judaism and Christianity tried to combine a belief in the immortal soul with hope for the resurrection of the dead by suggesting that when someone died their soul goes to an intermediate place and is then reunited with its body in the last days.

In 2001 there was a controversy in the columns of the *Jewish Chronicle* about whether reincarnation can be regarded as a legitimate Jewish belief. Some Christians were amazed that such a belief could even be considered Jewish. But in the Middle Ages the idea of reincarnation or the transmigration of souls came to be widely believed in some circles especially amongst the Kabbalists.

As far as this world is concerned there was a variety of beliefs amongst Jews at different periods about the coming of the Messiah, the establishment of his reign on earth, and the relationship between this reign and the life of the world to come, which was usually regarded as beyond space and time. Maimonides classifies five different types of belief in the Messianic age and the world to come, he himself laying most emphasis upon the union of the immortal soul with God.

Similar patterns are present in Christian history. Some have taught that Christ will return to earth and establish his reign for 1,000 years. Others have taught that the 1,000-year period is one of preparation just before the advent of Christ. Although the mainstream churches have treated such beliefs with great caution they have been influential in some forms of Protestantism since the Reformation and have taken root not only in the United States but in a number of forms of Christianity in the developing world.

As far as Judaism is concerned, Nicholas de Lange has said that if it is possible to condense the Rabbinic views about the hereafter into a brief summary, albeit one which is a gross oversimplification, it would go something like this:

After death the souls of the virtuous are despatched to the garden of Eden, while those of the wicked undergo a period of punishment in Gehinnom. The coming of the messiah will be preceded by various social and economic crises; then the prophet Elijah will return, a great trumpet will sound and the exiles will be gathered in; there will follow a cataclysmic war, known as the war of Gog and Magog, and after that the world will be renewed in the Messianic era, which will be an era of peace and harmony on earth. Eventually the dead will be resurrected and judged together with the living, and those who survive the judgement will live eternally in the Coming Age.[1]

In the modern world all these beliefs, both Jewish and Christian, have come under severe pressure. For many believers of both faiths, perhaps most, these particular aspects of their beliefs have been eroded away to a very uncertain 'Well there must be something after death but we don't know what it is.'

We now know that our physical body decays and becomes part of the earth before being recycled in another form. It is impossible to believe that we will clamber out of our graves like people in a painting

---

[1] Nicholas de Lange, *Judaism* (Oxford University Press, 1986), 130.

by Stanley Spencer, because whether we have been cremated, buried in a churchyard, or buried in a woodland as some people are today, the material out of which our bodies are made will disintegrate and become part of the material out of which other forms of life are made, forms of life which in their turn will disintegrate and be recycled. But belief in the immortal soul is no less secure from the acids of modernity than a belief in a resurrection of the dead. We know from neurological and other studies that there is a correlation between the thoughts of our mind and electrical impulses in the brain. Damage to certain parts of our brain, as for example in a stroke, drastically alters mental functions. From a philosophical point of view the idea of the soul as a kind of inner core of the person has not stood up to critical examination. As far as millenarian beliefs are concerned whether Jewish or Christian, these seem so far-fetched that they are not even entertained by the majority of thoughtful people, except by sociologists who see them in terms of compensation by marginalized and dispossessed groups.

All this having been said, hope remains fundamental for both Jews and Christians, hope for the individual, hope for God's world, and hope for the ultimate vindication of God's justice. If we get away from a literal account of traditional beliefs and regard them instead in terms of a symbolic realism, they all have something vital to say about the nature of this hope. By this term I want to suggest that the spiritual dimension is real, not simply a human projection. It is there in its own right independent of the way we perceive it. Nevertheless we can only grasp or point to this realm through the use of symbols and metaphors which always have to be qualified and then qualified again.

First, then, the resurrection of the dead looked at in this way. Several fundamental truths are safeguarded by this Jewish and Christian symbol. It reminds us that whatever comes after death is, like this life, the sheer gift of God. We have no right to a life beyond death; we cannot assume that we can automatically live on. God gives us this life as a gift and whatever comes next is also a gift from him. It is also a reminder that bodily life, physical life, is a good. The story of the creation of humanity in the early chapters of Genesis makes it quite clear that human beings are psychosomatic unities; body, mind, and spirit are bound up together in a whole. We are not immortal souls trapped in material bodies that are regarded as evil, as some ancient philosophies taught. Life in the body and life in the material world is a blessing. This means that we will take into the life beyond death all that has been good in our physical existence in a transfigured form. C. S. Lewis has an interesting speculation on how this might be so. He argued that it is not matter as such that really concerns us but our sensations. What the soul cries out for is the resurrection of the senses. Matter only counts for us because it is the source of our sensations. And we already have some feeble and intermittent power of raising dead sensations from the grave through memory. Memory brings the past into the present. By that Lewis did not mean that the dead will simply have the power of remembering earthly sensations, rather the other way round. Our memory now is but a foretaste, a mirage even, of a power which the soul will exercise hereafter. There will, however, be two differences. Our power to recall the past will not come and go but will be permanent. Secondly, memory will not be private. I can now tell you about the vanished feelings of my childhood only imperfectly and in words. Then I will be able to take you for a walk through them. It's a mistake, thought Lewis, to dismiss memories as being inferior to the original experience. If we went back to the wheat field we might see stalks of grain-bearing grass. It is the transfiguring power of memory that remembers our visits as 'Orient and immortal wheat', to use Traherne's words. This power of memory to glorify the past is the beginning of resurrection. This resurrection state may not happen all at once. We may first have to go to Lenten lands to be made ready but one day we will recover, in transfigured, glorified form, what time has borne away.

Then the new earth and sky, the same yet not the same as these, will rise in us as we have risen in Christ. And once again, after who knows what aeons of the silence and the dark, the birds will sing out and the waters flow, and lights and shadows move across the hills and the faces of our friends laugh upon us with amazed recognition.

Guesses, of course, only guesses. If they are not true, something better will be. For we know that we shall be made like Him, for we shall see Him as He is.[2]

[2] C. S. Lewis, *Prayer: Letters to Malcolm* (Fountain, 1977), 124.

Again, belief in 'the resurrection of the body' makes the symbolic point that persons need to express themselves in and through some medium. In this life it is flesh and blood. In the next life it is 'the stuff of glory', to use a phrase of Austin Farrer, whatever that might be. St Paul talked about being raised 'a spiritual body'. Whatever it is, the idea of a disembodied spirit, that is a spirit that has no way of being recognized by or communicating with, others makes no philosophical sense.

When it comes to language about the soul, I think both Jews and Christians will want to retain such language, not to assert the existence of an immaterial box within a box within a box, but to indicate that human beings have an inescapable spiritual orientation and destiny. Furthermore, although there is a correlation between movements in the brain and mental events, many philosophers would reject the idea that the one can be reduced to the other. In this life consciousness is a function of the brain but, having developed, it does not follow that consciousness has no independent role, or that within the providence of God it cannot exist independently of the brain. Mainstream Judaism and Christianity have resisted ideas about the pre-existence of the soul and the transmigration of souls. Rather each person is uniquely formed and develops gradually from conception, through birth to maturity. This is a unified process of physical, mental, and spiritual development. Language about the soul is important as preserving the spiritual dimension to that development, our orientation towards God.

Taking talk about the resurrection of the body and the immortality of the soul together we might say that when we die, although our knowledge seems to cease, the person we truly are, who is known fully only to God, is recreated or reformed in a manner appropriate to an eternal existence. We can be totally agnostic about the form that existence will take and the nature of our reality within it. But we can trust that the God who has given us this good life will share with us his own immortality. The Amidah, the prayer said standing in the morning service in the Reform tradition, now talks about God's power to renew life beyond death.

You, O Lord, are the endless power that renews life beyond death; you are the greatness that saves. You care for the living with love. You renew life beyond death with unending mercy. You support the falling, and heal the sick. You

free prisoners, and keep faith with those who sleep in the dust. Who can perform such mighty deeds, and who can compare with you, a king who brings
death and life, and renews salvation. You are faithful to renew life beyond
death. Blessed are you Lord, who renews life beyond death.[3]

That prayer expresses a hope shared by both Jews and Christians. It
does not depend upon a literalistic interpretation of the Bible or traditional beliefs. But it expresses a real hope.

When it comes to beliefs about the establishment of God's reign on
earth, whether in Jewish or Christian form, and this giving way to the
life of the world to come, here again if we discard literalism there are
important truths to be safeguarded. One is that God's purpose and
scope is not limited to the world of space and time that we know. His
purpose can be consummated beyond space and time, beyond the
material world. It is not limited by what we can conceive. Furthermore, given the fact that the universe as we know it is likely to come to
an end at some point, in however many billions of years in the future,
and the life of the earth will certainly have a terminus, it seems important to affirm that God's purpose is not limited by the universe we
know. Yet, at the same time there is a vital truth preserved in the pictures of a Messianic age or divine rule for a period on this earth. For it
is on this earth that God wills to establish his just and gentle rule. The
future of the earth and the peoples upon it matter. This is an important
corrective to the tendencies in some periods of both religions, but perhaps especially Christianity, to become escapist and other-worldly.

One aspect of belief which has of course traditionally divided Jews
and Christians is that of the messiah. Historically, Jews have kept alive
the hope of a messiah who will inaugurate a Messianic age. Indeed
from time to time in the early centuries of the Christian era, the Middle
Ages, and more recently leaders have arisen who have either themselves claimed to be the messiah or whose followers have regarded
them as such. There is a famous Hasid, Levi Yitzhak of Berdichev,
who is even said to have torn up the document announcing that his
son's wedding was to take place in Berdichev, furiously exclaiming to

---

[3] *Forms of Prayer for Jewish Worship* (The Reform Synagogues of Great Britain), vol. i:
Daily, Sabbath, and Occasional Prayers, 143.

the scribe that he should write, 'The marriage will take place in Jerusalem, unless the messiah has not yet come, in which case the ceremony will be performed in Berdichev.'[4] Even recently a particularly revered Rebbe, or teacher of Hasidic Judaism, has been regarded as the messiah. In the modern world Reform and Liberal Judaism have tended either to jettison or to spiritualize such a belief. But more recently there is some sign that even in liberal circles here is a truth that needs to be held on to. For example, Sidney Brichto has written:

The belief in a Messianic age must remain the essence of Jewish faith, not just for Jews, but for all mankind, whether achieved by a Messianic hero or by the collective efforts of humanity.

The Jew who does not live his life with this religious longing, who does not perform the Mitzvot to hasten the advent of the Messiah, forsakes the Jewish mission which was first accepted by Abraham and then by Moses and the prophets.

Only with a Messianic faith and the determination of Jews to bring that age of God's triumph over evil can Jewish history have a meaning and the personal lives of Jews a divine purpose.[5]

There is a particularly moving affirmation of this hope written by an unknown Jew on a wall in the besieged Warsaw ghetto. Translated into English this reads:

> I believe, I believe, I believe,
> with a perfect faith
> in the coming of the messiah;
> and in the coming of the messiah I believe.
> And even though he tarry
> I nevertheless believe,
> even though he tarry
> yet, I believe in him
> I believe, I believe, I believe.

Jews cannot believe that Jesus is the expected messiah, because his coming did not usher in the Messianic age. Indeed, it is all too obvious that the world continues to be beset by war, violence of various kinds,

---

[4] Quoted by Nicholas de Lange, *Judaism*, 133.
[5] Sidney Brichto, *Jewish Chronicle* (27 July 1990).

cruelty, poverty, and oppression. Christians continue to believe, despite all appearances to the contrary, that that age has been inaugurated in Jesus himself and those who are associated with him as part of his body, the Church. This age is characterized by the glory of God in humanity, the union of the divine and the human. This is why Christians continue to assert that they see the dawn of this age in Jesus and why they look for signs of that age in lives lived in loving union with God in the service of others. But Christians will certainly agree with Jews that this age has yet to be consummated. For both Jews and Christians there is a shared hope and a shared prayer that God's kingdom will come, that his will will be done on earth as it is in heaven. From this point of view there is a very great deal in common, as the proposed guidelines for Jewish–Christian relations in the Anglican Communion, already quoted, made clear. If there is a difference, it is one of emphasis, particularly the Jewish affirmation of the goodness of this life. Indeed as one teacher declared, 'Better is one hour of repentance and good deeds in this age than all the life of the Coming Age.'[6] Behind all these aspects of Jewish and Christian hope, there is a fundamental desire to affirm that in the end God's purpose will prevail, that his justice will rule. Traditionally this has been stated in terms of what Christians for example call the four last things, death, judgement, heaven, and hell, all of which have their counterparts in Judaism. Some aspects of the traditional picture need either rejecting altogether or radically reinterpreting. But the truth behind them is fundamental. We believe that it is a good God who has brought this world into existence. We believe that he would not, in his wisdom, have brought it into existence unless his purpose could eventually win through. We believe that his power, ceaselessly co-operating with us in bringing good out of evil, will in the end prove successful. One element in this links in very closely to the Jewish and Christian beliefs about the messiah. For Jews the messiah is a human figure. Whilst Christians believe that Jesus is, in the words of the creed, 'Very God of very God', they believe no less passionately that he is truly and fully human. It was these two boundary points which were staked out at the council of

---

[6] Quoted by Nicholas de Lange, *Judaism*, 130.

Chalcedon in 451. This means that God desires to achieve his purpose in and through human beings. He has delegated the task to us.

Another feature of the Jewish love for this life, in fact a converse of it, is the sense of loss ritually expressed when someone dies. Jewish mourning rituals are much more extensive than Christian ones. There is also great dignity as well as faith in the Kaddish, the prayer said by the chief mourner at a Jewish funeral. An English translation runs:

Magnified and sanctified be the great name of God
in the world which he created according to his will.
May he establish his Kingdom in your life and in your days,
and in the lifetime of all his people:
quickly and speedily may it come; and let us say amen!

Then continues blessing and praise of God. Not only is there a great dignity about this and an absence of false piety, it is focused on both God and his world, in the prayer that his kingdom may come. This fits in with what was said earlier about hope in the face of the Holocaust. We must, I believe, continue to have hope for those who perished so horribly. But this hope will very often be a silent affair, it will be expressed as much by what is not said as what is said. Meanwhile, there is work to be done.

On the grave of Karl Marx in Highgate cemetery are carved the words 'Philosophers have only interpreted the world, the point is however to change it'. It has often been suggested that Marxism is a Jewish heresy, with its belief that it is possible through human struggle to create a perfect society here on earth. That may be misguided. Even though they do not have a doctrine of original sin, Jews, like Christians, have a pretty realistic and robust sense of what is and what is not possible in the way of the perfectibility of life on earth. Nevertheless, many secular Jews, as well as observant ones, have been in the forefront of the struggle for human rights, and social justice in various contexts. There is a Jewish impulse at work here, even if the religious moorings have sometimes been left behind. Christians too, not least in recent decades, have been active in the field of social justice, particularly in relation to the great burden of financial debt being endured by so many developing countries.

In a remarkable sermon on the 50th anniversary of the founding of the Council of Christians and Jews already referred to, Donald Coggan, the former Archbishop of Canterbury, suggested that there were three stages of Jewish–Christian relations. First, there was the struggle in a world beset by antisemitism, to make it safer and more tolerable for Jews. Secondly, there has been the attempt to understand one another better. He proposed that we now needed a third stage, in which Jews and Christians stand together in the face of an unjust and secular world; that they work together to achieve some signs of God's rule on earth. There is a common task as well as a shared hope, a common task that arises out of that shared hope. For the hope that God's kingdom may come is at the same time a prayer that it may come in and through us as we work for a better world.

There is a remarkable and controversial German novel by Bernhard Schlink called *The Reader*.[7] The first half is about the erotic love of a schoolboy for an older woman. Then in the second half there is an unpleasant shock as the woman turns out to have been a Nazi guard who was responsible for locking a building in which scores of Jews were burnt to death. There may seem no connection between the two halves of the book, as there might seem no connection between the younger generation in Germany now and the older ones who are collectively guilty. But there is a connection. It lies in the attitude of the adolescent to the woman, the way he ignored her in public, was not willing to be seen with her on a bus, the way he failed to respect and respond to her as a human person. I think the author was trying to suggest that however terrible the things were which happened in the Holocaust, the actions of a generation which was not present then still have a crucial moral role to play. The moral dimension to human life is a seamless robe. How we treat others now has the same effect, for good as well as ill, as those in the past. In short, there is a particular responsibility on our generation, particularly the generation of Christians. This means radically rethinking our whole relationship with Judaism and in this book I have suggested ways in which I think this can and should be done without sacrificing Christian identity.

---

[7] Bernhard Schlink, *The Reader* (Phoenix, 1997).

Secondly, I hope it can mean that Jews and Christians can work together much more frequently than they have done in the past. We share a hope and, I believe, the task we have is in common: So to act that there are indeed signs of hope that God's rule on earth will come. As the Chief Rabbi has put it,

In the beginning, God created the world. Thereafter he entrusted us to create a human world which will be, in the structures of our common life, a home for the divine presence. That command still addresses us with its momentous challenge, the persisting call of faith.[8]

In Jewish tradition there is the wonderful theme of *tikkun olam*, repairing or healing the world. At any time or in any place we have the capacity and possibility to share in this work. One moving story which came out of the Holocaust was that of Charlotte Salomon, already discussed in Chapter 2, who painted a series of pictures. Even in the midst of evil, before she herself perished, she saw this activity as a way of playing her part in the healing of the world.

The purpose of God, as I understand it, is to create an inclusive, universal society characterized by a profound mutual care that draws on the depth of love within God himself. In order to further this purpose, God chose a particular people whose community life was to be a sign of what God intends for the world as a whole. Jesus came as a personal focus of God's purpose, to reconstitute or recreate human society around himself, under the loving wisdom of his heavenly father, as he called people to follow him in the way of love. Jews and Christians can work together to make their shared hope a reality for the world in which we are both called to be a light.

---

[8] Jonathan Sacks, *The Persistence of Faith* (Weidenfeld and Nicolson, 1991), 107.

The Council of Christians and Jews was founded in 1942, in the dark days of World War II, with the prime purpose of combating anti-semitism. It is easy for Christians who move in liberal circles to be lulled into thinking that antisemitism is a thing of the past. Alas, it is not. Moreover, it is now more in evidence than it has been for some decades. In France in 1998 there was only one violent attack on Jews. In 1999 there were nine, and in 2000, 116. Writing in the *Independent* and the *Guardian* on 28 February 2002, Jonathan Sacks, the Chief Rabbi, wrote, 'I never thought I would have to write about anti-semitism. Until recently I hadn't experienced it.' He then went on to suggest a thought experiment:

Suppose someone were to claim that there is a form of prejudice called anti-kiwism, an irrational hatred of New Zealanders. What might convince us he was right? Criticism of the New Zealand government? No. A denial of New Zealand's right to exist? Maybe. Seven thousand terrorist attacks on New Zealand citizens in the past year? Possibly. A series of claims at the UN Conference against Racism in Durban that New Zealand, because of its treatment of the Maori, is uniquely guilty of apartheid, ethnic cleansing and crimes against humanity, accompanied by grotesque Nazi-style posters? Perhaps.

A call to murder all those with New Zealand loyalties even though they were born and live elsewhere? A suggestion that New Zealanders control the world's economy? That they are responsible for Aids and poisoning water supplies? That they arranged the September 11 attack on the World Trade Centre? That they are a satanic force of evil against whom a holy war must be fought? By now we have moved from criticism to hatred to evil fantasy. But delete

'New Zealand' and insert 'Israel' and 'Jews', and all these things have happened in the past year. What more has to happen before an impartial observer concludes that antisemitism is alive and well and dangerous?

To put this in human terms and to take just one example, a student at Manchester University, where Jewish students have been under attack, said, 'For the first time in my life, I am feeling hated because of my religion. I feel hated because I have a Star of David on my necklace and hated because I go to a synagogue on a Saturday. There is a real sense of fear and unease for Jewish students right now. People don't even feel comfortable walking around the students union.'

If, as Conor Cruise O'Brien said, antisemitism is a very light sleeper, then unfortunately it has now woken up with a virulent hatred. It is the clear responsibility of all churches and all Christians to work with Jews in overcoming this hatred. It also behoves us to examine as searchingly as possible those aspects of our theology, tradition, or attitudes that might, even unconsciously, engender antisemitism. In particular, at the present time, we need to ensure that criticisms of Israeli government policies, which may be entirely legitimate, do not become a vehicle for displaced antisemitism.

In connection with this there is still much work to be done in striving for the most objective history possible of the founding of the state of Israel and what has happened since. Of course there will be differences of perspective and fierce disagreement. Nor can there ever be one final account, for history is a result of the continuing interaction of the present with the past. But at the moment the propaganda element is so strong and the myths so enduring it is difficult to approach the idea of an agreed history. Yet there is hope for this precisely because of the new generation of Israeli historians such as Benny Morris, already referred to earlier, who have done so much to rewrite the Israeli account of what happened in earlier years, thereby bringing it much closer to what has always been a Palestinian understanding.

There is not such agreement on why the peace process broke down. Benny Morris in a much publicized conversion has come to totally distrust the Palestinian desire for peace and believes that it was their responsibility almost entirely that the process resulted in failure. It is not only his ground-breaking role as a historian that gives him credibility. He favours an Israeli withdrawal from the territories and in 1988 served time in a military prison for refusing to serve in the West Bank town of Nablus. But he now says, 'I don't believe that Arafat and his colleagues mean or want peace, only a staggered chipping away at the Jewish state—and I don't believe that a permanent two-state solution will emerge.'

Abi Shlaim, a professor of international relations at the University of Oxford, however, takes a very different view about who was responsible for the breakdown. He refers to 'The latest national myth', which 'is that of the generous offer that Ehud Barak is said to have made to Arafat at Camp David, only to be confronted with a flat rejection and a return to violence.' He argues that what the Palestinian leadership rejected were proposals put forward by Barak in July 2000. In fact they accepted in principle proposals put forward by Clinton in December, as did the Israeli leadership, even though both sides had reservations. At Taba in the last week of January 2001 the two teams made considerable progress on the basis of the Clinton parameters and came closer to an overall agreement than at any other time in the history of this conflict. But as Shlaim says:

By this time Clinton and Barak were on their way out and Sharon was on his way in. During the run-up to the elections, Barak hardened his line on Jerusalem. At this critical juncture, as so often in the past, the peace process was held hostage to internal Israeli politics. With Sharon's election, all the progress made at Taba towards 'the agreement' was rendered null and void. A new and grisly chapter in the history of the conflict was about to begin.

In quoting Shlaim above, this is not to claim that his understanding is the last word. It is simply to applaud such efforts of Israeli historians to dispel widely accepted myths and to continue persevering towards agreed understandings of what happened.[1]

There are myths to be dispelled on all sides, in Israel, amongst the Palestinians, and amongst Christians. Some of the material I have seen from pro-Israel Christian groups seems not just partial but distorted.

---

[1] *Guardian*, G2 (21 and 22 Feb. 2002).

For reasons stated earlier in the chapter on Israel there is a natural Christian sympathy with Palestinians. This is partly because of the contact Christians have there with the wider Christian world, partly because Christian organizations like Christian Aid are working in the refugee camps and partly because in recent decades Christian theology has worked on the basis of a bias to the poor and Palestinians are perceived to be the weaker, suffering David in its struggle with American-backed Goliath. But the bare minimum of a Christian relationship with Judaism today, as Paul van Buren put it, is that disregard for Israel's 'safety and welfare is incompatible with concern for the Jewish people'. At times the debate between pro-Palestinian Christians and pro-Israel Christians has become very polarized. But it may be that in the Church of England now there is a better understanding of both sides of the conflict than has sometimes seemed to be the case in the past. An observer at the July 2002 Synod of the Church of England not noted for his support of the powers that be in the Church of England commented:

Sometimes the Synod debate will reach the heights, and that was certainly the case in the debate on the report *Israel/Palestine: An Unholy War* which was expert, thorough and evenly balanced. As one nurtured in the world of the Synod/WCC of the 70s and 80s, I was expecting speeches denouncing Israel (and of course the USA) and an absolute silence on the cruel activities of the suicide bombers.

I could not have been more wrong, for it named evil by whomsoever it was perpetrated in a manner that would have almost been shouted down in earlier days. As a result it was a valuable and valid Christian contribution in the face of an almost intractable situation, in a debate of which Synod can be truly proud.[2]

The resolution called upon the Israeli government to withdraw from the occupied territories, which it named as the root cause of the present conflict, and called upon the Palestinian authority to condemn suicide bombing. It was a resolution which probably fairly represented the mind of most members of the Church of England, and indeed other Christians, at this point. As an antidote to the potential polarization

---

[2] George Austin, 'Much Ado', *New Directions* (Aug. 2002).

amongst Christians I like this prayer which is based on one by a
Palestinian Christian:

> Pray not for Arab or Jew
> for Palestinian or Israeli
> but pray rather for ourselves
> that we might not divide them in our prayers
> but keep them both together in our hearts.

There is no glossing over the fact that on the Israeli/Palestinian
conflict there is a fundamental difference of perspective of genuinely
tragic dimensions. If I were a Jew who had come to Israel from a
country with a long history of pogroms and anti-Jewish persecution,
my overriding priority would be to build a secure state to hand over to
subsequent generations. If I were a Palestinian living in a refugee
camp, nurtured on stories of the family orange groves in Jaffa, it would
take a very great deal to dispel my bitterness at their loss. So it is no
good pretending that this fundamental, irreconcilable difference of
perspective is going to bring about any kind of easy harmony.
Nevertheless, both in order to achieve some kind of political compro-
mise, however uneasy, and in order to go beyond that uneasy com-
promise to a genuine living together, mutual understanding is
essential. If all ethics, as the philosopher said, is a training in sympathy, then an attempt to at least understand the perspective of the other
is an essential feature of any moral approach to this issue.

Shortly after Easter 2002 I spoke to the big solidarity with Israel
rally in Trafalgar Square. It was a highly fraught occasion, with
Islamic groups chanting in counter demonstrations, on the one hand,
and Benjamin Netanyahu, on the other, using the occasion for his own
political purposes.

In my speech I expressed solidarity with Israel and in particular
with those who have been injured or bereaved as a result of the suicide
bombings. I also said that, in my view, both the policy of Israel and of
the Palestinians was at the moment based on a sense of despair and
what we needed to recover was the politics of hope. I suggested that
when an 18-year-old girl straps bombs around herself to blow up herself and ordinary people going about their daily business in cafés or

buses, whatever else this was, it was an act of desperation—from the Latin *de spero*, without hope. This part of the speech was booed by a section of the crowd who shouted out, 'Not despair but hate'.

The correspondence I had afterwards brought home to me the extent to which Palestinian young people are subject to a propaganda of hate. Yet, sadly, a sense of despair and hate are not mutually exclusive. The one can reinforce the other. At the same time a fieldworker with Reform students commented afterwards, 'He was the first speaker to really say something I wanted to ecstatically applaud, because it highlighted the complexity of the issue and humanised the Palestinian people. . . . The booing of the people around me, directed at the Bishop of Oxford, coupled with the joyous chanting for Benjamin Netanyahu, left me feeling quite isolated.'[3]

I say this not to suggest that I got it entirely right in what I said at the rally but to indicate how difficult it is to get any of us to enter into the hearts and minds of those who appear to be our enemies. And this is why I am full of admiration for those members of the Jewish community, both within and outside Israel, who try to get their fellow Jews to understand the Palestinian plight and perspective and those Palestinians who try to help their fellow Palestinians enter into Jewish fears and insecurities.

And then there are the values on which the state of Israel was founded and how far it is possible to maintain these during a prolonged occupation. As the Chief Rabbi, Dr Jonathan Sacks, said in an interview to the *Guardian* on 27 August 2002, 'I regard the current situation as nothing less than tragic. It is forcing Israel into postures that are incompatible in the long run with our deepest ideals.' He went on to say that he was 'profoundly shocked' at the reports of smiling Israeli servicemen posing for a photograph with the corpse of a slain Palestinian. 'There is no question that this kind of prolonged conflict, together with the absence of hope, generates hatreds and insensitivities that in the long run are corrupting to a culture.' Dr Sacks is of course deeply and irreversibly committed to the state of Israel and the point he made, as not everyone saw, was perfectly

---

[3] Debbie Young, *Felafel*, the Newsletter of CCJ's Youth Section (June 2002).

proper expression of his commitment to the state of Israel's deepest meaning and life.

So if the first task of the unfinished agenda is to be aware of the rise of antisemitism again and to join with the Jewish community in combating it, the second is to care both about the suffering of the Palestinian people and the well-being and security of Israel in a way which is as prayerful, objective, and as constructive as possible in this enormously complex, tragic, conflict.

As I write this it is not possible to be very optimistic about the political process. So it is necessary to bear in mind some words of Vaclav Havel: 'Hope is not the expectation that things will turn out successfully but the conviction that something is worth working for, however it turns out.'

As far as Israel is concerned I go back to words of its founding father David Ben Gurion: 'The state of Israel will prove itself not by material wealth, not by military might or technical achievement, but by its moral character and human values.' The state of Israel was founded in hope and its national anthem *Hatikvah* means hope. Hope is not optimism. As Jonathan Sacks has put it,

Hope—not optimism—is what empowers us to take risks, to offer commitment, to give love, to bring new life into the world, to comfort the afflicted, to lift the fallen, to begin great undertakings, to live by our ideals.[4]

Away from the life and death issues of antisemitism and Israel, there remains the more rarefied but still crucial concern about truth. This involves both our general understanding of the relationship between our religion and others and for Christians and Jews the particular bond which both unites and distances them one from the other. Drawing on some of the points made in Chapter 5 I would sum up a possible approach as follows.

First, we hold to our own religion because we believe it to be true. It is not just the fact that we were shaped by it and it is part of our heritage. People opt out of their heritage and, in the modern world in Europe, very many do. We adhere to our religion, if we do, because in

---

[4] Jonathan Sacks, *The Politics of Hope* (Jonathan Cape, 1997), 267.

some way it has taken hold of us. We are attracted spiritually and morally by what it sets before us. It seems to make sense of life.

Secondly, this means that questions of truth cannot be side-stepped; however difficult to resolve, they matter. There is truth to be sought and found. Dr Rowan Williams, the Archbishop of Canterbury, drawing on the work of an American scholar, Katherine Sonderegger, has written:

> We need a way of articulating the fact that Jews and Christians *disagree* without claiming that one is a corrupt and illegitimate version of the other. If we cannot find such a language, we are left with 'pious sentimentality or dogmatic certainty'—or, we might add, crippling theological embarrassment and shame among Christians, afraid to sustain certain theological claims for fear of being accused of 'supersessionism', the belief that Christian revelation 'fulfils' Jewish history.

As Dr Williams goes on to say, again drawing on Sonderegger:

> The important thing is to recognise that Judaism and Christianity are now separate religions, *both* claiming legitimate descent from the religion of biblical Israel. This at least saves us from the implicit or explicit claim that Judaism has no post-biblical history, from the ignorant assimilation of contemporary Judaism to the polemical targets of the New Testament rhetoric, and from the unbroken reading of Jewish experience in exhaustively alien categories determined by Christian needs and interests.[5]

Thirdly, all that we mean by postmodernism brings home to us the fact that we have no bird's-eye view of the world's religions, no Archimedean point from which to judge them. We are bedded down in our culture and language and the religion of our time and place. If I had been born of Jewish parents the chances are I would be Jewish by conviction. If I had been born in a Roman Catholic family, again, the chances are that I would now be a Roman Catholic. However, this knowledge does not lead to the conclusion that there is no truth to be found, or that one tradition is as good as another because of the two points made above.

Fourthly, however, because of this third point it means that we will hold to our own position with a certain humility. From a religious

---

[5] Rowan Williams, *Sergiei Bulgakov* (T. and T. Clark, 1999), 300.

perspective it means that we are human with our tiny human minds and very limited capacities. God is God, beyond anything we can conceive or know. As St Paul put it,

O depth of wealth, wisdom, and knowledge in God! How unsearchable his judgements, how untraceable his ways! Who knows the mind of the Lord? Who has been his counsellor? Who has ever made a gift to him, to receive a gift in return? Source, guide, and goal of all that is—to him be glory for ever! Amen. (Romans 11: 33–6)

It is worth noticing that that moving passage of St Paul comes at the end of his long reflection on the place of Judaism in the providence of God and its relationship to Christianity.

Fifthly, the consequence of these points taken together is the need for a willingness to learn from one another. Jesus was reported as saying 'When, therefore, a teacher of the law has become a learner in the Kingdom of Heaven, he is like a householder who can produce from his store both the new and the old' (Matthew 13: 52). The point of this is that Christians are to be learners in the Kingdom of Heaven. We stand with all those others willing to learn, willing to learn from life, from the school of divine wisdom, from the nature of the Kingdom of Heaven. Elliot Dorff writes that those aspects of his Jewish tradition that make him most proud are its moral seriousness, its insistence on translating good intentions into actions, its compassion for the poor and its strong emphasis on education as well as its sense of community requiring Jews to care for all other members in the extended Jewish family.[6]

There is nothing here from which a Christian cannot learn and much that she or he ought to be enriched by. A Christian has a particular understanding of the nature of God and his purposes and we want to share this with others. But this does not preclude learning from others. Indeed, if we are wanting people to see life from our point of view we can hardly expect them to do that unless we are willing to see life from their point of view. At the Church of England General Synod in July 2002 there was a motion about the importance of sharing the

[6] 'Understanding Election', in Tony Bayfield, Sidney Brichto, and Eugene Fisher (eds.), *He Kissed Him and They Wept* (SCM, 2001), 75.

good news of the Christian faith with other people. An amendment was put forward also urging the importance of learning from others. The motion as amended was passed by 301 votes to 10. It read:

Urge all Christians to encourage sensitive and positive sharing of faith with people of all faiths and none whilst being willing to learn from and to be enriched by people of other faiths.

This possibility of learning from and being enriched by people of faiths other than one's own does not lead to the relativity of truth. On the contrary, dialogue and the possibility of mutual learning is based on the premiss that there is a truth to be sought and entered into more deeply. We cannot approach that truth from some neutral, detached position. We stand on a particular foundation.[7]

All this applies with special force to the relationship between Christianity and Judaism. From a Christian point of view, the relationship with Judaism is not simply with one religion amongst others. Nor can we lay down in advance what might be learnt. It is the nature of a learning process that the future is open and the insights are genuinely fresh. Reading the scriptures together, with Christians enjoying the benefit of Jewish exegesis of familiar texts, may be one way, as Jonathan Magonet and John Pawlikowski have shown.[8]

Reading the scriptures brings to the fore, for a Christian, how those scriptures are to be interpreted in a way which does not reinforce anti-Judaic prejudices. At a Sunday by Sunday practical level this is a crucial issue. What is being taught and preached from Christian pulpits?

The prevalence of anti-Jewish polemic in Christian teaching and preaching down the ages is now universally recognized. But what about the New Testament itself? Eliezer Berkovitz has written that:

Christianity's New Testament has been the most dangerous anti-Semitic tract in history. Its hatred-charged diatribes against the Pharisees and the Jews have

[7] I have explored this point in relation to certain particular people in ch. 7 of *God Outside the Box: Why Spiritual People Object to Christianity* (SPCK, 2002). I have argued the case in relation to discovering common ethical truth in 'Tuning into the world before turning it upside down', *Crucible* (April–June 2001).

[8] *He Kissed Him and They Wept*, part IV, 'The Context of Partnership'.

poisoned the hearts and minds of millions and millions of Christians for almost two millennia.[9]

Other scholars, however, have denied that the New Testament is inherently anti-Judaic. Tom Wright, for example, has argued that Judaism at the time of Jesus was pluralist and the different groups all engaged in disputation about the true meaning of Judaism in a style and tone that we today would regard as polemical. The fact that the first Christians argued for the truth of their understanding of Judaism as it had come to a head in Jesus does not make the New Testament any more intrinsically anti-Jewish than the writings of the Dead Sea scroll sect or the Pharisees. However, whether one takes the view that antisemitism is inherent in the New Testament or that its attack on certain expressions of Judaism can be paralleled in other Jewish writings at the time, or that antisemitism rests on a misinterpretation of the New Testament, the fact is that we *hear* the New Testament today as being anti-Jewish so we need to do all we can to counteract that tendency.[10] The situation may be likened to the failure to use inclusive language. A few years ago everyone took it for granted, for example, that the word mankind meant humanity. The use of that word and similar ones now strike us as being sexist. We have been sensitized to the issue in a way that does not allow us to go back to a time when people heard words differently. So, whatever the historical context in which the New Testament grew up, which may well have been polemically pluralist, we hear certain phrases and sentences in the New Testament today as anti-Jewish. So those charged with the responsibility of teaching and preaching Christian truths need to do all they can to counteract this tendency. Very special care is needed, particularly with certain texts.

There is, however, a problem that is more fundamental than any particular text and which lies behind all the difficult ones. It is that so often the good news of Christianity has been preached in contrast to the bad news of Judaism. Christianity has been the good guy and

[9] Eliezer Berkovitz, 'Facing the Truth', *Judaism*, 27 (1978), 325.

[10] *Sharing One Hope? The Church of England and Christian–Jewish Relations: A Contribution to a Continuing Debate* (Church House Publishing, 2001), 5–7.

Judaism the bad one. It's as though Christians have defined them-selves in terms of the fact that they are not Jewish. The problem is so fundamental because it goes to the very heart of Christian identity. There is of course a universal propensity for human groups to define themselves in relation to others. Particularly in times of conflict and war they bond strongly together in opposition to a common enemy. The inclination to say about another person or group that they are 'not one of us' is not confined to the followers of Mrs Margaret Thatcher in the 1980s. The issue is also vital for Christian mission today. For if the good news of Christianity is defined simply in terms of its contrast with Judaism, it will cut no ice in a world that does not share the pre-suppositions of Judaism, most notably about the moral law.

This basic attitude has expressed itself in a number of continuing stereotypes.

One stereotype that Christians have so often reinforced is that of Judaism as a legalistic religion, concerned with the minutiae of obser-vance rather than the basic principles of love and justice and obsessed with outward practice rather than the inward, spiritual heart of the matter. But Jews do not see the Torah as a burden. Rather, it is God's revealed way of helping his people flourish and find fulfilment. Psalm 119 puts it,

> O, how I love thy law!
> It is my meditation all the day.
> Thy word is a lamp to my feet
> and a light to my path.
> Therefore I love thy commandments
> above gold, above finest gold.
> Therefore, I direct my steps
> By all thy precepts.

Furthermore, practical detailed guidance is not to be lightly dismissed. Christianity developed the whole tradition of moral theology precisely because in so many situations it is not at all clear what we should in fact do and how the great principles of love and justice should be applied where there are conflicting claims. Then it is quite untrue to say that Judaism is only concerned with outward observance and not right intention. It was many years ago that T. W. Manson drew attention to the very strong emphasis in Pharisaism on the importance of right motive.[11]

Closely connected with the stereotype about the law, is the stereotype about the Pharisees. Indeed, the very term Pharisee has become a smear word.

A balanced reading of the New Testament shows that not all aspects of the relationship between Jesus and the Pharisees was polemical. It is Pharisees who warned Jesus of the risks he is running (Luke 13: 31); some Pharisees are praised, for example the scribe of Mark 12: 34; and Jesus eats with the Pharisees. (Luke 7: 36 and 14: 1). Jesus shared with the majority of Palestinian Jews at that time some Pharisaic doctrines such as the resurrection of the body, their forms of piety, such as almsgiving, prayer, and fasting, and the liturgical practice of addressing God as Father. Not least he shared their priority of the commandment to love God and our neighbour. He also used methods of reading and interpreting scripture which were common to the Pharisees at the time. Particularly noteworthy is the fact that the Pharisees are not mentioned in accounts of the passion. The Pharisee Gamaliel defended the apostles at a meeting of the Sanhedrin (Acts 5: 34–9).

Pharisaism was in fact a complex and diversified movement with a range of continuing debates. There are criticisms of some types of Pharisees within Rabbinical sources themselves. So criticism by Jesus of some Pharisees or some forms of Pharisaism need not and should not be taken as a criticism of Pharisaism as a whole, to which in some ways Jesus was close. He was probably closer to them than any other contemporary Jewish group.

Pharisaism, far from being an ossified form of legalism, was a creative movement. Looking back to the great prophets of the eighth century with their call for social justice they sought to make the great principles of the law a reality in daily life. They began to internalize the Torah, making it a matter of personal and inward response. Their distinctive institutions, the oral Torah, the Rabbinate, the synagogue, and their emphasis upon table fellowship in the home led, even before

---

[11] T. W. Manson, *Ethics and the Gospel* (SCM, 1960).

the destruction of the temple, to a religious way of life of great vitality. Although Jewish scholars warn against seeing later Judaism simply in terms of the Pharisees it was out of Pharisaism that some of the most distinctive features of Judaism emerged and Jesus should be seen within that tradition rather than implacably opposed to it.[12]

A Jewish scholar, Hyam Maccoby, shows in some detail how the teaching of Jesus fits into a Pharisaic context.[13] For example, on the issue of Jesus' healing on the Sabbath he points out that healing was not one of the 39 forms of work expressly forbidden. Indeed it was encouraged if it was a matter of saving life, for danger to life overrode all other claims. Even that apart, however, it would seem that the form Jesus' healing took, which did not involve work such as grinding up herbs, would not in any case have infringed Sabbath regulations. In relation to another incident where Jesus and his disciples are reported to have plucked corn on the Sabbath and the example of David is appealed to, Maccoby points to Rabbinic interpretations which argue that David was entitled to take the shew bread, which no one not even priests were allowed to eat, because his life was in danger. Similarly Jesus and his disciples, constantly on the move and perhaps on the run, were in dire need and necessity, above all the necessity for safeguarding life and this rightly overrode the law of the Sabbath. Jesus, according to Maccoby, argues like a Rabbi and gives a Rabbinic justification.

As for the Torah itself, E. P. Saunders, who has done as much detailed work on Judaism and the New Testament as any modern scholar, has written about the attitude of Jesus to it: 'We find no criticism of the law which would allow us to speak of his opposing or rejecting it.'[14]

St John's gospel, from a Christian point of view, is the most profound and sublime of all the writings in the New Testament—or that at least has been the judgement of many Christians down the years. Yet today St John's gospel makes Christians feel very uncomfortable

---

[12] John Pawlikowski, *What are they saying about Christian Jewish relations?* (Paulist Press, 1980), ch. 4.

[13] Hyam Maccoby, *Judaism in the First Century* (Sheldon Press, 1989).

[14] E. P. Sanders, *Jesus and Judaism* (SCM, 1985), 269.

on one point. For it keeps referring to 'the Jews', who are invariably depicted as hostile to Jesus. But who are these Jews? Raymond Brown in his great two-volume commentary on St John's gospel argues that it uses 'the Jews as almost a technical term for the religious authorities, particularly those in Jerusalem, who are hostile to Jesus'.[15] According to Brown, in many instances the term 'Jews' has nothing to do with ethnic, geographical differentiation. And in some passages the term 'Jews' is interchangeable with references to the Chief Priests or the Pharisees. Brown argues that after the fall of Jerusalem in 70 CE the differentiation between different groups in Judaism at the time of Jesus had disappeared. The Pharisees alone remained and Judaism was Pharisaic Judaism. Furthermore, at that time Christians who had until then remained practising synagogue goers were under pressure from the synagogue to leave. It was from about the year 85, for example, that we have the curse on minim or heretics. So John in part writes to support such Christians and to encourage them to profess their faith even if it did mean expulsion from the synagogue.

I have argued in earlier chapters that Jesus did indeed bring something challengingly new to the Judaism of his time. He proclaimed the nearness of God's rule in human affairs. After his death the Christian movement arose proclaiming that, despite all appearances to the contrary, that rule had indeed been inaugurated in Jesus himself and that he would return shortly in mercy and judgement. We know from the New Testament that the majority of Jews did not respond to this interpretation of what had happened and that serious controversy arose. Nevertheless, there is now widespread agreement among New Testament scholars that the strength of this disagreement has been heightened by the split between the Synagogue and the early Church. 'The parting of the ways', as it has often been called, means that a great deal of the New Testament reflects subsequent hostility rather than what actually happened at the time. The important and valuable Vatican document *Notes on the Correct Way to Present the Jews and Judaism in Preaching and Catechesis of the Roman Catholic Church* has stated:

---

[15] Raymond Brown, *The Gospel according to John* (Geoffrey Chapman, 1971), vol. i, p. i.

Hence it cannot be ruled out that some references hostile or less than favourable to the Jews have their historical context in conflicts between the ancient church and the Jewish community. Certain controversies reflect Christian–Jewish relations long after the time of Jesus.[16]

All this means that teaching and preaching needs to be very aware of the historical context of the gospels. Not least of course is this true in relation to the readings for Holy Week which, historically, have had a particularly devastating effect on the Jewish community.

I think it is very possible both to be true to the Christian gospel and affirmative of God's gracious action in and through the Jewish people. If you will forgive a personal anecdote, I preached not long ago at a confirmation where one of the candidates, an Oxford academic, was being confirmed as a Christian from a Jewish background. His Jewish parents, who had never been in a church before, were there, extremely apprehensive. I did not know beforehand that one of the candidates was Jewish nor that his Jewish parents were to be there. Nevertheless, in preaching on the summary of the law by Jesus I stressed the role of this in Judaism, the importance of the *Shema* and the continuity of the teaching of Jesus and Judaism on this point. The candidate was kind enough to say that both he and his parents were very appreciative that this had been said. I was simply glad that I had not known the background of the candidate beforehand because it would have made me much more self-conscious in mentioning the continuity with Judaism. As it was, it was simply what needed saying, whoever was to hear it.

Behind the question of how we understand and interpret particular texts for today, is the more fundamental issue of what we understand by the good news of Jesus Christ. Too often, as I pointed out earlier, when Christians have thought of the good news they have puffed themselves up with the thought that they, in contrast to Judaism, believe the good news. It is worth quoting Martin Luther on this point. Although he was responsible for some of the most devastating anti-Judaic teaching and preaching in history, he also said:

---

[16] 'Notes on the Correct Way to Present the Jews and Judaism in Preaching and Catechesis of the Roman Catholic Church', *Catholic Jewish Relations: Documents from the Holy See*, introduced by Eugene Fisher (Catholic Truth Society, 1999), 43.

Now there are not a few who preach Christ and read about him that they may move men's affections to sympathy with Christ, to anger against the Jews, and such childish . . . nonsense. Rather ought Christ to be preached to the end that faith in him may be established that he may not only be Christ, but the Christ for you and me.[17]

One of the major problems faced today is the growth of biblical literalism. What is not always realized is that fundamentalism, as James Barr has repeatedly shown, is not, as its adherents think, a true interpretation of the Bible but an interpretation using a particular grid or set of assumptions and presuppositions. The fundamentalist brings a number of notions to bear in the light of which he or she interprets the text. We can't approach the Bible without certain assumptions. What is vital is that we realize what these are and subject them to examination. The Bible itself is a series of texts which interpret one another and Christians stand within a tradition of continuous reinterpretation. Unfortunately anti-Judaism infiltrated that tradition at an early stage and has been part of it ever since. It needs to be exposed to view and decisively rejected. The eyes through which we see and interpret scripture must be simply Christ himself and the gracious love of God which is disclosed in him. Surprisingly, given his hostility towards Judaism, it is Martin Luther that can guide us at this point. He said, 'The scriptures point to Christ alone'. The scriptures must be 'understood in favour of Christ, not against him. For that reason they must either refer to him or must not be held to be true scriptures.'[18] Even more strongly Luther argues that if adversaries 'press the scriptures against Christ, we must urge Christ against the scriptures'. (*Urgemus Christum Contra Scripturam*).[19] As Gareth Lloyd Jones has put it,

In the context of Jewish–Christian dialogue, this means that texts which are manifestly antagonistic to Jews should be interpreted in the light of the gospel, because ultimately they stand under its critique. If they do not 'point to Christ', if they do not make plain the unconditional love of a gracious God to all people, if they do not promote justice and righteousness in society, in short,

[17] Quoted by Clarke Williamson and Ronald Allen, *Interpreting Difficult Texts: Anti-Judaism and Christian Preaching* (SCM, 1989), 61.

[18] Theses concerning faith and law, *Luther's Works* (Philadelphia, 1960), xxxiv. 112.

[19] Ibid.

if they contradict the 'good news' of God in Jesus Christ, are we not justified in repudiating them?[20]

As Clarke Williamson and Ronald Allen put it, 'On occasion, we may have to preach *to* or *against* the text. We are free to do so, even obligated to do so, provided we responsibly proclaim the gospel.'[21] It is the Roman Catholic Church above all that has pioneered a new approach to Judaism. Vatican II published its historic document *Nostra Aetate* in 1965. Affirming a common 'spiritual patrimony', it said that the passion of Christ 'cannot be charged against all the Jews' and affirmed that the relationship between Jews and Christians 'concerns the *Church as such*'. This was followed up in 1974 by *Guidelines and Suggestions for Implementing the Concilia Declaration Nostra Aetate*. This in turn was followed up by *Notes on the Correct Way to Present the Jews and Judaism in Preaching and Catechesis of the Roman Catholic Church* in 1985. This was particularly important because it set out practical ways in which this new relationship with Judaism could be fostered by correct teaching.[22] In addition to the authoritative Vatican documents and guidelines produced by individual dioceses there has been the work of SIDIC (Service International de Documentation Judéo-Chrétienne), which has produced regular teaching documents from Rome to help priests and teachers avoid negative images of Judaism. There has also been the work of individual Roman Catholic theologians and teachers who have sought to build this new teaching into the curriculum of seminaries and schools.[23]

As a result of this some impact has been made on individual Roman Catholic priests, teachers, and congregations. However, I suspect that very little of this new understanding of the relationship between Christianity and Judaism has permeated the curriculum of Anglican theological colleges or the colleges of other denominations. There is a huge task still to be done.

[20] Gareth Lloyd Jones, *Hard Sayings: Difficult New Testament Texts for Jewish–Christian Dialogue* (The Council of Christians and Jews, 1993), 47.

[21] *Interpreting Difficult Texts: Anti-Judaism and Christian Preaching*, 62.

[22] All these documents are contained in *Catholic Jewish Relations: Documents from the Holy See*.

[23] See Eugene Fisher, *Seminary Education and Christian–Jewish Relations: A Curriculum and Resource Handbook* (The National Catholic Educational Association, Washington, 1983).

This anti-Judaism has persisted in some surprising quarters; not only in some mainstream German biblical scholarship in the intermediate post-war period but in more recent liberation theology from Latin America in such writers as Gustavo Gutierrez and Jon Sobrino.[24]

Rabbi Hugo Gryn was one of the best-loved Rabbis of our time. Against all the odds he survived Auschwitz. Later he wrote how one day in Auschwitz he saw jet streams, probably from experimental V2 bombs, in the sky and he believed that God himself was about to intervene to put a stop to the terrible evil that was happening. Later however, trying to keep Yom Kippur, the Day of Atonement, as best he could in the camp he found himself sobbing for hours.

Never before or since have I cried with such intensity and then I seemed to be granted a curious inner peace. Something of it is still with me. I believe God was also crying. . . . I would like you to understand that in the builder's yard on that Day of Atonement, I found God. But not the God I had churlishly hung to until those jet streams dissolved over Auschwitz. People sometimes ask me 'Where was God in Auschwitz?' I believe that God was there Himself—violated and blasphemed. The real question is 'Where was man in Auschwitz?'[25]

Hugo Gryn's insight that God was there in Auschwitz, not as the great deliverer but as one who shared the suffering and torment, reiterates powerfully one of the main themes of Chapter three. It also recalls us to our responsibility as human beings. As Christians we have a particular responsibility to create a new, constructive relationship with Judaism and this involves serious, continuing attention to every aspect of how we preach and teach the faith. For Jews and Christians together it means standing side by side in combating every form of racism and violation of human rights, whenever they occur.

---

[24] John Pawlikowski, *Christology and the Jewish People*, paper prepared for the Council of Christians and Jews, London, 2002.

[25] Hugo Gryn with Naomi Gryn, *Chasing Shadows*, (Penguin, 2001) 251.

Index

233

Index

Index

Jerome, St 18, 156, 158
Jerusalem: in Christianity 155–60
  in Islam 160–2
  in Judaism 162–3
  religious significance 154–66, 216
Jesus Christ: and covenant with human-
    ity 89, 95, 96–7, 111, 125–6
  and covenant with Israel 97–100,
    104–5, 107, 176–7
  and forgiveness 69, 71–3, 77
  as God sharing suffering 59–60, 61–2,
    133, 190
  as Jew 169–70, 188–90, 199, 229
  Jewish attitudes to 167, 172, 176–7,
    180–1, 183–4
  as Messiah 119, 121, 124, 190, 194–5,
    209–10
  and Messianic Judaism 119, 127,
    137–8
  and Pharisaism 101–2, 103 n.15, 105,
    203, 226–8
  and relationship with God 106
  resurrection 99, 133, 192–4, 196, 199,
    203
  as Son of God 96, 106, 191, 194–6,
    199
  as Son of Man 73, 190, 193–4
  as word of God 191–2
Jews: massacres 19
  Messianic 119, 124–5, 127, 136–8
  mission to 4–5, 97, 117–39
  seen as depraved 19
  seen as eternally reprobate 19
  seen as killers of Christ 17, 18, 20–1,
    159–60
  will to survive 30–3, 48, 108
Jews for Jesus 119, 124, 136, 138
Job (book), and suffering 42, 44–6
John the almsgiver 158
John of Damascus 91–2
John Paul II, Pope 132
Judah Halevi 50, 167–8
Judaism: attitudes to Christianity 116,
    167–87
  beliefs shared with Christians 111–12,
    176, 202–12
  and common task 129–30, 212–13
  and covenant 88–92, 94, 97–100, 107,
    110, 132–3, 142–3, 148, 176
  and forgiveness 65–70, 72–80, 84–7
  and Gentiles 96–7, 104–6, 116, 126,
    176
  Hasidic *see* Hasidism

and Jerusalem 156, 162–3
as living religion 8, 99, 108, 126, 132
and mission 117–18
and problem of evil 25–32, 178–9
as religion of Torah 95, 97, 101,
    105–7, 113–15, 126, 137
and repentance 70–1, 73, 75–6, 78, 85
and 'Righteous Gentiles' 10–12, 62
seen as legalistic 2, 105, 225–6
and suffering 25–37, 38–55, 58–64,
    175, 183–4
and theology of Christianity 104
see also Rabbinic Judaism; superces-
    sionism
justice, divine 54–5, 57, 60, 63, 82–3,
    205, 210

Kelly, J. N. D. 18
Kingdom of God: and fulfilment of
    God's purposes 29, 52, 97, 189
  Jewish witness to 132, 178
  in life and teaching of Jesus 102,
    189–90, 193, 203
  and repentance 72
  as shared belief 112, 121, 210
Kraemer, David, *Responses to Suffering in
    Classical Rabbinical Literature* 39

Lambeth Conference 1988 3–5, 118–24,
    128, 147
Landau, Yehezkel 164–5
Langmuir, Gavin 16
law: international, and state of Israel
    147–8, 150
  Jewish *see* Torah
Lawrence, D. H. 112
Leaman, Oliver, *Evil and Suffering in
    Jewish Philosophy* 39, 44–6
learning, mutual 120–2, 222–3
Levi, Primo 30
Levy, Isaac 7
Lewis, C. S. 206
liberation theology 26, 54, 232
life after death *see* afterlife
Littell, Franklin 20, 60, 131, 136
Lloyd George, David 149
Lloyd Jones, Gareth 230–1
Longley, Clifford 127, 167
Luria, Isaac 32
Luther, Martin 15, 19, 139, 229–30

Maccoby, Hyam 127–8, 137, 197, 227
Magonet, Jonathan 223

Index